PENGUIN BOOKS

THE WRONG STUFF

Bill Lee was born and raised in California, where he attended U.S.C. After his apprenticeship in the minor leagues, he came up to the Big Leagues in 1969 with the Boston Red Sox and stuck with that strangely perplexing team for ten years. Bounced from Boston, he went on to grace the Montreal Expos in 1979.

A native of New York City, Dick Lally has written for numerous New York newspapers and magazines and is the author of *The Bartender's Guide to Baseball*. He lives in Manhattan with his wife, Barbara Bauer, who is also a writer.

The WRONG STUFF

Bill Lee
with Dick Lally

Penguin Books

PENGUIN BOOKS
Viking Penguin Inc., 40 West 23rd Street,
New York, New York 10010, U.S.A.
Penguin Books Ltd, Harmondsworth,
Middlesex, England
Penguin Books Australia Ltd, Ringwood,
Victoria, Australia
Penguin Books Canada Limited, 2801 John Street,
Markham, Ontario, Canada L3R 1B4
Penguin Books (N.Z.) Ltd, 182–190 Wairau Road,
Auckland 10, New Zealand

First published in the United States of America
by Viking Penguin Inc. 1984
Published in Penguin Books 1985

Printed in the United States of America by
George Banta Company Inc., Harrisonburg, Virginia
Set in Aster

To Pam and Barbara from the Rover Boys

• • •

The authors wish to acknowledge gratefully the assistance and encouragement of the following: Cork Smith, Bill Strachan, Chuck Verrill, Gary Zebrun, Bill Shannon, Billy Altman, Robert F. Moss, and our fabulous agent, Julian Bach.

The **WRONG STUFF**

God, it's dark. I am sitting in the lotus position on the floor of the office of Montreal Expo president and general manager John McHale. There is not another soul around. It is early morning, the lights are out, and the room is as quiet as a crypt. That may seem spooky to some, but I find it rather relaxing.

I had been summoned to these executive chambers for an audience with a presumably upset McHale. I was presuming he was upset with me. Less than twenty-four hours earlier I had walked off the Expos in protest over the unfair treatment and eventual release of our second baseman, Rodney Scott. The walkout lasted four hours; I had gone back to the clubhouse before that afternoon's game was over. Upon returning, I was informed by manager Jim Fanning that I had been indefinitely suspended, was about to be fined, and had to see McHale the next day. I assumed that it would be then that the shit would really hit the fan.

I had stopped off in the clubhouse before going up to McHale's inner sanctum. The only player there was John Milner. Milner was a psychic. Had to be. He had spent most of his career with the Mets, Pirates, and Expos as a lefthand hitting outfielder–first baseman, playing against right-handers or sitting on the bench in a state of advanced readiness. Life as a platooned player breeds an ability to perceive events long before they actually happen. So, on the morning of May 9, 1982, as we both sat in that clubhouse, and he handed me a fried egg sandwich, I'm sure we both knew that he was giving me something more than just an early snack. He was giving the condemned man his final meal. I thanked him, ate it, and made my way to the door, pausing only to grab a bagel. Slobbering it with peanut butter and cream cheese, I thought to myself, What a time for us to run out of spareribs.

I went directly to McHale's office and, seeing no secretary around, decided to let myself in. I made myself comfortable on his floor and quickly reached a meditative state that was beyond transcendental. This wasn't the first time I had crossed swords with management; I was always matching wits with authority. Pondering over my past and present hassles, I began to wonder why my life had taken the direction it had. What cosmic forces had led me to this precise moment that saw me, once again, dancing on the rim of the volcano? The answers started to come to me as my life flashed before my eyes. I think it all started when I was arrested as a pyromaniac.

I was five years old.

It was a tree that got me into trouble. My grandfather owned a walnut ranch, and he had hundreds of beautiful walnut groves. I loved to sit and look at them. There were similar ranches all around his spread. One of them was cursed with this horrible-looking tree. It was gnarled, twisted, and diseased. I was only five, but even then I had an appreciation for the beauty of nature. I decided the best thing anybody could do for this poor wreck was to put it out of its misery. I grabbed a book of matches and held services for it. I always liked the idea of cremations. Very neat and clean. I had whipped up a pretty good pyre when suddenly the air was filled with the sound of sirens. Somebody had seen the smoke and sent in an alarm. When the fire engines arrived they were able to put out the flames in a couple of minutes. There really wasn't much damage: the tree was hardly marked. I didn't fare as well. A fire marshal collared me and hauled me off to the firehouse. My parents had to come and get me. I really caught it for that one. The tree enjoyed a perfect revenge because for the next two weeks my butt developed a severe inability to come in contact with wood. Or any other hard surfaces.

I really didn't get into much trouble when I was a kid. I spent my formative years in California, living first in the San Fernando Valley and then moving to Marin County when my father received a transfer from the telephone company. We had a real *Leave It to Beaver* sort of family. I was Wally and my younger brother, Paul, was the Beave. There was some sibling rivalry there. As a child he was much prettier than I was, so I took a scissors and cut off all his curly locks. Transformed him into a normal mortal and robbed him of his strange powers. I used to jump in whenever he was involved in a fight. Everyone would turn on me and start swinging. Paul would back off and start rooting for the other kids. I guess he really liked those curls.

Looking back, I suppose there were some omens that my destiny had already been laid out. When I was seven years old I had to go to First Holy Communion practice, and it really made me nuts. It was so boring! I mean, all you really had to be able to do was kneel down and open your mouth. How much practice does that take? We would do it every day for hours. I just couldn't take it. It had become the Catholic version of the Chinese water torture. One day I took my Roy Rogers handcuffs and locked myself to my bedpost. Those were really good cuffs—this was 1955, in the pre-Taiwan era of toys—and they had a key, which I had carefully hidden. It took my mother hours to get me unshackled. I spent the whole time watching television and missing out on Sister Merry Christmas's inspirational chidings. This was an immediate tip-off on how resourceful I could be. I was too small to overpower anybody, so I outsmarted them. It was the sort of thing that would later help me compensate for the lack of a good fastball.

The Lees were an athletic family. I grew to six feet three inches, getting my size from my mom. Dad was an average height but had amazing reflexes. He had played a lot of sandlot ball and fast-pitch softball. He was a teammate of Don Drysdale's father, Scotty. Don was their bat boy. They used to play their games in Canoga Park, which is situated right near the orange groves where Jack Nicholson almost got his ass blown off in *Chinatown*. I used to jog through there with my friends, and the farmers would fire rock salt at us. I never got hit. Even as a kid I had good lateral movement.

My grandfather William F. Lee, Sr., was one of the top infielders in Los Angeles in the early 1900s. He used to get fifty dollars a game to play. That was a lot of money back then, and he didn't have an agent. The Lees always did their own negotiating. Still do. He probably could have been in the majors, but he had a family to support and he knew that there was neither money nor security in playing baseball, so he pursued it only on weekends.

He must have been a real scrapper. Grandfather used to cut the leather out of the center of his glove and just leave his bare palm, in order to make the double play quicker. He said modern ballplayers were pussies because they wore those big gloves; he claimed it robbed them of their manual dexterity. The Japanese have gone back to the small glove, knowing my grandfather was right. They're not afraid to combine modern technology with age-old traditions. That's why we're all driving Toyotas.

When my grandfather played there was a real scarcity of gloves. When you came off the field you usually left your mitt at your position, allowing a member of the opposing team to use it. The other side's shortstop would come out and have to wear this little glove with the middle cut out of it. He could not handle it. He would end up making a lot of errors with the same glove my grandfather was using to turn all those double plays. Bill, Sr., wasn't unaware of the advantage this gave him. In telling me about it, he always made sure that I understood the very valuable baseball lesson he was trying to teach me: Always look for an edge.

My brother, Paul, was a better athlete than I, very quick, but he severed his Achilles' tendon while playing football against West Texas State and separated his shoulder in another ball game. Paul got carried off the football field so often that by the time the baseball season started, he looked like a pile of uncooked hamburger. These and other injuries he received on the playing field forced him to look away from sports as an occupational avenue.

The best athlete in the family—and I mean the best baseball player in the family, including me—was my Aunt Annabelle Lee. She was called Lefty and was one of the biggest influences on my life. She threw harder than I did, even when I was in high school, and could really bring it. My aunt pitched the first perfect game in the history of the Women's Semi-Pro Hardball League in Chicago and had a lifetime ERA of 1.17. That was her idea of the Equal Rights Amendment. Any man who did not consider her an equal could try hitting against her. Annabelle was a Pete Rose—type player, sliding head first and playing with a burning intensity. She wouldn't give an inch on the field to anyone, man or woman. I like to think I got my competitive nature from her.

When I was eight years old, my brother and I were near the highway close to home when a bum came over and tried to grab him. He wrestled free, and we jumped over a fence into some orange groves and started pelting the bum with oranges. I nailed him in a vulnerable spot. Right in the flask, breaking it into a hundred pieces. That's when I knew I was born to be a pitcher.

I got my first taste of organized ball in Little League. My father was the coach. He really hadn't encouraged me to become a ballplayer. He felt that a person had the right to develop his own interests without the bias of parental supervision influencing his choice. This somewhat modern approach to parenting caused him to wait until my mother was three months' pregnant with me before he bought me my first fielder's glove.

Actually, both of my parents encouraged my brother and me to pursue whatever interests we had. They were great. My father was an excellent coach, very good at imparting baseball fundamentals. He used to crowd the entire team into a '50 Chevy and drive us out to the park for practice. That's a great way of learning the team concept. You really get to know your teammates when you're crammed into a car with about a dozen of them.

My father taught us all to hustle, and he made his pitchers throw strikes. He hated walks. We lost two games in four years and went one two-year stretch without a loss. There was a lot of talent in that league. Tim Foli was on one of the teams. He was feisty and temperamental, and always seemed ready to mix it up with someone. He was a good player, but his father would at times chastise him in front of the other kids when he did poorly. I thought those chewing-out sessions would turn him into a wreck. When he finally made it to the majors he had earned the nickname Crazy Horse. He hadn't changed. Later on he got religion and mellowed out, trading his boxing gloves for a Bible.

Al Gallagher was another guy who played in that league and made it to the majors. Even back then he was known as Dirty Al. He reminded me of the character Pigpen from the *Peanuts* comic strip. You could be at a black-tie banquet, and Al would show up looking like he just stepped down from a tree. He was a real challenge to interview. I saw him give a live radio interview during halftime of a Santa Clara basketball game. The announcer gave him a tremendous introduction and commended him for having a good season. Al thanked him, saying, "Yes, I did have a good year. I really hit the shit out of the ball." The radio guy nearly swallowed his microphone.

My father was an extreme conservative. Still is. He believes FDR gave everything away and caused all the economic problems we are having now. He's a Republican and a devout Catholic. I view that as a contradiction in terms. It was my religious beliefs that caused me to take a liberal stance on issues. I believe in the corporal acts of mercy, in giving to people who don't have anything. If you take care of those around you, you end up taking care of yourself, because you establish a good pattern of karma.

It was my maternal grandfather's love for the environment that helped shape my concern for the earth's well-being. Grandfather was an ecologist of sorts and was very intense about it. He used to run litterers off the road with his car. He also felt motorboats were polluting the lake near his home, so he used to sit on the shore and root for the water skiers to crash into each other. I had a lot of conversations with him, and he taught me a great deal about life, passing down the things he had learned from my great-grandfather Rockwell Dennis Hunt. Great-grandfather was a historian and dean of the USC graduate school for thirty-five years. His intelligence was awesome, but he did, to some degree, inhibit my learning experiences as a child. He used to sit me on his knee and tell me how he would hunt swans on the Sacramento River in the 1880s. That was his favorite story, and after the tenth retelling, it started to get to me. Pretty soon, every time someone picked me up and put me on his knee, I automatically figured, uh-oh, here comes the swan story, so I would wink out and not hear a word they said. This probably closed off a whole avenue of education for me.

My father always told me, "Ask a lot of questions or you'll never learn anything." But I was unusually quiet in grammar school and throughout most of high school. I never had any girl friends back then. Two missing front teeth were part of the reason. They made me shy and embarrassed; I developed the habit of talking with my hand in front of my face. I was honestly afraid of girls and couldn't play any of their games. They wanted to go to movies and dances. I just wanted to run around trees. Making out just didn't seem to be a very productive way to spend time. I made up for that later. Actually, that shyness was probably a good thing. If I had gotten my sexual aggression out earlier, I never would have made it as a ballplayer. I would have fallen by the wayside and had three kids of my own by the age of seventeen.

One of the reasons I didn't, besides my own bashfulness, was the attitude of coaches toward sex. We were taught to fear sex as something that would rob us of our stamina. The word was, "Tiger, if you let women drain away your life's essence, you'll never be able to go nine." Some of that mythology has carried over to the pros. The Red Sox brass were always telling Sparky Lyle that if he kept screwing around he would lose his fastball. They claimed it would float right out of his dick. Later he told me they were right, but that they forgot to mention how it would add all sorts of movement to his slider and carry him to the Cy Young Award.

My early formal education was really quite ordinary up to high school. I had been in a three-year junior-high-school program in Southern California and transferred to a four-year high-school program in Northern California in my sophomore year, enrolling in Terra Linda High.

Coming to Terra Linda was a traumatic experience that actually paid some dividends later on. When I arrived there I found their system wasn't in sync with the one I had just left. They told me that even though I was old enough to be a sophomore, I still had to take some freshman classes in order to fullfill their requirements. So half my classes were on the sophomore level and the other half were for freshmen. I ended up caught between two cultures. My soph class was made up mostly of fifties rockers, while the freshmen were the eventual flower children of the sixties. It was like being stuck between two time warps.

I also went through some culture shock. All the kids in Northern California wore really tight pants with cuffs up around their ankles. Very punkish. I found out later that the reason for this style was the wind coming in off the Pacific. It would blow up their legs and freeze their nuts off in winter. We never worried about cold weather in Southern California. People in the north would huddle in groups for warmth and would end up sharing thoughts and concepts. Down south we didn't care for crowds. Too sticky. We preferred one-on-one relationships. Being exposed to what was essentially a whole new world while still in my teens helped to raise my consciousness. It made me more tolerant of others and more open to change in myself.

Another big difference between the two cultures was their attitudes toward war and violence. Northern California was dove country; the southern part was populated by hawks. Most of my freshman class would later become part of the peace movement in the sixties. They made me aware of a life outside my own. I started to read political literature and began to listen to music in a new and different way. A group of us would go to concerts at the Fillmore West. I remember seeing Jim Morrison and the Doors there. It was extraordinary, watching him as he swayed back and forth, clutching the microphone as if it held the secret to life. He was the Lizard King holding court. I liked his sense of poetry and the way he delivered his songs. The voice was shot, really wasn't there anymore. But there was something awesome in the way he paused. It was as though he would set himself in a trance, view a world only he could see, and then come back to earth to report on it. The Joshua Light Show was going on in back of him, swirling amoebas on a screen, and after a while it looked as if my brain cells were bleeding out of my eyes. When we left, we watched as sparks flew out from under our shoes. They had sprinkled phosphorus on the floor. I hadn't done any drugs, didn't really know what they were yet. Didn't matter. Just being in there got you high, like being a nonsmoker at a cocktail party. It was one of those San Francisco nights that helped shape my formative years.

I started to look for messages everywhere, in songs, books, and movies. I realized everything had its own message. In 1969 I saw *Easy Rider* with several members of the Red Sox. They thought it was a movie about drugs and sex, but I knew otherwise. It was a movie with a very specific message: Don't ride a motorcycle through Georgia while wearing an American flag as a jumpsuit. That's something I've never quite forgotten.

The sports program in high school was very limited. All we had was baseball and basketball. We couldn't have any other sports; the school was only two years old, and we only had freshman and sophomore years to draw talent from. I didn't go out for basketball that first year—I just didn't have the confidence. That's a shame, because I really grew to love basketball, almost as much as baseball.

I did try out for the baseball team right away and had no trouble making the squad. I was able to throw strikes right from the start. The team came in second in our conference, surprising a lot of people. No one expected us to do that well with the small universe of players we had to draw from. I had one of the better records in the conference, but no one seriously scouted me because I didn't throw hard. That was a problem. Scouts, on both the pro and the college level, just love to see those big studs who can throw the ball through the wall. This often causes them to overlook the finesse player who really knows how to pitch. I was your basic fastball, curveball, changeup pitcher. The breaking ball was my biggest asset and had been for a long time. My father had taught me how to throw a curve and a knuckler when I was eight.

He also taught me to change speeds, preaching that hitting was timing and that the successful pitcher could upset that timing. Since I could change speeds and get my breaking ball over, I was able to win a lot of games in high school.

It was about this time that I became aware of the preferential treatment that athletes automatically receive, even on the high-school level. We could cut certain classes and get away with a little bit more than the average student. Or even the above-average student. It's no wonder that our priorities got screwed up. Just because a person can throw a ball harder or hit it further than most ordinary human beings, he is placed on a pedestal at an early age. I don't think there is anything wrong with admiring an exceptionally skilled person, but the hero-worship we shower on athletes goes beyond that. This is a part of the tribal influence handed down by our ancestors. Man has always been lionized for his physical prowess. An Indian brave did not have to pass a math quiz in order to become a chief, he just had to tear the ass off some bear. And the twelve labors of Hercules did not include a Regents' exam. Society has tended to find its heroes in the most obvious arenas, and I don't regard that as a healthy thing. We should find our heroes in the bathroom mirror each and every morning.

Graduating from Terra Linda in 1964 brought me face to face with the first big decision of my life. I had to choose a college. I was not yet seriously considering a career as a ballplayer. The odds were too great against it, and I wasn't sure it was what I wanted to do with my life. I had worked part-time with my Uncle Grover as a locksmith. He was a good friend of Howard Hughes and used to do a lot of work for him. Hughes would call him up at three in the morning and have him change all the locks in one of his studios. One time I went with Grover on a job at one of Gene Autry's hotels. We changed 165 locks and charged $8,000. The materials cost $150. I took one look at that and said, "Shit, who needs baseball. This is great." But by the time the summer was over I decided that locksmithing would just be my safety net, something to fall into if some other things didn't work out.

My mother was pushing for me to become a dentist, but I didn't think I could handle that. That's a profession with a very high suicide rate. Which is understandable. You spend hours on your feet digging five-day-old frankfurter out of somebody's mouth, and you're bound to get depressed. I wanted to be a forest ranger. I had a yearning to sit up in one of those towers and look after thousands of evergreens. That seemed peaceful and worthwhile. But in the back of my mind, I did want to give baseball a fair shot. I considered going to Humboldt State College because it was the only college in California that had a forestry program. My family wouldn't hear of it. With a great-grandfather who had served as dean at USC and a lawyer uncle who was still a leading member of their alumni association, I was expected to uphold the family tradition and go to the University of Southern California. The only problem with that was the university didn't have a forestry program. I was at a crossroads. Would I become a forest ranger and live forever with pent-up guilt over not pursuing a baseball career? Or would I become a baseball player with pent-up guilt over my failure to protect the sons and daughters of Bambi? I thought I could compromise by going to the University of Oregon and exploring both possibilities, but my father straightened me out, saying, "Son, face the fact that you want to be a ballplayer. Now, do you want to be a big fish in a little pond? Or, do you want to go to SC and be a little fish in a big pond and accept the challenge of eating your way up into becoming a big fish." I liked challenges, so I went to SC and gobbled up people left and right. And I still didn't get scouted.

I was hoping to get an athletic scholarship, but the school wouldn't grant me one. I had gone up to speak to the baseball coach about it the summer before my admission. That was my first meeting with Rod Dedeaux. After hearing the reason for my coming, Rod shook his head, saying, "Tiger, tiger, you have to prove yourself here. Nobody buys a car sight unseen. Get on the freshman team, win some ballgames, and then we'll see what we can do for you." Rod called everybody Tiger. I don't think he knew anybody's first name. If he did, he wasn't letting on. Fortunately, I was able to get an academic scholarship because my grades were high and I had gone to a progressive school. Terra Linda was considered progressive because we didn't have any school bells. We just floated around the building from class to class.

During that first year I made the team and went 9–2, but my grades were dropping and I was placed on probation. My ERA and my grade-point average were exactly the same: 1.92. I was in predentistry out of deference to my mom, but I couldn't hack it. I lost my academic scholarship but was switched over to an athletic one because I could get people out. After a semester of staring at pictures of decayed molars and inflamed gums, I also changed my major to geography.

My early days at SC were mildly upsetting. It was my first time away from home, and the dormitory was in the middle of Watts. All we kept hearing about was how tough the neighborhood was and how high the crime rate was. The statistics really struck home on the very first weekend, when my friend Freeman and I were all set to cruise Hollywood in his '63 Impala. We were dressed to kill, with our best jeans and sports jackets, hair slicked back with Brylcreem, and two quarts of Aqua Velva between us. We were ready to tear the town up. Racing from the dorm, we felt like modern adventurers out of *Route 66*. We flung open the doors of the Impala, jumped into the car, and fell into Freeman's trunk. Someone had made off with his interior. There was nothing left, not even an ashtray. We ended up driving along the Sunset Strip, sitting on orange crates.

I have to admit to homesickness those first couple of weeks, but I was lucky. The baseball was a calming influence. I had never seen anybody like Dedeaux. By our first game I was convinced he was the greatest manager who had ever lived. He was a good friend of Casey Stengel and had learned a lot from their association. Casey taught Rod to be a master psychologist, able to convince his team that there was no way they could lose. Dedeaux used to tell us, "Don't be concerned with winning. That's not good enough. Play to achieve perfection." He figured winning was the by-product of the quest for perfection.

My first time on the mound he taught me another important lesson. I was in the process of semi-intentionally putting the winning run on base, confident I could get the next hitter out. Before I threw my second ball Rod was racing out to the mound, demanding to know what I was doing. I told him I thought I would have an easier time with the next batter. He put his arm around me and said, very seriously, "Tiger, that's where you're making your first mistake. Never think. It can only hurt the ballclub."

Dedeaux is from Louisiana and has a French background, but he always had us singing "McNamara's Band" after each victory or before a crucial game. He had heard Dennis Day sing it years ago and once had his team belt it out before an important series that they went on to win. He's been using it ever since. There are many times that I am convinced he's just a frustrated Irishman.

It's only in the last ten years or so that people outside of California have become aware of him. That's because, despite a great record at USC, Rod was never much interested in self-promotion. All he cares about is promoting baseball in general and Trojan baseball in particular. He's a great man. He could probably command an astronomical salary from any major college, but at SC he works for nothing. Rod is a very successful businessman, and he donates his time to the school gratis. That's how much he loves the game. Rather than take money out of the baseball program for himself, he prefers to use it to make sure that his boys travel first class all the way. I've heard more than one of his players say that, in a lot of ways, going from SC to the minor leagues is a demotion.

Rod always had good teams, so good that when Don Buford played for him he wasn't really a starter. He was what Rod called a Double X'er, which is the same thing as a utility man in the majors. This is the same Don Buford who starred on three American League championship teams with the Baltimore Orioles, batting lead-off and playing left field.

The secret to Dedeaux's success was his strict adherence to fundamentals and his ability to maximize a player's strengths while minimizing his weaknesses. I have a quirk in my body: I can't throw two pitches in a row at the same speed, no matter how hard I try. I also can't throw the ball straight; it either dips or rises. Rod knew I wasn't about to overpower anybody, but he saw that I had a good command of my pitches and that I had pretty good stuff. I might not be able to throw the ball by too many people, but I could break your bat with a sinker. Rod continued the teachings of my father: Throw strikes and keep the ball low. He also made me work on my fielding, realizing that I threw a lot of groundballs and would have to be able to help myself with the glove.

Dedeaux was known as the Houdini of Bovard because USC played their home games at Bovard Field and his teams were always pulling off miraculous escapes from defeat at the last minute. Years after my time SC was playing the University of Minnesota in a semifinal round of the College World Series. Dave Winfield was pitching for Minnesota, and he had a one-hit shutout and a 7–0 lead going into the ninth. The only hit off him had been an infield roller. SC got up in the bottom of the ninth and scored eight runs for the ballgame. They got five consecutive pinch hits in the last inning. I was pitching for the Red Sox against the Angels in Anaheim that night, and they were carrying the linescore for the SC game on the electric scoreboard. Everyone went nuts when that big eight went up. Didn't surprise me. That was Rod. This was just another example of his team's knack for coming back and ripping out the opposition's heart.

Of course, I had seen Rod's influence firsthand, the way he made you believe you were in a temple the moment you stepped in between those white lines and how he had everyone do his job with maximum effectiveness in order to get positive results. It paid off. In each of my four years at SC, we always were able to field a competitive squad. We were eliminated in the National Championships in 1966. Barely. The next year we didn't make it, having been beaten out by UCLA. They had a first baseman named Chris Chambliss who used to eat my lunch. He was the same kind of hitter then that he is now, an alley hitter with line-drive power. The thing that impressed me most about him was his uncanny ability to wait on the ball. I guess that's why he would kill me; I wasn't quick enough to put the fastball by him. He'd fight it off and hit jam shots over second. Or, if I hung a breaking pitch, he'd step back and... *yak-a-tow!* There it went over the far reaches of the Pacific Ocean.

A lot of great players came out of SC. Guys like Freddy Lynn, Steve Kemp, Steve Busby, Rich Dauer, and Roy Smalley. Ron Fairly was a Trojan superstar long before I got there. After joining the team, I found myself on one of the best pitching staffs in college history. I was there with Jim Barr and Brent Strom. The three of us went to the majors. And for one season we had Tom Seaver. He had transferred over to USC from Fresno Junior College. Dedeaux loved him, calling him his "Phee-nom from San Joaquin."

Tom didn't have much of a breaking ball back then, but he threw very hard. He was just starting to mature and was more of a thrower than a pitcher. His personality was strictly laid back, very Fresno. But underneath that placid exterior was a great competitiveness. He exuded confidence without opening his mouth. One look at him told you that he had a future of big cigars and long limousines. On the other hand, it was quite obvious to people who met me that I had a future of six-packs and canoes. And that after drinking enough of those six-packs, I would probably slip out of the canoe, fall into the water, and drown.

Seaver pitched only one year for us—1965—but an extraordinary thing happened to him in that short time. When we got him, he wasn't very big. Then he must have gotten exposed to some gamma rays, because he just suddenly filled out and got those big legs that resulted in that patented Tom Seaver delivery and turned him into a human dynamo. He had so much intelligence and adapted to changing speeds so quickly that you just knew he couldn't miss. It was too bad he pitched with us for only one season. He got drafted to Cleveland, was stuck in a dispute over whether or not they had signed him illegally, and ended up being unable to play ball anywhere. He had to sit out a whole year. I felt sorry for him, but he ended up with the Mets and, by 1967, was the National League Rookie of the Year.

When I first saw Jim Barr, he had a shaven head and a four-day growth of beard on his face. You couldn't tell if his head was upside down or not. He looked like a twenty-eight-year-old Marine just down to play some pick-up with the college kids. I didn't know he was only a seventeen-year-old freshman. When he took the mound he looked like a fixture out there; it was as though he had been pitching for about one hundred years. Brent Strom, who was a year behind me, ended up breaking all my records at SC. With guys like this around I felt privileged to get a start once in a while. It became obvious to me that the environs of Southern California were conducive to good pitching. I think the reason is all the good Mexican food available down there. I believe in it as a staple for pitchers. It puts a fire in their bellies and protects their arms from harm. You never read about Pancho Villa having a sore wing.

By the middle of my first year on campus I had loosened up, become less of a loner. This made my academic life a little tough. All the drinking and carousing that was part of being one of the guys made it difficult for me to get oriented. But it would prove to be excellent training for the major leagues.

I had geography class at night, and all the football players would attend it. You could tell who they were; they were the guys in the back with the girls on their laps yelling and screaming. It was really very hairy. Our professor used to show us slides of California geography, and every twentieth slide or so he'd slip in a nude to make sure the guys were awake. I started hanging around some of them. Big mistake for a naïve kid from Marin County.

Mike Battle and Tim Rossovich were in that group. Battle was the guy who played on the Jets, hung out with Namath, and ate shot glasses to help him get up for a game. He used to challenge ski jumps with his motorcycle and would show up for scrimmages covered with cuts and scratches. Mike would get hurt more before practice than during it. Didn't care though; he seemed to enjoy pain.

Battle and Rossovich were the dynamic duo. Tim was worse than Mike. Stoned soul crazy. One afternoon he was with a girl who was a Kappa Kappa Gamma. They were upstairs in her bedroom in the sorority house when they heard the house mother coming up the steps. Tim jumped out the third-story window in his shorts and bare feet. Landed on the pavement like a cat, took off, and dashed through the parking lot to his frat house. Later that night we asked him if it was worth it. He said, "Not really. I had her Kappa Kappa off and was all set to grab her Gammas when we got busted."

On pledge night Tim and Mike headed an expedition to the Olympic Auditorium to watch the professional wrestling card. After two matches Tim started to complain that the whole thing was a fake. He got very emotional about it and started ripping out chairs from the ground. Then he ran up to the ring and creamed one of the wrestlers, knocking him on his butt. A free-for-all broke out. This was an excellent example of one of my reasons for not joining a fraternity. It didn't seem as if it would be conducive to my maximum potential for survival. I still went to all their parties, though, and I would usually wake up the next morning on a beer-sodden couch with a pledge pin stuck to my chest. Not my shirt, just my chest.

Rod didn't go in for this sort of behavior. His idea of a wild time was to have rookies on the team walk through a crowded airport terminal while wearing inside-out blazers and red fright-wigs. I got that treatment once, but I foxed him. Instead of walking through the terminal I jumped on a baggage chute, slid down to a side door, and had a taxi drive me to the team bus. Nobody saw me in that getup except the cabbie.

Aside from minor hazing, Rod was a stickler for discipline. But he was not omipresent. So when the team went down to San Diego to play in a tournament, it was not too difficult for several of the more enterprising members of the squad to slip across the border into the legendary oasis of sin and debauchery known as Tiajuana.

The first place we would head for was the Blue Ox Cafe, the sort of place where you walked around with your hand over your drink. This precaution was necessary unless you wanted to spend the evening straining pubic hairs out of your beverage. It was really wild in there. One girl would be taking on a donkey, while another girl would move about picking up the coins that grateful spectators had showered onto the stage. And she never once used her hands. Talk about dexterity—she would have made a great shortstop.

On one trip we almost lost a good part of the team. One of our infielders and I were coming out of the Ox one afternoon. We were fried. We were in the middle of a discussion on the finer points of the hook slide, when he decided to give me an on-the-spot demonstration. Racing up to the corner, he hurled himself into a perfect slide just as a cop was rounding the corner. My buddy took him out. The cop got up, brushed himself off, and arrested him before he had a chance to explain. I couldn't understand why; I thought it was a hell of a play. I spent the next several hours scrounging up bail for him and was able to gather more than enough. Good thing, too, because when I got down to the jailhouse I found that one of our pitchers had also been locked up. He had tried to engineer our teammate's release with words instead of money, and when he was rebuffed he protested the treatment of the prisoner by urinating in the police station parking lot. I got them both out, and I don't believe either of them has been back to Mexico since.

It was during this period that I first smoked marijuana. My first encounter with drugs had been with St. Joseph's aspirin when I was four years old. Up until my second year at SC I hadn't done anything much stronger than that. Marijuana was completely foreign to me; I had never even heard of the stuff in high school. It introduced itself to me one afternoon when I was sitting in a friend's apartment and some people came over to listen to records. Somebody lit up a joint, passed it to me, and said, "Here, smoke this." I gave it a hit and wasn't very impressed. I had worked part-time as a janitor for the telephone company during high school and had started smoking Camels on the job.

Woo! I used to have to sit down for twenty minutes after smoking one of them. That was the strongest stuff I ever inhaled. Marijuana never hammered me like a good Camel.

After a few more tokes I did have to revise my initial assessment. I began to feel displaced. Something was definitely happening to me. I just sat around and did a lot of thinking. I would watch what was going on around me and then my brain would start clicking into another dimension or time-warp. None of my senses were distorted, merely highlighted. It was as if everything was in 3-D, and I could visually grasp all three sides at once. Aside from that, I didn't get much of a buzz. It never incapacitated me or caused me to lose control.

I believe the thing about marijuana that causes a stoner for people is that the majority of the population is right-handed. This means they think with the left side of the brain. When they get high they become aware that they are using the wrong side of their gray matter, and this tends to disorient them. But lefthanders, such as yours truly, are used to using the right side of the brain. The correct side. The smoke puts us totally in sync with nature, and we have no trouble handling it. A writer once asked me if marijuana was the only drug I experimented with in college. I don't know what he meant. I never experimented with pot, I just took it. I didn't sit down, do a few hits, and say, "Well, now my pulse is accelerating and the red lines in my eyes are being caused by the dilation of the capillaries." I just passed around the pipe.

We did not use greenies—the code word for amphetamines—on our team. Rod ran a very tight ship. But some of us did use DMSO, an anti-inflammatory that is well-known now but was virtually unknown back in the sixties. It worked so well we wouldn't tell anybody about it, especially Rod, figuring it just had to be illegal. There were rumors back then that if you used it you could go blind or become sterile. Or both. But you could throw a two-hitter with it, despite a sore wing, so nobody cared about the risks. Our supply came from Canada, and we used it for muscle injuries. All you had to do was rub it over the affected area. After a while it would start itching like hell, and it gave you oyster breath. On a ninety-five-degree day you were not the most popular boy on campus. You'd walk into the cafeteria for dinner and four hundred people would make a mass exit. It was great stuff if you didn't mind dining alone. It got rid of the inflammation right away. Personally, I didn't have much cause to use it. I never threw hard enough to get hurt.

There wasn't any sense in burning myself out trying to impress people with speed I didn't have. I always saved something for the late innings. Strikeouts, from my perspective, are boring things. Nothing happens. They are fascist weapons. I prefer the groundball out and view it as the perfect symbol of democracy. It allows everybody a chance to get into the game, gives the crowds an opportunity to see some dazzling work in the infield, and has virtually the same effect as a strikeout. Only better. A groundball can be converted into a double play, my idea of the ultimate two-for-one sale. Groundouts also take less of a toll on the arm than strikeouts. It's a far, far better thing to get a batter out with one pitch instead of three. I'd never pay to see a big whiff artist like Nolan Ryan pitch. I'd much rather watch Larry Gura or Tommy John. Those guys are artists, like Catfish Hunter and Mike Cuellar were.

Cuellar was the closest thing I had to a pitching idol. He was the great lefthander who played on those championship Baltimore clubs in the late sixties and early seventies. They used to bring him out to the mound in a sanitation truck and drop him out of a Glad Bag, looking like an Apache Indian chief in a baseball uniform. He was amazing. Once the game started he would begin serving up his garbage: "Here's a grapefruit for strike one. Take a swing at this toilet seat." You ever try to hit an empty beer can for distance? That's what hitting his screwball was like. It was awesome. He'd win twenty games every year. Just when the batters figured they had his slow stuff timed, he'd rip a 90 mph fastball at them and it would finish them for the rest of the game. That's what I call pitching.

It's obvious that I've always had a bias for guys who could pitch with their heads. Dedeaux did, too. He taught me the geometric approach to pitching, pointing out that we had a spherical object and that there was this plate with corners. We had to be able to make the ball cross those corners at various heights and speeds in order to avoid having it intercepted by a round wooden object. He told us, "Throw strikes, Tiger. I hate walks."

During the '67—'68 season we looked unbeatable. We also horsed around more than ever. During an exhibition game against the Army in Hawaii we had to sit through a rain delay. It got tiresome, so to liven things up, Strom bet me five dollars that I wouldn't go out on the field and do ten pushups while wearing nothing but my jock-strap. Five bucks was two six-packs back then, so I grabbed that bet. Going out on the field practically naked in front of ten thousand people was no big thing. The hard part was doing the ten pushups. I had spindly arms, and it took a great deal of effort to lug my big ass off the ground. The real bitch of it was that I went out there almost balls-naked and nobody noticed. That didn't say very much for my body.

I don't know if Dedeaux ever got wind of it. If he did, he didn't say anything about it. I was going too good at the time. It was my senior year, and I think I ended up 14–4, with a low ERA. Everyone on the team was having a good year; we were tearing people up.

When we made it to the regional playoffs—the first step to the College World Series—I was in the bullpen. I guess I had done something to get into Rod's doghouse, but whatever it was, he didn't keep me there for long. Barr was supposed to start the opener of the first tier of the playoffs against Washington State. They were a tough team and Jim wanted to get at them, but he had hyperextended his elbow and couldn't pitch. Rod knew if he caged me up for any length of time that I would come roaring out, so he gave me the ball. I threw really well. Early on in the game this little bowlegged, gimpy guy got up to the plate, and I thought, Jesus, do they expect this guy to hit me? I threw him a slider inside. Boom! Double off the leftfield wall. It was Ron Cey. I watched him slide into second and thought to myself, Holy shit, imagine if this guy had two legs. I'd really be in trouble. He dragged his legs around the basepaths and eventually scored. We beat them anyway. After the game, we flew to Portland to play the University of Oregon. I started again and got the win as well as four hits, including a home run and a triple. Now we had to take two out of three from Cal State L.A.

We were very cocky for that series. Everyone figured, "Hey, Cal State, no problem. State school, small budget." They nearly kicked our butts. I beat them on a Friday night, which meant we only had to take one game of a Saturday doubleheader to win the set. They murdered us in the first game and were leading 4–1 in the ninth inning of the second game. Then they made a fatal mistake. They messed with the pride of the Houdini of Bovard. At the start of the ninth they had already started to pop open the champagne in their dugout. Dedeaux made a big show of pointing that out to us. He didn't have to say anything; the message was clear: Let's shove those bottles right up their asses. And that's exactly what we did.

I had been sitting in the dugout when Rod told me to get up and get loose. I had pitched nine the night before, so I didn't want to leave too much behind in the bullpen. I threw four pitches and came into the game. I got to the mound, threw three more warm-ups, and proceeded to get the side out in order, striking out two and getting the final out on a comebacker to the mound. Then, it was our turn.

The Cal starter got our first two batters. Chuck Ramshaw, our shortstop, was our last hope. He hit a line drive to right for a base hit. We followed that with a couple of walks, and then the dam burst: five straight hits, all with a two-strike count and all coming with two out. We scored four times to win the ballgame. Al Campanis, scouting for the Dodgers at the time, later said it was the greatest comeback rally he had ever seen. The Houdini of Bovard had struck again.

Dedeaux really got us geared up for the College World Series. He put a tight lid on all forms of fooling around and imported a couple of hard-throwing freshmen to pitch batting practice to the regulars. One of them was this tall, gangly kid from someplace in Oregon. We had put him on the team toward the end of the year and had used him in the outfield. He was awful. I had never seen such an uncoordinated fielder in my life, and he was so big there was no place we could hide him. He had a great arm, though, so Rod had him take the mound against us. The kid drilled all our righthanded hitters with a 100-mph sinking fastball in on their wrists. We're going for a championship, and this kid is nailing our best hitters! Dedeaux went out to the mound, collared him, and said, "I don't ever want to see you anywhere near the ballfield again. Ever!" The kid stalked off, really pissed. He stepped over to the batting cage, grabbed a bat, and hit a shot five hundred feet over the centerfield fence. Rod watched it go out, turned to the kid, and said, "Not so hasty, son. Come back here for a minute." The kid was Dave Kingman. He was incredible. He could throw hard, run like a deer, and was the strongest human being I had ever seen. Didn't have a clue what the game was about, though. He just wanted to hit the ball over the wall.

We won the Series that year with another patented Dedeaux miracle. It was getting monotonous. We played

Southern Illinois in the finals and were trailing 2–1 in the deciding game. With two men out in the ninth and two strikes on what could be our last batter of the season, we had the opposition right where we wanted them. The batter worked out a walk. The next batter beat out an infield roller for a single, and then our first baseman, Pat Kuehner, tripled both runners home. Game. We went nuts! Everyon was grabbing each other and jumping up and down That night we got two weeks of severe curfew out of our system.

We had decided to go to the nearest town and party all night long. On the way in, one of our players jumped out of the car as we stopped near a Texaco station and started to drink right out of the self-service pump High octane. I don't know why he did it. I guess there wasn't any beer left. Guzzling that stuff didn't have any effect on him at all for the first few hours. We got to town and hit a few places. Around midnight he finally passed out on a table. One of the girls who had joined us looked at him and said, "Boy, is that guy ripped." I said, "No. He just ran out of gas."

We got a hero's welcome when we came back home. I thought this was it for me. Even though I had gone 28–8 the last two years and had pitched well in the Series, I still didn't view myself as a possible major-leaguer. Al Campanis had already given me his assessment. I saw him at a party and he said, "Lee, you'll never pitch a day in the majors. You don't have an overhand fastball like Koufax, you don't have an overhand curveball like Koufax, and..." I finished it by saying, "...and I'm not Jewish. So I guess that's three strikes." I think Al had passed by the punch bowl a few times too many that night. He seemed so intent on shooting me down. Meanwhile, in another part of the room, Tommy Lasorda was busy telling my father that he was certain I was going to be a major-league pitcher. That picked me up. Of course, now I realize that Tommy tells that to every father, even those who don't have sons.

Neither of those two unofficial scouting reports meant much to me. I wasn't even too impressed when I got the word that I had been picked by the Boston Red Sox in the secondary phase of the free-agent draft on the day after the College World Series ended. They picked me in the twenty-second round, so you can forgive me if I didn't get too excited. All I did was think a little bit more about becoming a forest ranger. After all, when you get right down to it, there were about three hundred guys chosen ahead of me. That can make a man think.

Boston sent a scout, Joe Stephenson, to sign me. He had a son, a pitcher with the Red Sox, who was a punk rocker before his time. He dyed his hair green, a color that eventually clashed with the pink slip the Sox ended up giving him. Joe wanted to meet me in Los Angeles to discuss a contract. I said sure. My father warned me not to go and not to sign anything. That was a mistake. The best way to get me to do something is to tell me not to do it. I had no time to follow Dad's advice; I was in a hurry. Not in a hurry to play ball, just in a hurry. I think I've always been in a hurry, but never really knew what for. That's the story of my life.

When I got to see Joe, he gave me the big smile and the quick handshake and acted like the Red Sox were doing me a big favor. He draped his arm around my shoulder and said, "Hey, you're really too old for a rookie minor-leaguer. You spent too much time in college and we really shouldn't sign you. But, you look like a pretty fair pitcher, so we thought we'd give you a break."

I was a has-been at twenty-one, and Boston was going to sign me out of pity. He finished by saying, "By the way, we also can't give you any money. As it stands right now all the bonus money is gone." I asked, "Can't you at least pay for my continued education?" He thought about that for a minute, smiled and said, "I guess we could come up with about four thousand for that." I grabbed it. After the assessment he had just made of me I wanted to dash out and invest it in a life-insurance policy, because it was obvious I didn't have very much time left on this planet.

When I got back home my father didn't seem upset that I had signed a minor-league contract. I think he was just proud to have me in the Red Sox organization. The next day I packed my bags and got ready to leave for the club's minor-league affiliate in Waterloo, Iowa. Class-A ball. My father drove me to the airport and wished me luck, giving me a hug and some more good advice. "Son," he said, "you're joining the Boston Red Sox, a fine organization. Now if you can pitch like we both know you can and you can keep your mouth shut, you'll end up being with them for a long time."

![2]

I wasn't nervous when my plane took off for Waterloo. Being a geography major, it seemed like an excellent opportunity to study the climate and terrain of Iowa. The fact that I was going to get paid to play professional baseball was just an added inducement. I thought it would be a nice way to spend the summer. I was a little put off at first when Stephenson handed me my plane ticket. Ozark Airways. It sounded as if Wilbur and Orville would be taking turns at the throttle, and the passengers would be lying six across on each wing. I still hadn't made a firm commitment to pursuing a career in baseball. I just wanted to compete for that summer—it didn't matter where, just as long as the competition was challenging. More than anything I was anxious to see what the Midwest looked like. God, was it flat!

One of the team executives met me at the airport, greeting me with a speech about how happy the club was to have me and how they were certain I was a major-league prospect. There wasn't much conviction behind these words. His eyes were glazed over, and he sounded as if he was reading from a cue card. I couldn't blame him. He had probably given the same spiel to twenty-one other kids in the last two weeks and had just finally winked out.

We drove straight to the ballpark, where I met my first professional manager, the immortal Rachel Slider. Nobody called him Rachel; it was not considered a name that inspired manly fear or confidence. He was called Rac (as in lack). Rac Slider. It sounded like the name of a comic-book hero. "The Adventures of Rac Slider and his Wonder Dog, Frito." When I arrived at the stadium Rac was on the field, hitting double-play grounders to his second-and-short combination. The poor sons of bitches had messed up a play during a game that afternoon. Slider was up to what seemed to be his three hundredth grounder, and the infielders looked as if they had taken root. Their legs had died long before they finally broke for dinner. Later they had to come back and play the second half of a day-night doubleheader, and Rac couldn't fathom why their range was severely curtailed in the nightcap.

I knew immediately that I was not dealing with another Dedeaux here. After the workout I was brought into Rac's office and introduced as his new lefthanded starter. He looked me over from top to bottom, his eyes settling on my feet. For a moment it appeared as if he was trying to decide which shoe he was going to splatter with tobacco juice. Finally he looked up at me, fixed me with a vacant gaze, and said, "We'll see." Every now and again, in times of darkest crisis, I still recall those stirring words of inspiration: "We'll see."

While dressing for that evening's game, I met my new teammates and found that, despite the manager's frigid reception, the club was excited about getting me. Well, not me, specifically. They were just excited about getting a lefthanded pitcher. Any lefthanded pitcher. The only other one they had was Roger Moret, a young skinny kid from Puerto Rico who could throw the ball hard. He and I were supposed to be the lefthanded pitching strength of the club.

Roger had a tough time of it in the minors. He was very superstitious, having been raised in an area of Puerto Rico that dictated he be brought up with a heavy Catholic background tinged with a smattering of mysticism. That was his double-edged sword. Moret carried every religious icon possible, plus a lot of good-luck charms. Everybody thought that was strange, but I believed it showed good sense. None of us is certain of what awaits us in the next life; Roger was just covering all the bases. His teammates gave him a hard time about it. It's doubtful he would have lasted very long in the States if it hadn't been for a local widow who took him under her wing. She had three kids of her own, and she let Roger stay in her house, teaching him English and how to dress. That was a big help. People were always poking fun at his inability to communicate in anything but his native tongue. At times we would go out to eat together. He would order two eggs, and when asked how he wanted them done, he would say, "Over large." On another occasion, after being asked what he would like, he opened the menu and pointed to the bottom, where it read, "Thank You For Allowing Us To Serve You."

My first professional appearance came a few days after joining the club. Coming on in relief, I gave up an unearned run that tied up a game we eventually lost. Rac was all over me for that. He was very intense. Any time a player made a mistake he would jump on him and then have him come out to the park and work on it. Rac didn't like me, having pegged me as a smart-ass college boy. He had figured that out before he laid eyes on me, hence the cool reception. The fact that I was not averse to expressing my opinion also did not sit well with him. I told him he was crazy for working his players to death and then expecting them to have something left for the game. After a week he wrote a report telling the Sox I was a fat, out-of-shape hot dog, and that I couldn't get anything on my pitches. I had just thrown twenty-seven innings in a six-day period during the College World Series. All I needed was a little rest. Rac was quick to oblige.

He didn't let me pitch at all, not an inning. Then, as the schedule tightened up, he was forced to pitch me on and off in relief. I never started. Still, I liked playing in Waterloo. The local diner gave us credit, and if you hit a home run, you got a free steak dinner. As I recall, it was a good little diner, although when you're young the quality of food is relatively unimportant. You have the Frankenstein attitude toward nourishment. All food is good; only lack of food is bad.

Waterloo did not offer much in the way of entertainment, however. There was a theater in town that showed a new feature every leap year, and there was always the local tavern. We did spend a lot of time watching meter maids give out summonses. This was a slow town. There were groupies there, but most of them were interested only in the big-bonus boys with the brand-new Mustangs. I traveled on foot, so I didn't fare too well. That didn't surprise me. Cars made big impressions on young girls in the sixties. I had gone out with a beautiful lady at USC. She was my steady for about three weeks, which was about all the time a classmate, Alan Ladd, Jr., and his Ferrari needed to snake her away from me. From that time on I've hated all forms of elitism. I wouldn't knock myself out to get a set of wheels just so I could score. It said a lot about my principles, but it didn't do much for my sex life. Occasionally we would meet a girl wanting to do the whole bullpen, but I didn't go in for that. I was too much of a loner.

We did try to liven things up. The team had a standing bet that revolved around a contest. All you had to do was drink a gallon of milk in one half-hour sitting. If you kept it down you won a hundred dollars. No one could do it. A player would guzzle almost to the bottom of the carton and then suddenly race from the room while doing some heavy projectile vomiting. It was like something out of *The Exorcist*, and it never failed to break the boys up. Great waves of white would come flowing out of a guy's mouth.

Watching our centerfielder, Charlie Day, throw up white was one of the most exciting things that ever happened down there. It was great seeing his belly get distended, like Paul Newman's did in *Cool Hand Luke*. Even greater fun was to have some guy's stomach bloat up like that and then have someone cannonball off the top bunk onto his belly. Like Old Faithful, it was one of life's unforgettable experiences.

Carlton Fisk and I shared an apartment in town with a couple of outfielders from Massachusetts. Fisk was always late, the last one to get to the ballpark, the last one to leave. Very methodical. He was also slow at putting down signs. I used to think, Jesus, what's taking him so long? I've only got two pitches. I had my revenge later on, when we were both on the Red Sox. During one game I shook him off six consecutive times. He came out to the mound and yelled, "How the hell can you shake me off six times! I've only got five fingers!" My point exactly.

Carlton still catches the longest games in the majors. That's because he takes things in stride and likes to consider all options. He'll live to be a hundred and five, there's no doubt about it. Fisk comes from hardy stock and never gets frazzled. Funny thing, in the minors he was a fine receiver right away, but he didn't look like much of a hitter and he didn't have much power. He had a great arm, though, and despite being sluggish off the field, he was very fast on the bases. When the club signed him he really wasn't a catcher by trade, but he sure learned in a hurry. That Waterloo club wasn't too shabby. It had Fisk, Moret, Nagy, McGlothen, and me. We would all be up in the majors within four years. Our best player, though, was Charlie Day. He never spent a day in the big leagues, but he could hold down more milk than the rest of us.

After I went a month without a start, Neil Mahoney, one of the big honchos of the Boston minor-league operation, came down. When he asked why I wasn't pitching, Slider reiterated his assertion that I wasn't in shape and didn't have a good fastball. Mahoney didn't buy it. The next day, I started against the Yankees' minor-league affiliate. My frankness in dealing with the manager made this a pressure ballgame. It was one of the few times I can recall being nervous before taking the mound. If I screwed up in this game, it would be *sayonara*, smart-ass. Matters weren't helped any when I gave up a single to the first batter I faced. I could see Slider sitting on the bench, a big grin on his face, with visions of my butt being shipped to the local *gulag* dancing through his head. I could also see that the baserunner was taking a long lead off first. Too long. I picked him off and then retired the next twenty-six hitters in a row. After pitching this one-hitter, a coach came up to me and said, "Abner Doubleday must have been watching over you today." He knew what had been at stake.

As it turned out, Slider was able to get rid of me anyway, but not by choice. Twenty-four hours after pitching that game, I was on a plane heading for Winston-Salem in the Carolina League. It was a promotion. The Carolina League was still Class-A ball, but it was on a slightly higher level than the league I had just left.

After arriving at the team's boardinghouse on a beautiful Sunday morning, I headed to the ballpark for an afternoon game. The first member of the club to greet me was the trainer, Pio Di Salvo. He was the brother of the Boston Strangler. I discovered that when he came over to me and introduced himself, saying, "Hi. I'm Pio Di Salvo and my brother was the Boston Strangler." I didn't know what he meant at first; I thought his brother was a professional wrestler. When I found out who his brother actually was, I thought, Holy Jesus, where have the Red Sox sent me? Turned out I had nothing to worry about. Pio was one of the nicest guys I ever met in baseball, a very hard worker. That introduction was just his way of getting any questions about his infamous relative out of the way. It certainly did that.

Bill Slack was my new manager. That was a blessing. He had been a pitcher and really understood my needs. The day after my arrival, I started and got jocked. He took me aside and said, "Don't worry, you had good stuff. You'll get them next time." That gave me confidence. Bill left me alone, and I pitched well for him. I was still basically the same type of pitcher I had been in college, but I was getting more strikeouts. I had a pretty good breaking ball, and the kids in Class-A ball didn't get to see many curves. I split six decisions that year and had an ERA of 1.72.

When the season ended I went back to school to complete my education. While there I took an aptitude test. It recommended I become an undertaker. With that in mind, it wasn't very hard for me to continue playing ball for a while. I also decided to get married.

During the summers of 1966 and 1967, I had played ball in an amateur league in Alaska. It was there that I met Mary Lou. I married her the moment I set eyes on her. She was tall and blonde, a former Miss Alaska with a sensitive soul, a good sense of humor, and tons of brains. She also had great legs. Adding all this up, I knew she was for me. My friends were surprised when we got married, figuring I wasn't the marrying type. That didn't faze me; I knew it was the right move. I had a temperament that dealt only in extremes, while Mary Lou had the level-headedness that balanced me out. We were Yin and Yang.

We went to spring training together in 1969, a first for both of us. We lived in a duplex in Ocala that was a small slice of heaven. Outside our door was the river that fed Silver Springs. Mary Lou and I would go to the river's edge and fish for bass. When we finished, we would head over to the Ocala Inn for an evening of Lowenbrau. It was during this time that I first discovered that Mary Lou couldn't cook. I didn't care. It was our honeymoon; I wasn't into cooking.

The Red Sox had listed me on their Double-A roster. I thought I was doing well, but midway through camp they put me back on the Winston-Salem team. I was pissed, but before I had a chance to sound off, one of the coaches grabbed me and told me to keep cool, that it was only a temporary condition. Apparently the front office just had to do some roster juggling, and I was odd man out for the moment. Turned out to be a worthwhile move for me, because without it I might have missed out on a chance to start a game against Bill Faul.

Faul was a curveballing righthander who had been up to the big leagues with the Tigers and Cubs and had become something of a living legend. This status had nothing to do with his pitching. Faul was a guy who used to prepare for games by ripping off the heads of live parakeets. With his teeth. Then he would put himself in a trance and go out to throw a shutout. When he wasn't decapitating birds he was swallowing live toads, claiming they put an extra hop on his fastball. None of these tricks bothered anybody, and after a few performances their novelty wore off. What did upset some people and helped gain Faul undying notoriety was his habit of grabbing someone's attention by picking him up at the ankles and holding him upside down. From outside the fourth-story window of his hotel room. Up to this point in my career, Bill was the craziest guy I had ever met or heard of. With the possible exception of the Marquis de Sade, there was nobody else in his league.

Faul and I matched up well against each other, but I was able to beat his team, 2–1. Four days later the Red Sox gave me a start against the University of Florida. I won that game, too, and my timing couldn't have been better. Those two wins came right before camp ended, and they must have convinced someone in the front office to take me off that Winston-Salem roster. I departed Florida as a member of the Pittsfield club. This was an important step up. Though Pittsfield was only Double-A, it was located in

Massachusetts, not far from Boston. Whenever the Sox had an injury they generally brought players up from there instead of their Triple-A club in Louisville. We had a good group of guys in Pittsfield. Billy Gardner was the manager, Fisk caught, and Ivy Washington kept us laughing.

Ivy was a big righthander with a good fastball and a back-breaking hook. He could bury a batter with curveballs. I could never figure out why he didn't make it to the majors. Whatever he lacked, it wasn't a sense of humor. Ivy was equipped with the world's greatest vocabulary. One day he sat at his locker, moaning, "This club is going nowhere. It can't win. The trouble with this club is there's too much *decision* on it." The consensus was that he meant "dissension." Another time he ambled up to me and said, "You know, Bill, you and I are both pitchers, but we're not the same. I get them out with smoke, while you finance them." I'm not sure if he meant "finesse them" or if he actually believed I was paying hitters off to miss the shit I was throwing up there. My pride allowed me to settle on the former.

Ivy could be particularly devastating on the back of the bus. Minor-league life revolves around long boring bus rides with baseball games played in between. In order to quell the monotony of an endless trip, we would take part in an initial quiz. One guy called out a set of celebrity initials and everyone else would try to guess who the person was. When it was Ivy's turn, he stumped everyone for the duration of the trip. His entry was B.D.K. No one could get it. We spent the better part of an hour on it. Finally, as the bus pulled into the parking lot, Ivy said, "C'mon, that one's easy. It's Billy De Kid." I'm still not sure which was funnier, that answer or the fact that at least three guys walked off the bus shaking their heads, saying, "I knew that was it," over and over again.

I pitched well at Pittsfield. Two games stand out in particular. The first was a game against Salem that almost got me killed. I had come on in relief, runners on first and third, with Salem's big home-run hitter at the plate. I threw him the sinker and he hit a combacker up the middle. Catching it behind my back, I turned and threw a perfect strike to start a game-ending double play. I didn't catch the ball in back of me to show anyone up; the way I follow through with my delivery made it impossible to catch it any other way. Don Hoak, the Salem manager, didn't see it that way. He was all over me, yelling and screaming at me from the clubhouse to the team bus. If he had a gun, so help me, he would have shot me. He yelled, "Lee, you fucking lucky son of a bitch, you can't get away with that shit. You can't make a play like that to beat us." I looked at him and said something bright like, "Well, I just did." He dived off the deep end trying to get at me. He started punching at the bus window and kept pounding and screaming until we pulled out. I just stayed in my seat, shaking my head and saying, "Now, now, Tiger, it's only a game." A few years later Hoak died of a heart attack. Boy, you could see that coming.

The other game I remember featured a magic moment. We were playing against Manchester. I wasn't pitching that day, but the manager called on me to pinch-hit in the last inning. I represented the winning run. The pitcher threw me two breaking pitches high and outside that I took for balls, and then came in with a fastball down the chute. I cold-cocked it, hitting a long fly toward the center fence. *Adios, amigo.* As I rounded first and got ready to go into my game-winning home-run trot, I looked up just in time to see the center-fielder jump up and fling himself over the fence to make a great catch. Unbelievable. I started screaming like a madman, feeling pain, joy, denial, and excitement all at once. And then I became two people. While half of me went through all those emotional transitions, the other half stepped back and watched, thinking, God, isn't this fun. Everything that baseball is was wrapped up in those precious seconds.

That near homer took on added significance, since it came in what turned out to be my last appearance in a Pittsfield uniform. The next day, June 24, 1969, I was called up by the Red Sox. Jim Lonborg had gotten hurt, busting up his toe badly while attempting to lay down a bunt. That's one of the hazards of being tall; it's a long way from your eyes to your feet, and you can't always watch out for them. I'd had a feeling something was up. The night before our manager had told me that I wasn't going on our next road trip. Explaining that we were going to be gone for only three days and that I wasn't scheduled to start anyway, he suggested that I might as well stay home. He had this big smile on his face all the while he was telling me this. I went home to my ski chalet in South Hancock and found a message to call the Boston front office. When I did, one of the brass got on and said, "Bill, Lonnie's hurt and Bill Landis and Sparky Lyle are on Army duty. We'd like you to come up and give us a hand."

I liked that. They made it sound as if I had a choice. Actually, I wasn't too anxious to leave. I was throwing well, and we had a great ballpark. The sun set behind the centerfield fence on a low angle, and if you kept the ball down, as I always tried to, no one could hit you. But on the other hand, I had never seen Boston or Fenway Park, and I was always interested in broadening my horizons. I told him I'd be happy to do whatever I could to help the club. The last thing he told me before hanging up was that I shouldn't pack a heavy bag, because I wasn't going to be up for too long. Nine years and 102 days later, I was gone.

Driving down the turnpike into Boston, I caught my first glimpse of the lights of Fenway and of its notorious leftfield wall, the Green Monster. The stadium was so close to the highway you could almost touch it as you rode by. A sign warned me that the next exit was about two hundred fifty yards ahead to the right. I figured, Great. All I have to do is get off here and cut back to the ballpark. No problem. It took me two and a half hours. In my entire life I had never seen streets like they have in Boston. They call the city "The Hub" because it's laid out like a wheel, with spokes. The problem is none of those spokes lead anywhere. It was nuts. I drove around, all the time able to see the stadium lights but unable to find a way to reach them. This did not seem like a good omen. The thought occurred to me that I might have crashed, died, and gone to hell without realizing it. I was condemned to drive an eternal highway that would only bring me past the ballpark without ever letting me enter its gates. I kept looking in the rearview mirror, expecting to find out I had just crossed over into the Twilight Zone. Just as I was about to panic I got hold of myself and adapted. Deciding that this was a foreign environment and that the only way to conquer it was to submit to it, I humbled myself in surrender to the Boston topography and became caught in its spiritual flow. I also stopped and asked for directions.

I got to the park in between games of a doubleheader with the Cleveland Indians. I had just enough time to get into uniform, introduce myself to manager Dick Williams, and run out to the bullpen before the start of the second game. I got to pitch right away, throwing four innings and giving up only one run. It wasn't easy. I walked the first two guys I faced, and a single thought immediately flashed through my mind: I am fucking this up. After putting runners on first and second, I had to face Hawk Harrelson. Hawk had been a big hero in Boston only the year before, leading the league in runs batted in and named American League Player of the Year by *The Sporting News*. He had been dealt to Cleveland at the start of the season in an unpopular trade, and the fans were going crazy when he came up to the plate. I got him in the hole right away with two strikes, and then I threw him a sinker. Hawk hit a two-hopper to third, and George Scott made a great stab in the hole, throwing to second to start a 5–4–3 double play. Max Alvis struck out to end the inning. It was really fun. The Indians had some hitters on that team—Harrelson, Tony Horton, and Jose Cardenal—but I wasn't interested in who they were or what they were hitting. They were just meat to me. Tom Satriano, a Dedeaux disciple from SC, was my catcher, and I just threw whatever he called for. I hadn't had time to go over batters with him or anything like that. I had just finished meeting everybody in the bullpen, when the coach turned to me and said, "Kid, you're in there." Williams was like that. He'd get somebody and then he'd use him right away so he could find out what they were made of.

Dick was a lame-duck manager at the time, though few people knew it. Yastrzemski hadn't run out a groundball, and Dick fined him something like a thousand bucks. Carl didn't like getting drop-kicked in the wallet, and the Red Sox owner, Mr. Yawkey, didn't like having his favorite player shown up. The incident polarized the club. It became the Williams cartel against the Yaz and Yawkey cartel. Yaz was the highest-paid superstar in the game, and Yawkey signed the checks. Williams was just the manager, and before the season was over he was history. The press made a big deal out of it—Dick was good copy and popular with the writers—and for two years the fans were so incensed that they booed Carl religiously. I came up after their run-in, so I had no idea who was right. But I do know that Carl and Mr. Yawkey were very close. Yawkey was often seen with him, picking his brain in order to find out what the club needed. I have to believe Yaz exerted some influence.

Most of the players weren't crazy about Dick. If a player

made an error, Williams would conduct his postgame interview right near the guy's locker and point out how horseshit he was. While the press gathered around, he'd stand there and look at the player and say, "Yeah, we had a pretty good little game going until Andrews fucked up that groundball." Not too many players appreciated that. Dick hated losing. I guess we all do, but Williams was a little more vocal about it than most. He had an acid sense of humor, quite funny actually, but it rubbed a lot of guys the wrong way. I think it affected Carl to the point where he couldn't play hard for Dick.

Darrell Johnson was our pitching coach. He didn't say much to me. What pitching advice I did get came from my peers. Lee Stange or Ray Culp would discuss certain situations with me or the tendencies of certain hitters, what they liked to swing at on a particular count. The best piece of advice I got was given to me by Ron Kline. Ron had been in the majors for seventeen years and had led the league in saves in 1965. But now that he was at the end of the road, I used to sit next to him in the bullpen, hoping to grab any bits of information he would occasionally drop. One afternoon he educated me on the various grips he employed, showing me how he held his fastball, his curve, and even his spitter. When he reached the end of the lesson, he cautioned me to pay strict attention because he was about to reveal the most important grip of all. Holding out two fingers and a thumb semicircled in front of his lips, he proudly announced, "This is how I hold my shot glass."

I actually surprised a lot of people on the club. When they got me they had heard I was a control pitcher. So I finished the season 1–3, with twenty-eight walks in fifty-two innings pitched. My only win came in relief against Detroit on September 20. I was really horseshit, but I did manage to get forty-five strikeouts. I was throwing a lot of fastballs. Dick was using me in short relief, and I never had enough time to work my breaking stuff in. I was getting so pumped up for the brief time I was in there that I was throwing the ball by hitters whenever they weren't walking or kicking my ass. By the time I had calmed down enough to throw my proper stuff, I was pinch-hit for. I must have been very nervous, though I wasn't aware of any preconceived anxiety over being in the major leagues. When Boston signed me the only thing I worried about was doing well in the minors. There was never any thought given to the majors; I took each day as it came. When I suddenly got called up to the Red Sox, I found myself psychologically unprepared for the jump. So I threw too hard. Ted Williams has said that pitchers are the dumbest people on earth, and I guess he has something there. Nobody had to tell me that my strength was hitting the corners and keeping the ball low. But there were days when the adrenaline would be racing and the ball would say, "Come on, Bill, throw me through that wall," causing me to rear back and do my Sandy Koufax impersonation. It would work for about two batters. I'd blow both guys away, walk the next batter, and then give up a satellite to a .220 hitter. That would drive Williams and Johnson nuts. Once Johnson came out to me and said, "How can you keep throwing those fastballs when they keep getting creamed?" I told him I was stretching out my arm. He reached down, grabbed his nuts, and said, "Oh, really? Try stretching this!" He was right. I had no business going away from my strength, especially when it caused me to play right into the hands of my weakness.

A lefthander's first good look at the leftfield wall, the Green Monster in Fenway, is an automatic reason for massive depression. And that's when it's viewed from the dugout. From the vantage point of the mound it looms even closer. I felt like I was scraping my knuckles against it every time I went into my motion, and I was always afraid that it would fall down and kill Rico Petrocelli at short. That wall psyched out a lot of good pitchers. Great control pitchers would come into Fenway and suddenly not have it that day. They'd pitch too fine, walk a few guys, and then be forced to stand back to watch the rocket's red glare. It could be demoralizing. Everybody talks about the advantage righthanded pull hitters like Petrocelli gained there, but lefthanded hitters do almost as well. Ted Williams, Yaz, and Freddy Lynn won batting titles playing there, and they swing from the left side. It's just not a park built with the welfare of pitchers in mind.

The key to pitching at Fenway, whether you are right-handed or lefthanded but especially if you're a lefty, is to keep the ball outside and away on righthanders and down and in on lefthanders. Make that ball sink to lefthanders. Your lefty hitter is going to try to shoot your pitch the other way so he can jack it against or over the wall. If he can't get the ball up he's going to hit a two-hopper to the second baseman. You can make the temptation of the wall work for you. The Monster giveth, but the Monster can also taketh away. You just have to know what to feed it. I had some success with it. When I started winning big for the Sox, the writers compared me to Mel Parnell, the lefty who pitched for Boston in the forties and fifties. I checked up on him and discovered that Parnell had a smashed middle finger that caused him to throw the ball off his index finger, making his pitches sink. That was interesting. I was always having the callouses shaved off my index finger. Obviously, we both threw off the same digit and were able to keep the ball on the ground, enabling us to win a lot of games in Boston. I also found one legend about the Monster that should be exposed as a lie. The markings claim it is 315 feet from home plate at its nearest point. Not by my measurements. I once threw a screwball to Luis Aparicio while he was still with the Chicago White Sox. He dented the wall with it. Without the benefit of a tape measure, my ego will not permit me to believe that there is any way Luis could hit my screwie 315 feet on a line. Somebody is lying.

It did not take long to get used to life in the majors. I was never overawed by ballplayers, and everybody on the club treated each other as equals. Yaz was the biggest name on the team, but he was one of the first to introduce himself to me. He really tried to make me feel at home. The guys on the club would good-naturedly get on his case in a heartbeat. Everytime the team bus passed a junkyard, someone would yell, "There's Yaz's Ford on the left." They were constantly making fun of his clothes. He had this mock London Fog raincoat that cost him about ten dollars. We spent hours trying to hatch new plots to steal it and put it out of its misery. Someone would confiscate it and stick it in a garbage can. You really couldn't tell it apart from the rest of the stuff in there, but Yaz would always find it. He'd go digging through the trash, haul it out, smooth out the wrinkles, and put it back on. I think we finally had papers served on it. We had it deported as an illegal alien.

The big chuckle when I first joined the team came over Big Yaz Bread. I'm not crazy about ballplayers doing commercial endorsements, but if you're going to do them, you had better be well paid, because your teammates will give you nothing but grief for it. And then try to get a free sample. Free or not, I wasn't going near that bread. It looked like there should have been a surgeon general's label on the side of it, warning, "This bread contains no vitamins known to man." I believe you could take a whole loaf, grind it up, and then use it to make one good golf ball. It would explode in your stomach and force your throat to expand like an accordion. I'm not sure, but I think it might have been Phil Gagliano who delivered the best line I ever heard about the stuff. Phil bit into a slice, spit it out, made a face, and said, "We should feed this to the Orioles. Then we'd win the fucking pennant!" That was the sort of line that was guaranteed to break up everyone. Especially George Scott.

Scott was great. He loved to laugh and play baseball and he *loved* to hit those long taters. Everybody knows what a great first baseman he was, but he was also the best third baseman I'd ever seen. He played a lot of third the year I joined the club, and he was awesome. The only reason he wasn't used there regularly was because he was an even better first baseman. George deserved every Gold Glove he ever won. Once Bert Campaneris, while he was still a short-stop with Oakland, bunted the ball on me down the first-base line. He pushed it, but he didn't quite get it past me. I came in and made the play in one motion, but I got off a bad throw, skipping the ball through Campy's legs. George went inside the bag on the foul side of the line and picked the ball cleanly from between Campy's legs for an out. That was remarkable.

The Red Sox were blessed with a lot of power when I came up. Yaz hit over forty homers that year, Reggie Smith hit twenty-five, and Tony Conigliaro hit twenty. That was the year of Tony's comeback. He had been beaned by Jack Hamilton two years earlier, an accident that nearly blinded him. He hit the ball well for us that year, but there was always something crazy happening to him. The weirdest episode occurred when he hit a home run against Seattle and wrenched a back muscle while doing it. By the time he reached second base he was in such agony that he had to be replaced by a pinch runner, who finished the trot home for him. I had never seen that happen before.

Tony's brother Billy came up in '69. He was a good ball-player who did everything well and made good contact at the plate. But everybody expected him to be another Tony C, and he wasn't big enough. He didn't have Tony's power. I think living in his brother's shadow hurt him. He would have been much better off if he had come up in a different organization.

The spirit of our club was Petrocelli at short. He was a fire-eater. Rico was in his last seasons as a shortstop, even though he would hit forty home runs that year. The club had already started experimenting with him at third. It seemed everybody in the infield, except Scott, was losing their range at the same time. Mike Andrews was at second and he was another good hitter with power, but by 1970 he couldn't move two steps to his right or left. It was as if he was nailed down to the bag at second. He and Rico were both scrappers. Petrocelli had a temper. He was very quick to drop his gloves, and he knew how to box. Whenever a brawl broke out on the field, most players pushed and pulled and did their best to keep from getting hurt. Not our Rico. He'd be out throwing left jabs and overhand rights with no concern for life or limb. Petrocelli could be in the whirlpool when a fight started and he'd just jump up, wrap a towel around his middle, run out, and get a piece of somebody. He just loved to mix it up, especially against the Yankees. Rico had been involved in at least one memorable on-field brawl with them before I joined the club. Some of the guys on our team told me that it was something to watch. It seemed as if every time Rico threw a punch, a pinstriped body would hit the ground.

Looking at our roster, people would shake their heads and wonder why we didn't walk away with the pennant. The Red Sox had a lot of big names, and they were a liberal organization when it came to salaries, especially after they won the pennant in 1967. Mr. Yawkey was so happy he was giving the money away in wheelbarrows.

Players told me a story about Gary Bell. After winning thirteen games in '67, Gary went to Dick O'Connell, the team's general manager, to talk contract. While waiting outside Dick's office, Gary had a lot of time to ponder what kind of money he would ask for. He reached a figure he could live with, then went in and asked O'Connell for an amount fifteen thousand dollars higher than that. Dick didn't bat an eyelash. He just turned to his secretary and said, "Mary, type up another one."

It was that easy. That sort of thing gave rise to the portrayal of the Red Sox as a country club, a label that was supposed to explain why we didn't win the pennant despite all the talent we had. We were too pampered by management. I view that as a misreading. Mr. Yawkey was a compassionate man who cared about his players more than he cared about winning. He didn't mind winning; he just never crucified you if you lost. But the high payroll and his treatment of players didn't curtail anyone's hunger for a pennant. Our problem wasn't attitude. It was a lack of pitching, speed, and a deep bench. People would look at our starting eight and say, "Jesus, these guys should win the division by ten games." They didn't realize that it takes more than eight players hitting twenty home runs each to make a winner. Baltimore didn't win because of their hitting. It was their pitching and defense that made them a great club. Their hitting merely combined with their other assets to make them unreal. In 1969 we finished in third place, twenty-two games behind them, yet we had a good ballclub. The problem was that Baltimore was better.

No matter where we finished, for whatever reason, the Red Sox fans were incredible. They always turned out to support us. Sox fans are a special breed, living in a state of constant denial. Even when the team's going good, they can't allow themselves to be lulled into a false sense of security. They keep waiting for the other shoe to drop, knowing that it usually lands on their heads. New York fans let it all hang out, never worrying about tomorrow because they know tomorrow may never come. In direct contrast, Boston fans figure no, let's worry about tomorrow because the odds are it probably will get here, and when it does, it's going to rain. They realize that death is lurking in the background of every celebration. It can't be avoided. Their city is filled with famous old cemeteries. Every corner you turn, there's John Adams or John Hancock. And they're all dead.

I became acutely aware of the difference between the majors and the minors in that first season with Boston. Some of the contrasts were obvious. The accommodations up here were all first class, the pay was better, and the media attention was intensified one hundredfold. The minute you put on a uniform you were a celebrity. But the biggest difference was the women. They were everywhere, and they would come at us in swarms. Guys in the bullpen did particularly well when we hit Comiskey Park in Chicago. The visiting bullpen was right near the bleachers, and any knowledgeable female could gain access to it through the ground crew's entrance. A woman could come in through the back, go underneath the stands, and trip the light fantastic with one or more of her heroes. The best part about this was that if a player worked out his positioning properly, he could get it on and still watch the ballgame, elevating his enjoyment of the National Pastime to heights never before imagined. The first time I sat out there and checked out this sexual circus, I thought, Now I know why everyone is so hot to get up to the big leagues. I also realized what Dick Williams meant when he admonished us to keep our heads in the ballgame while we were out there.

Dick got fired before the season was over, and Eddie Popowski, our third-base coach, took over the job on an interim basis. He gave me my first major-league start during our final season series in Washington. He left a note in my hotel room one afternoon, informing me that I was starting. Unfortunately, that was the day I had picked to walk up and down the Washington Monument, followed by an on-foot tour of the Capitol. I came back to my room exhausted and found his message. I went out that night and was okay for six innings. Then the roof fell in. Mike Epstein hit a moon shot off me—I got whiplash watching it fly out—and Del Unser crashed a triple with the bases loaded. Even a couple of bat boys got up and hit ropes. By the time Popowski came out to get me, I was speaking in tongues, a victim of shell shock. Turning philosophical after the game, I figured things could never get any worse than that. Wrong again. Four days later I received a notice from the draft board, notifying me that my student deferment had gone down the tubes. I had been reclassified 1-A.

After I notified the Red Sox of my change in classification, they immediately got in touch with an Army Reserve office in Boston. The team had a lot of pull. The day after I took my physical at a base in Oakland, I caught a plane to Boston and enlisted in a reserve unit. When I got back to California, a letter was waiting for me advising me of the date for my formal induction. I went down to the Selective Service office and said, "Thank you for the invitation, but you can't have me. I've enlisted in the Reserves." That pissed them off no end, but there was nothing they could do about it.

Mary Lou and I were able to get to spring training with the Red Sox, and I made the team again, a totally unexpected development. Eddie Kasko was our new manager, and I really liked him at that point. I would reverse that opinion a bit later. We opened the 1970 season against the Yankees in New York. Gary Peters beat them, 4–2, and I came in to pitch three and two-thirds scoreless innings to get the save. I also received my first taste of the intense rivalry between the Red Sox and the Yankees. On my way in from the bullpen, while riding one of those golf carts that transported us to the mound, I got smoked in the chest with a beer bottle. That will wake you up and take the edge off you. You realized that the Yankee batters couldn't possibly damage you any more than that bottle did. I thought New York should have signed up the fan who tossed it. He didn't have overwhelming velocity, but he threw a heavy, sinking bottle for a strike. The guys had warned me about Yankee rooters, so I wasn't amazed when I got hit by an object. I was surprised that the fan had such good control on the first day of the season, though.

I pitched with the club for about two months, leaving them in early June. While playing an exhibition game against the Montreal Expos in Jarry Park, I received a telegram ordering me to report to Fort Polk, Louisiana, for the start of basic training in the Reserves. I had tried to get my induction delayed. Mary Lou was almost seven months' pregnant with our son Michael, and she was too big to travel. Unable to swing it, I ended up at Fort Polk and Mary Lou went to Jackson, Mississippi, to live with her mother. My base was close enough to Jackson, so it worked out pretty well. I was supposed to do six weeks there, and then do the rest of my time near Boston.

My army aptitude test indicated that I would be a crackerjack clerk-typist. I couldn't type a word, but that was the Army. Their test results were geared more toward what they needed than what a person could actually do. My unit needed someone to do their paperwork, and I had been nominated. Lonborg, Dalton Jones, and Ken Brett were medics, and a few other players were in the motor pool. Our captain put me on the fort baseball team as soon as he found out who I was. We played other bases down there and beat them all. We did so well that he tried to keep me down there, but the higher-ups wouldn't permit it. That made my final weeks with him tough. He was so pissed off he wouldn't let me play, and his officers really tried to make life miserable for me, assigning me eternal guard duty. I didn't mind. I found it very peaceful, watching the armadillos and the rabbits as they played cards at four in the morning.

Military life was interesting, a mixture of perfect logic with a huge helping of the absurd. We received our immunization shots on our first day. Lining us up single file, they had us walk into a room that offered no clue as to what dangers it held until you were just about to enter. The first thing you saw was two nurses standing across the room. And they looked great. You sauntered through the door, gave them your best smile, and froze just long enough for two medics to grab you and nail you with four shots in each arm. You never knew what hit you. Then you were slung on a cot, where you spent the rest of the day throwing up.

The Army had a clever way of inducing you to get into top physical shape. We had one guy in our outfit, Ken Livesgood, who was a skinny little runt when he first signed up. They fed him like a horse, exercised him until near death, and he came out like Mr. America. They put me in the best shape of my life and taught me a new respect for punishing my body. When I got in I couldn't do a chin-up. I had a weak upper body and a big ass. By the time I left basic, my ass had gotten smaller and my chest and arms had expanded. I was overweight when I came in, and Ken was underweight, but we both came out the same. The Army accomplished these miracles through the strategic use of clothing. If you were big you got a tight uniform, little you got a baggy one. The uniforms were all the same size, and you were expected to mold your body into them. That made sense. They attacked us through our fashion consciousness, getting us to work our butts off while at the same time holding down their clothing bill. They simply bought one or two sizes in bulk. It worked well, convincing me that our society would be better off if we had special agents riding about in unmarked cars. They would be like specialized dog catchers. Every time they spotted someone who was obese or smoking too much, they would hustle him off to a variation of boot camp for six weeks. It would put people in terrific shape and return the sparkle to their eyes. Could be disconcerting, though. If some overweight businessmen went into Macy's to buy socks and suddenly vanished for six weeks, it could cause a small panic. Of course, I believe this is already being done on a much smaller scale. I suspect those video games are part of a plot. I'm certain the Army has a trap door in front of each machine. Whenever a kid registers an unbelievably high score, he types in his initials and the door is automatically sprung, causing him to drop down into the waiting arms of a drill sergeant. Then the kid is transported via an underground railroad to the Pentagon. Three years later, he's driving a computerized tank through Europe.

I fit in well in the Army. I wasn't rebellious, but I did get into trouble for helping Pineapple, an asthmatic kid from Hawaii. We were on a field march with full gear when he passed out, falling into an irrigation ditch. He was in the midst of drowning when I pulled him out. A sergeant came running over, yelling, "Leave him there! People fall by the wayside all the time, but we have to press on!" Somebody forgot to tell this hero that we were still in the States. He thought we were in the heart of Cambodia. He noticed that I had placed my rifle on the ground, or, to use military jargon, had dropped my weapon. He went bonzo, and it led to a very bizarre scene. Pineapple was lying in the ditch, turning seven shades of blue, and this guy is screaming, "Where's your weapon? You must never drop your weapon in the field, it's your top priority!" He was like the Robert Duvall character in *Apocalypse Now*, the one who kept checking the break of the waves for surfing while the world was being blown up around his ears, and who says, "I love the smell of napalm in the morning. It smells like...victory." The sergeant ended his tirade by lecturing me on Army procedure, telling me that I should have kept my ass in gear and let our trucks pick Pineapple up. I don't know about that. Pineapple didn't look like he was in the mood to wait for any rides unless they were showing up in a hurry. That little episode got me a week of KP.

My son Michael was born on July 24, the day I was supposed to go out on bivouac. Bivouac was an excellent opportunity to go out and sleep in the woods while being assaulted by various spiders and snakes. I got to miss that, receiving a two-day pass and getting to the hospital in Mississippi two hours before his birth. He was a cute little butterball, and when I looked at him I got dizzy. Seeing what Mary Lou and I had made was better than pitching a no-hitter.

It was amazing how many people I met in the Army who were really borderline. There was a whole group of guys from Chicago and two-thirds of them never made it out of high school, and the ones who did were functionally illiterate. The Army didn't care. It was a lot like baseball. They weren't interested in having to answer too many questions. It would have been chaos to have a bunch of recruits from MIT come in, saying, "But Sergeant, we really think you should do it our way. It would lead to greater productivity." You lay something like that on them and you were looking at four weeks of latrine duty. The Army wanted us to keep our heads down, our eyes open, and our mouths shut. At all times. In my whole time in the Reserves, I never once let on that I had been to college. They get a college boy in the army and they try to make him out to be the biggest asshole the world has ever seen. Whenever I was asked about it, I just said, "No, sir, I did not get out of junior high school."

At the end of basic, orders came down, transferring me to Fort Worth, Texas. After six weeks on base I had learned at least one thing. The warrant officer could get my orders changed. Fortunately for me, ours was a heavy baseball freak who knew who I was and was able to get me stationed in Massachusetts, in a fort not far from Boston.

When I got there, they tried to make me an MP. I lasted about a day. Our first sergeant came up to me and said, "Look, you don't want this job. It's got late hours and it's risky. Let's find something else for you. We have to protect that left arm." He attached me to the adjutant general's office. I spent my day answering the phone and typing letters. Whenever a congressman wrote protesting some boy's induction, we sent him a form letter. I also typed a lot of letters informing the parents of dead soldiers where and when they could pick up their son's medals. They had a choice. The medals could be sent home or the parents could come to the fort on a Saturday to view a parade and receive the medals in a small ceremony. Those notices hit me hard. I was a privileged character by virtue of the fact that I could throw strikes; no one was shipping me overseas. I'd get off work at four o'clock, get to the park by five, and throw batting practice. Since I wasn't on the club's active roster I couldn't get into a game, but I could stick around the press box for a few innings and then go back to the fort. Other guys were coming back to the fort, too, only they were coming back in green bags.

I thought I was doing a good thing, coming to Fenway and throwing batting practice. It seemed like a fine way to show the Sox how much team spirit I had. Later on, I found out they hadn't wanted me around. They were having trouble with the military at the time, because one of our players had allegedly told an officer to shit in his hat and the officer told him, "I'm going to have you and the rest of these ballplayers walking point in Quang Tri." That really hurt the club's relationship with the Army. That player hadn't messed around. He didn't tell this to a sergeant or a second louie. He picked on a colonel. Somebody later told me that player had been Tony Conigliaro. That made sense—old spur-of-the-moment Tony. I had to stop showing up at the park when people started asking, "What's Bill Lee doing here? We thought he was supposed to be in

Fort Worth, learning how to type."

I finished my military commitment for the year just as the baseball season was ending. Coming out of the Army, I found myself in great shape, but with my feelings about armed conflicts clarified. I was opposed to the war in Southeast Asia because of my moral convictions, the chief of which was that I did not want to get my ass splattered all over Nam. I knew the war was immoral and illegal. The writings of Colonel Thompson had convinced me that it was also unwinnable. Thompson was a British officer who had served in Malaysia. He had conclusive proof that the only way to win a guerrilla war of the type that was taking place in Viet Nam was to have maximum air support and a ten-to-one manpower advantage over the enemy. He knew one thing about the Viet Cong that the American public hadn't been told: they had shovels. They could just dig in and let their pursuers exhaust themselves trying to find them. I built a political science paper around that theme at SC. It got a D-minus. The professor was a conservative, and he said my paper showed a lot of imagination but that it was based on a false premise. He also wrote across the top of it that this country would never lose a war. Seven years later Saigon fell.

Coming out of basic, I was hungry to pitch. When I received an offer to play winter ball, I packed up Mary Lou, Michael, and my equipment, and headed south to warm climes and balmy breezes. I went down with the illusion that only my baseball skills would receive a stiff test while I was there. Little did I know that my military training would also come into use. Thanks to a fastball thrown in the general direction of Ellie Rodriguez's body, I was going to be involved in a different kind of war in Puerto Rico.

3

I had lost my top four front teeth when I was a kid, the result of an ill-advised attempt to take a bite out of a football helmet that, at the time, had a speeding linebacker underneath it. Eventually, they were replaced by a dazzling three-tooth bridge with a cap on one side. If you don't believe it was dazzling, just take a look for yourself. All you have to do is take a trip to Tigres Stadium in Caguas, Puerto Rico. It's imbedded in the cement somewhere in front of the ballpark.

I was pitching winter ball for Mayaguez and was the starting pitcher on a Sunday afternoon that saw us hosting Caguas, a bitter rival from a neighboring town. Eliseo Rodriguez, a major-leaguer with the Milwaukee Brewers, was the Caguas catcher. I knew very little about him and had no recollection of ever having faced him before. No matter. We were about to become well acquainted.

It was a slider that got away from me in the seventh inning that brought us together. Rodriguez was hanging over the plate, guessing sinker. When the ball ran in on him, he was unable to get out of the way, and it clipped him on the elbow. Stepping out of the batter's box, Ellie rubbed his arm and started yelling at me in Spanish. I didn't comprehend a word of it, so I just shrugged, hoping he understood that the hit wasn't intentional. I don't think he got the message. Dropping his bat, he took two steps toward first base, turned, and charged toward me on the mound. I had an immediate understanding that he was not coming out to tell me what great stuff I had that day. Especially since his entire team had emptied the dugout and was following behind him. I felt like Davy Crockett at the Alamo. As Rodriguez reached the mound he lunged at me. Stepping to one side, I set myself and caught him with a quick left lead, laying him out on the mound. My manager, Cal Ermer, later told me it was the best lefthand he had ever seen.

The fans went crazy, and both teams started duking it out on the playing field. Rodriguez, after finally regaining consciousness, picked himself up off the ground and went berserk trying to find me. He kept diving in and out of the pile of players, shouting, "Lee, I get you!" He was so insane he didn't realize I was standing right next to him, watching as he tried to penetrate the perimeter of the mob. When order was finally restored, we were both thrown out of the game. The next day the headlines read: MAYAGUEZ LOSES, BUT LEE TKO'S RODRIGUEZ IN THE SEVENTH. That was embarrassing for Ellie, who was a former light heavyweight Golden Gloves champion of Puerto Rico. I had damaged his elbow, his jaw, and his pride, and that was something he would not easily forget. Or forgive.

Four days after the incident, we were scheduled to go to Caguas. All my teammates told me to say behind. Rodriguez had a reputation as a madman, and everyone was certain he would be out for my blood. I couldn't believe that. I also didn't want to miss my start that evening.

I had completely forgotten about Ellie by the time our team bus reached Tigres Stadium in downtown Caguas; I was too busy thinking about the game I was about to pitch. After unloading my gear I stepped off the team bus and started to make my way toward the players' entrance. I was just about at the door when, out of the corner of my eye, I saw a muscular midget creep up from my right side. It was Ellie Rodriguez, looking a lot different out of uniform. As I turned to face him, *bam!* I got hit in the back of the head and found my face being rammed into a steel pole. That's the last thing I remember. Rodriguez had two other guys, apparently relatives, with him, and while I was unconscious they really did a number on me. While his cohorts held me down, Rodriguez sat on my chest and punched my face into pulp. He might have killed me if Ron Woods, an outfielder with our club, hadn't come out and grabbed him. Moments after Ronnie jumped in, the *policia* showed up and tried to arrest me. I guess they were going to charge me with assaulting the sidewalk with my face and bleeding on public property. Our club owner talked them out of it, and I was sent back to the team hotel. The most amazing thing in all of this was the reaction of the Caguas townspeople. Hordes of them came to the hotel, saying, "Oh, Bill, please don't hold this incident against our town or our country. We are not all this way." That was unnecessary. I already knew that. I did find it funny, however, that one soulful gentleman kept telling me how peaceful they were down there, and then finished his monologue by offering to kill Rodriguez and his entire family. I said no thanks.

As much as I wanted it to, the incident would not go away. I flew back to Boston for a few days to get fitted for a new set of choppers, and when I returned to Mayaguez I was met at the airport by the club's general manager. He seemed very excited, and when I asked him what was up, he said, "Bill, how would you like to make three thousand dollars?" I asked him what I had to do, and he replied, "You're going to fight a three-round preliminary against Ellie Rodriguez before next Thursday's game." I said, "You got to be shitting me! I'm scheduled to pitch that night. I can't fight three rounds and then go out and pitch a ballgame." Pondering that for a minute, he said, "No, no. You're right. Okay, you don't have to pitch that evening." I told him there was no way. Fighting Rodriguez on the mound was merely a case of self-defense; he had attacked me. But I wasn't about to get into the ring with him. Lacing up those gloves would have been playing right into his hands. Then again I guess I could have handled him for three rounds. I v ıld have danced and counterpunched. But we'll never find t. I had come down to pitch, not to fight, and I wasn't about to forget that. Deep in my heart I wanted to get back at Rodriguez, but I also knew that I would be seeing him ın the States. Whether or not he knew it, he had just made my list.

My life underwent a drastic change in 1971. My commitment to the military consisted of only one weekend a month and two weeks out of the year, so I knew I would get to play my first uninterrupted season of major-league ball. I had a great spring and had made the club as its primary long reliever. I also became good friends with Gary Peters and Sparky Lyle, the two renegades who were responsible for starting me on the road that has taken me to where I am today.

Gary Peters was my hero. Talk about being able to handle the call of the bright lights—this guy could do it all. He could drink a half bottle of VO and show absolutely no ill effects from it. There was at least one time, though, when he was forced to pay the piper. After spending a good part of the evening pumping villainous potions into his body, he had to drag himself to the ballpark and run through a series of windsprints in killing ninety-degree heat. By the time he was finished he had punished himself so badly that he could barely crawl from the field into the clubhouse. When he finally got to his locker he collapsed in a heap. I thought he had died, but after a few minutes we noticed his eyelids were fluttering open. Picking up his head, he just barely managed to get his mouth open. When his words came, it was as if they were arriving from the grave. "Please,"

Gary implored us, "don't anybody light any matches near me, or we're all going up in smoke."

Peters was an eight-year veteran, and he took me under his wing. He once told me that as I got older I should become aware of any young lefthanders who might take my job, that I should find out their weaknesses and take them to that bar. After the season commenced Gary had a few bad outings, and he started biting me on the left elbow. I took it as a compliment.

Peters introduced me to Lindell's AC in Detroit, a great bar with a heavy sports atmosphere that served as the backdrop for some of baseball's funniest moments. God, I loved that place. Lindell's owner had a cigarette lighter that looked like a .22 pistol. You pulled the trigger and a flame would come out of the barrel. One night Norm Cash, the Tiger first baseman, was up there with several players, and they started messing around with the gun. They pointed it at each other and then aimed it at their own heads. Finally one of them took out a cigarette and went to light it. Pulling the trigger, he managed to put a bullet hole through the office wall. Wrong gun. When Cash realized what had happened, he paled out. He looked like a cadaver and ended up going into a slump for about a month. That was the kind of story that could put Peters in stitches for the rest of the season. He seemed to have a taste for the absurd.

Gary was always into something. He had a benign violent streak. Once he was in a nightclub in Minnesota when he, Yaz, and Aparicio started tearing each other's clothes off. Luis was an impeccable dresser, and it started when Gary tore the lapel off one of his Oleg Cassini suits. Yaz grabbed Gary from behind and ripped his shirt to shreds. Naturally, Gary and Luis united and turned on Carl. They used to do that all the time. Carl, of course, always made sure to wear one of his twenty-dollar suits, which gave him a big advantage in these confrontations.

On this particular evening, after having his jacket converted into a heap of rags, Yaz did not come back with an immediate retaliatory response. Waiting until he got back to the team hotel, he got his revenge by throwing together a pile of clothes belonging to Luis and Gary and setting them on fire. He nearly burned a hole through their hotel-room floor. Back at the nightclub, everything had calmed down when Reggie Smith decided to get involved in the fun. But Gary was tired of the whole thing, and he let Reggie know it before he even had a chance to grab a cufflink. He did this by holding a steak knife to Smith's throat, telling him that if he moved he'd cut out his Adam's apple. Reggie not only didn't move, he didn't breathe for what seemed like fifteen minutes.

Smith was Gary's favorite victim. Reggie was into scuba diving. Once, while on a road trip, a bunch of us were sitting in the restaurant of the Holiday Inn ordering breakfast, when a girl came running in, shouting that we had to see what was going on in the pool. Once out there, we found Reggie sitting at the bottom of the hotel pool in full scuba gear. Gary made note of this, and a few months later took Reggie on an expedition to the underwater caves in Freshwater Springs, Florida. They dived down with searchlights and tanks filled with about thirty minutes' worth of oxygen. As soon as they got deep inside of one of those caverns, Gary stole Smith's light and took off. He came back five minutes later and found Reggie praying. Smith had about four minutes of oxygen left, and they had to use the buddy system to get out of the cave.

Though Gary was a starter, the bullpen was really his domain. He was adept at keeping us loose out there. Whenever the team was down by a few runs, he would grab Lew Krausse in a headlock, announcing, "I'm going to squeeze Lew's head until we score or he turns blue." He'd get Lew to the point of coma before he'd let go. Krausse must have thanked God that we had a good-hitting ballclub. Peters did that to him twice, and the team was able to rally both times.

Lyle was our short man, and he was the greatest, befriending me the moment I joined the club. He was the sort of guy who would give you the shirt off his back if you asked him for it. Sparky was a man of simple philosophy. He believed that water was to be used as a mix, never a staple. One night in New York, Sparky got so blind he couldn't stand. He was leaning against a wall, calling for a taxi at four in the morning. Finally one stopped. Unable to move, Sparky just looked at the driver and said, "Cabbie, I want you to take me to the Biltmore Hotel." The cabbie poked his head out the window, looked at Lyle, and said, "You're leaning on it." Following his and Peters' examples, I formulated the Bill Lee exercise program: Take a Jack Daniel's in your left hand and a bottle of Molson's in your right. Do two sips of the beer, down the Jack Daniel's, and then chase it with the rest of the brew. Do a minimum of eight reps and then pass out. Not only is this a wonderful way to improve flexibility, it also relaxes tension.

I found a lot of drinking going on in the majors, especially on the road. I was doing more than my share. The partying begins at the airport. We usually get to the airport early, so we kill time in the terminal lounge. Many times the flight doesn't take off as scheduled. The longer the delay, the longer we're in that lounge. When we finally do board our plane, the first thing they do is start pounding drinks into you. There are usually open bars on board, and we had our methods of getting a little bit more than our normal allotment of liquid refreshments. I was often designated to distract the stewardess while the guys went in and grabbed all the two-ouncers of Scotch they could carry. While I set up a screen with the stewardess, another scouting party would be sent to keep management occupied. If you're ever on a plane with ballplayers and you see a bunch of them involved with their coaches in an intense discussion about the subtleties of the slider, you know the alcoholic supplies are being raided. By the time the plane touches down most of them will be severely hammered.

The games present us with excuses to take a drink. If we have a good game, we want to celebrate. If we were horseshit, we want to forget. Young players drink to fit in, to take part in the camaraderie and relieve the boredom. When a player sees his career coming to an end, it's a more dangerous time. He tends to drink a lot more than he used to, knowing that his days in the sun are almost at an end and there's nothing he can do about it. That's one of the offshoots of being unable to separate the game from your life. You drink out of fear, mindful that when you get off that bar stool and walk out that door, the Grim Reaper is waiting with a pink slip and a greeting: "Hello, Jim. You gave up that home run with the bases loaded last night. You're gone."

Alcohol and baseball go hand in hand, and whether or not the powers that be care to admit it, it's a marriage that baseball condones. Bowie Kuhn was quick to preach about the evils of alcohol and drugs, yet he allowed breweries to form a major portion of baseball's advertising. He made statements for public consumption that lauded the work baseball is doing in the area of addiction rehabilitation, but I noticed that after doing all this terrific p.r., he looked the other way when a ballplayer hit a home run and the team announcer celebrated with a plug for beer. Some may call this a contradiction; the commissioner and the owners call it economics.

Alcohol is like anything else. It's only as bad as the person it's being poured into. If it's used to heighten an occasion, or to take an edge off stress, I don't see a problem. Trouble starts when you either lose control and let the bottle run you, or when you believe its promises of immortality. You realize that no matter how much you punish yourself, you always seem to wake up the next day. Pretty soon you're convinced that you will never die. When that happens I guess it is time to look for help before your life becomes one long, lost weekend. You can lose sight of the dangers because athletes are treated as an elite class. It's rare that one of us gets called to task for anything. While I was in Boston, a story was making the rounds that Wayne Cashman of the Boston Bruins had been picked up on a misdemeanor. He was brought down to the police station and told he was allowed to make one phone call. Wayne called a Chinese restaurant for some take-out and had it delivered to the precinct house. As far as I know, he probably had the cops pay for it.

Alcohol never hurt me. I never showed up drunk at the ballpark, and I was never incapacitated to the point that I couldn't perform the day after the night before. I've pitched through a few hangovers, but I've always been one who believes that, quite often, the worse an athlete feels, the more menacing he becomes. Juan Marichal was the same way. When he was feeling sore with a bad back or stiffness in his joints, he was amazing. When he felt super, he got jocked. Unfortunately, by the time he joined our club he was feeling super most of the time. There were days when I would get my nine hours of z's, get up with the dawn, do some calisthenics, have a great breakfast, and get to the ballpark early. I wouldn't make it past the first inning. On the other hand, there was many a time when I got to the stadium with my head on fire, still smelling of last night, and I'd go out and twist the opposition into pretzels. I guess what they say about "no pain, no gain" has some truth to it. When you're hurting badly enough you don't think about pressure. Your body is like an open wound, so your instincts take over, and this is still basically an instinctive game. Managers try to make you live right and watch *Patton* before each ballgame, hoping to get you psyched. Your adrenaline reaches an early peak and explodes like a premature ejaculation. When it comes time to romp, you can't perform. But guys like me who can sleep standing up, or like Bernie Carbo, who would nod out in the bus racks on the way to the park, are ready when the bell rings. You show me a bunch of guys who come dragging into the stadium, and I'll show you one dangerous ballclub.

The front office had made a lot of moves prior to the start of the 1971 season, in an attempt to restructure the ballclub. Boston was haunted by its history of teams boasting .290 club batting averages, which would lead the league in home runs and runs scored and still finish fourth. They had ticket-takers who could hit .270, but they never won anything. To reverse that trend, we traded Tony C to the Angels for Ken Tatum, a hard-throwing righthanded reliever, and Doug Griffin. Tatum had already had two great seasons with California, but everyone knew that Griffin was the key to the deal. Doug was a minor-league second baseman who, our scouts claimed, was the second coming of Bill Mazeroski. That deal allowed us to ship Mike Andrews and Luis Alvarado to the White Sox for Luis Aparicio, the best shortstop in baseball. After moving Petrocelli to third on a permanent basis, it became quite clear that we had radically changed the complexion of our ballclub. These moves beefed up our team's speed and defense, the two areas that formed this club's Achilles' heel. A lot of people screamed that we had sacrificed too much power in surrendering Conigliaro and Andrews, but as a groundball pitcher, I thought the deals were great.

Aparicio was amazing. Everyone says his glove got him into the Hall of Fame. They don't have to convince me. When he joined the Red Sox he was thirty-seven years old. At least that's what he admitted to. He had lost a step, but he had the greatest hands I had ever seen, and he knew where to play everybody. He could no longer steal a lot of bases; he was saving his legs for more important things—

like walking. Based on how good he looked when we got him, I would have loved to have seen him in his prime, when he was swiping bases and moving at full throttle in the field. He must have been unreal. He and Griffin shored up our infield. Griffin was everything the scouting reports said he was: fast, with good range and soft hands. He was excellent on the double play, and I sure appreciated that. When you have guys like Aparicio and Griffin making plays that other infielders couldn't, and turning double plays that you have no right to expect, it really means a lot to a team. They save runs, not only the runs they cut off with great stops, but the ones a tiring pitcher might give up later on. They cut down on the number of pitches needed to get twenty-seven outs, and that can make a difference in a tight ballclub.

Dougie was a battler. He once got beaned by Nolan Ryan, which is about as scary a thing as can happen to you in baseball. Ryan throws one-hundred-plus miles per hour. He got Doug in the skull with his express, and I mean he crushed him. Griffin's head was lopsided for three weeks. His first game back from the disabled list was against the Angels, and Ryan was on the mound. Doug went out and smoked him for two hits in four at-bats. I'm telling you, it was one gutty performance.

Aparicio was a big help to Griffin that first season. There wasn't anything he didn't know about positioning, and he was a very canny player. Luis was always looking for that edge. While with the Orioles he played an exhibition game against the St. Louis Cardinals in which Julio Gotay was the opposing shortstop. Gotay had a lot of religious idiosyncrasies. Taking advantage of this, Luis laid tongue depressors in the shape of crosses on the second-base bag. In the very first inning Aparicio was on first with one man out, and the batter hit a perfect double-play ball to Gotay. Crossing to his left, Julio got ready to step on second, saw the crosses, and jumped into the air, screaming. He wouldn't go near the bag until the tongue depressors had been removed. He was like Dracula. Naturally Luis and the batter were safe, and they both scored when the next hitter tripled. I asked Aparicio if he ever tried that trick again. He told me no, explaining that he wanted to save it in case he played against Gotay in a World Series or an All-Star game.

Tatum was a disappointment for us. He came up with the Angels in 1969 and just blew people away for a season and a half. He was unhittable until the middle of the 1970 season, when he beaned Paul Blair of the Orioles and almost killed him. Blair was on his way to superstardom when it happened; he was never the same ballplayer after that. He could still go get them better than anybody in centerfield, but he really dropped off at the plate. That was understandable. A lot of guys turn gun-shy after getting hit a lot less badly than Blair did. That particular beanball hampered two careers. Tatum was never the same pitcher after he threw it. He hadn't been trying to hit Blair. He was just a guy who had so much velocity, he didn't have a clue where the ball was going. After beaning Blair he didn't throw quite as hard as when he first came up. It was as if he was afraid of skulling someone again. Changing his pitching pattern, he stopped coming inside and lost his speed. Then his control, never great to begin with, vanished. By the time we got him, he was almost useless. I thought the tip-off on him came in spring training. I noticed he never spent any meal money and that he was always taking the uneaten toast off the players' tables. Those are always signs that a player sees the end of the road coming up.

We got off to a good start in 1971 and it looked like we might finally put it all together. Baltimore got off slowly, and by late May we were leading the American League East. Oakland was on top in the West, and when they came in for a visit on May 28, the club got its first glimpse of the season of them and Vida Blue. Blue had come up with the A's at the end of the 1970 season and pitched a no-hitter against the Twins. I had faced him in the minors. He threw B-Bs that day and nobody on my team wanted to hit against him. In 1971 he opened the season for Oakland against Washington, got jocked, and then won his next ten decisions. Five of those wins were shutouts, and he had been striking out a man an inning. Vida was the hottest thing in baseball. When I got to the park that evening, I nearly freaked, having never seen anything like it. The media crush was tremendous; there were reporters hiding under second base hoping to get an exclusive with Blue. Traffic was snarled outside the park, and Fenway was packed almost full by the time we finished batting practice. It was like a carnival. All of Boston was turned on because both teams were in first place, Dick Williams was managing Oakland, and the Red Sox were sending Sonny Siebert out to face Blue. Without one-tenth the publicity that Vida had received, Sonny was already 8–0.

When I got into our locker room, all the talk centered on what a light show this evening had become. Everybody except Petrocelli was impressed. Rico just sat at his locker, a look of contempt etched into his features, telling everyone, "Blue's just another lefty who throws hard. We'll take him over the wall a couple of times and have him out of there before he knows what hit him." Rico never gave an inch to anybody. In the first inning, with us trailing 1–0 and Reggie Smith on first base, Rico hit a Blue fastball into the centerfield bleachers. In the bottom of the sixth he hit a Blue slider over the leftfield wall, putting us ahead to stay in a game we would eventually win, 4–3. That game would be the highlight of our season. Right after it we went into a slump and never recovered.

Everything fell apart simultaneously. Our defense held up, but our starting pitching failed us, especially when Sonny got hurt late in the season. And our hitting just died. We still scored runs, but we seemed able to score them only in bunches: ten runs in one game and then nothing for the rest of the week. Billy Conigliaro had replaced his brother in right. As soon as it became apparent that power was not part of Billy's game, Kasko tried platooning him with Joe Lahoud. Joe must have hit 757 home runs in batting practice, but he couldn't get his average over .230 when it came to the real thing. Griffin and Aparicio were as weak at the plate as they were strong up the middle. The biggest mystery, though, was Yaz. He went into an early-season slump and never got out of it. No one could understand why. I thought hitting forty homers in both '69 and '70 might have hurt him, causing him to try to pull everything, whereas he had been successful hitting the ball to all fields. Pitchers do have a grapevine, and once it got around that Carl was no longer going with the pitch, everyone pitched him away. The end result saw Yaz hitting a lot of groundballs to second. We started calling him "Four to Three." As his slump wore on, the fans got on him, and that only made it worse. None of these things mattered much. Even if we had been able to correct all our inadequacies, there still would have been one insurmountable obstacle left: Baltimore. We just couldn't beat the Orioles. We'd go into Baltimore, or they'd come to Fenway, and each game would be like a videotaped replay of the one before it. We'd get a lead, hold it for six, and then...here come the Robinsons! In the seventh, eighth, and ninth, Frank and Brooks would realize they were in a ballgame and it would be all over. We just couldn't beat them, and we knew it. Boston was always lacking that righthanded reliever who could get the Orioles' big righthanded hitters out. That's why the club dealt for Tatum, but he couldn't do the job.

In one game when we had a lead in the late innings, we brought Bob Bolin in to pitch to Frank Robinson. Bob loved to knock hitters on their ass. In this game he threw one of the most hellacious knockdown pitches I had ever seen.

Robinson's hat went in one direction, his bat in another, and his legs went so high off the ground that for a few seconds he seemed suspended in space. His body was completely parallel to the ground. I watched him fall back to earth, get his gear together, and stalk back into the batter's box. He was exuding so much obvious determination up there that I remember thinking to myself before Bolin delivered the next pitch, that we should have let sleeping dogs lie. Bob threw another fastball inside, and Frank stepped back and tomahawked it five hundred feet for the ballgame. Bolin wasn't sorry. He said the only mistake he made was in not hitting him. But I never saw him throw at Mr. Robinson again. And Baltimore still beat the crap out of us. We finished the season eighteen games out of the hunt, languishing in third place.

I thought Kasko handled us very well that season. He got the most out of his pitching staff, considering what he had to work with, and he never got too high or low. I also liked his sense of humor. Once, he was in the shower with George Scott, watching Scott wash his hair. George loved to lather up with about half a bottle of shampoo. The totally bald Kasko would look over at Scott's bottle and say, "What a coincidence. That used to be my favorite brand." George would spend fifteen minutes trying to rinse the stuff out of his hair.

I had gotten close to Aparicio, and, when the season was over, he asked me if I wanted to play winter ball again. Luis was going to be managing a team in Venezuela, and he needed lefthanded pitching. I figured as long as it would be as far away from Ellie Rodriguez as possible, it would be fine. I was not making much more than the major-league minimum, and I could not afford another pair of dentures.

There must be something about the balmy breezes of South America that induces visitors to part with small portions of their sanity, because one week after arriving in Venezuela my brain began to slip out of my right ear. I was ready for the fudge farm, and I was not alone. There was an entire group of us that became certifiable.

My first day down there, everybody was talking about how easy it was to procure greenies. It was amazing. Greenies are amphetamines and act as an anti-depressant, just the thing a ballplayer needs after an evening on the trail of Jack Daniel's. They are verboten in clubhouses in the States, though players still find a way to get them. One way is to play winter ball. In Venezuela and the Dominican Republic they're sold over the counter. Guys would load up and return to the States with buckets full of them, enough to last the whole season. You have to watch what they sell you, though. While I was down there, one of our pitchers came to my room with a fresh supply. Turning me on to one, he told me how he had already done two that day, and how they were the most incredible things he had tried. I took one taste and told him, "These are not amphetamines. These are a placebo." He said, "A placebo? Is that what they're called in Spanish? Back home we call them greenies." When I tried to explain that they were only sugar pills, he wouldn't listen, telling me, "But I paid good money for them and they got me fried!" I finally gave up arguing and proceeded to prove my point by taking two more and going to sleep. That didn't faze him in the least. He took them and thought they were God's gift. That proved to me that a lot of fatigue is mental.

I've done greenies, but for the most part I tried to stay away from them. For two reasons. One, they made you feel stronger than you really were, making you believe you could blow the ball past people. For a control pitcher like me who didn't have a whole lot of velocity, that could be fatal. Secondly, you never know when it might rain. There's nothing worse than dropping a greenie before a ballgame and then having the contest washed out. That's when you see entire teams of players chattering away at each other while doing six hours of Nautilus.

One of my teammates was a pitcher who really liked to pound the pavement. He was relentless. He also was the owner of a bad case of jock itch, which was eroding his nuts so badly that he had to have them painted blue with silver nitrate. One night we went to a whorehouse in Caracas. He grabbed the first girl he saw and headed for a rear room. They weren't back there three minutes when she came running out, screaming, "Blue balls! Blue balls!" My friend came out, wearing nothing except a big grin, and said, "Hey, no problem. I'm royalty."

Dropping into a cathouse wasn't a sexual thing. It was just a chance to grab another one of life's experiences. God knows we didn't have to go looking for women, they came looking for us. I remember one in particular. She followed me for days, although, as it turned out, not for reasons gratifying to my ego. She was a beautiful woman who was skating with the Ice Capades, and I first noticed her in a bar after one of the games. She didn't say anything to me; she just looked interested. She started coming to the ball-park, sitting near the bullpen. She still hadn't made a move, but I was always catching her out of the corner of my eye, staring at me. She finally did approach me in a café near our hotel, joining me at my table as I was having lunch. For the first couple of minutes she didn't say anything. She just watched me eat. I was about to ask her what she wanted, when she reached into her pocketbook and took out a hundred-dollar bill. Placing it on the table, she looked deep into my eyes and said, "I will give you this and the best blow job you've ever had if you hit Rod Carew in the balls during tomorrow's game."

For the first time in memory I was speechless. I couldn't think of anything to say until I decided that it might be a good idea for all concerned, especially Rod's gonads, to talk her out of this foolishness. I told her it wasn't a good idea. Not only was getting hit in the balls painful, it could do a lot of damage that people aren't usually aware of. In some cases, a shot in the cubes could be fatal. That gave her pause. She took a few sips from her drink and stared down into the glass, looking as if she was deciding what to do. It didn't take her long. She looked up at me again and said, "You're right. I hadn't realized the dangers. Well, in that case *could you just nip him in the cock?*" That's when I made for the door, knowing this woman had to be crazy. I mean it was true I could pitch to spots, but how good did she think my control was?

I just barely managed to keep out of jail while I was in Venezuela. Jim Rooker, Joe Keough, and I had gone into a Caracas restaurant after Rooker had taken a tough loss in that evening's game. He was upset, and Joe and I decided to cheer him up by stuffing ourselves with good food while getting hammered. Somehow we never got to the good food. First we drank to each other's health. Then to the health of our families. Each individual member of our families, going back four generations. As the bar bill got heavier, our heads got lighter and our toasts got louder. Soon we were being asked by the proprietor to quiet down. A wedding party was going on in the back room, and we were upsetting the celebrants with our uncouth behavior. We didn't mind, having too much class to stay where we weren't wanted. Rooker did get a trifle pissed, though, on the way out. He overturned a table that was loaded down with beautiful, intricately designed ceramics. Kicking the legs out from under it, he sent the pottery crashing into several thousand pieces.

Once outside, we decided we were hungry. A perfectly natural discovery, since we hadn't eaten in twelve hours. We went to an open-air café, directly across the street from the bar, but it was closed. Now we were all upset. We did some very adult things, like banging on the doors and knocking over tables. After getting no response, Rooker picked up a chair and chucked it through the plate-glass window of a store next to the café. A jewelry store. I wasn't that drunk. Seeing that glass shatter told me it was time to get my ass out of the vicinity. The three of us did the mile in three minutes flat and didn't take a drink for the rest of the month. We had heard the alarm bells go off and the wail of the sirens as they cut through the night. Just the thought of a Venezuelan jail was enough to put the fear of God in the three of us. It was better than the threat of a year of daily AA meetings.

Winter ball was a vacation for me. I played ball, basked in the sun, and got paid for it while people back in the States were freezing their tails off. The Latin American fans were very intense. Their love of baseball borders on the fanatic. Cal Ermer had told me the story about the time he had played for the Rochester Red Wings in a game against the Havana Sugar Kings in Cuba. This was in the late fifties, right after Castro had kicked out Batista. The Kings were up by one run, and the Red Wings had the tying run on third with no one out. One of Fidel's soldiers stood up and trained his rifle on the runner at third. He said if the guy tried to score, he would shoot him. And nobody, except the Red Wings, seemed to think this was a particularly bad idea. I guess everyone figured, Hell, they closed down all the casinos. The war is over. There's nothing else to do, so why don't we just shoot a couple of ballplayers. Things weren't quite this hot in Venezuela, but the rooting did seem to be a thin skin over an underlying violence. I also noticed some paranoia on the part of the club owners down there. They were always afraid that the players from the States were going to skip out on them. It was such a fear that did a great deal to damage my relationship with Aparicio.

I had done a good job for Luis, and I felt the experience had been mutually rewarding. I could always change speeds and throw strikes, but now I had learned how to pitch to a batter's weakness and how to pace myself to go nine. I was grateful for that, and Luis seemed to appreciate the hard work I had done for the club. We had an excellent rapport. So I had no compunctions about asking his permission to go to Aruba, giving Mary Lou and me a chance to visit her great-grandfather's gravesite. He had been the governor of the Dutch Antilles.

There shouldn't have been any problem. The Venezuelan All-Star game was coming up, and that meant a three-day holiday for all those who hadn't been selected to play. When I asked Luis if I could leave, he said, "Fine. That won't be any trouble." Except there was trouble. Luis split for a holiday of his own without giving me the necessary papers that would allow me to leave the country. I was detained at the Maracaibo airport and told that I wasn't allowed to leave. Stunned, I asked what documents were needed for our departure, but no one seemed able to help me. Ozzie Virgil, a coach from the States who was managing down there, came along just in time. After hearing about my difficulty, he explained exactly what I needed, telling me that the only thing standing between me and Aruba was a letter of permission to travel from my general manager. I took a cab back to the stadium, went up to the g.m.'s office, and asked him for that crucial piece of correspondence. He looked at me as if I had three heads. He said, "No, no, no. You are not going to leave. I know what will happen. You will get on the plane and not come back. We want you here for the second half of the season. You're not going to skip the country."

I thought he was joking. I knew some players had walked out on their contracts. Most of them were homesick or couldn't handle the food and water. Others went into culture shock. But I liked it in Venezuela. I pointed out that I was leaving my clothes here in an apartment that was paid up until the end of the season. He said it didn't make a difference. Others had claimed the same thing, and then didn't return. After his refusal, he did something sadistic. He picked up a piece of paper, waved it in front of my face, and said, "This is what you want, and you're not going to get it." It was my letter. He had already filled it out and signed it, but he wasn't going to give it to me. He stuck it in his desk. Pushing him out of the way, I grabbed the note and hightailed it back to the airport. By the time I got there, it was too late for us to catch the flight to Aruba, so I got screwed out of that adventure. But Mary Lou and I did get to spend three days in Curaçao.

When we got back, Aparicio was angry with me. Luis claimed I made him look bad by leaving the way I did. We didn't get along too well after that, and I did end up going before the season was over. I felt bad. I had looked forward to playing winter ball, but Puerto Rico and Venezuela had been somewhat disappointing. I still would like to play at least one more season in Latin America, though. I always wanted to go to Cuba, study their baseball program, lay some slow curves on Castro, and then go body-surfing in the Bay of Pigs. It's one of my many unfulfilled fantasies.

Upon returning to the States, I started to hear rumors about how the Red Sox were going to back up the truck and make some drastic personnel changes. Scott, Lonborg, Culp, Conigliaro, and Peters were all supposedly on the block. And Boston was also reportedly entertaining thoughts about dealing away young, promising, charming, and handsome Bill Lee. To the New York Yankees.

4

I would have left baseball if that trade with the Yankees had gone through. Having grown up hating their cold, corporate image and their strutting glorification of elitism, there was no way I would have put on pinstripes. I would have headed for Japan. The Yankees, though, weren't all that interested in getting me. Their manager, Ralph Houk, wanted Lyle for his bullpen. Boston countered by offering me instead, and New York, bless their hearts, turned them down. The Red Sox gave in and sent them Lyle for Danny Cater. I'll never forget how I felt when I first heard the news about the deal. Relieved. I also remember thinking, Jesus, how could we let Lyle go? You would have thought this team had learned its lesson after it got suckered out of Babe Ruth!

It was a frustrating time. I thought the Red Sox were on the verge of becoming a force. We had made a terrific trade with Milwaukee, sending Scott, Lonborg, Billy Conigliaro, and Lahoud to the Milwaukee Brewers for Tommy Harper, Marty Pattin, and Lew Krausse. Harper was an outfielder who could flat-out motor on the basepaths and hit with some power. He would give us our first real base-stealing threat since the Reconstruction. Krausse could pitch, and I thought Pattin would win twenty games for us just by showing up. While hating to lose Scott, I knew that getting

Harper would allow Yaz to move to first, and that the deal would give us the speed and pitching help we needed. I really liked the look of our roster after that deal. Then we had to go and blow it by trading Lyle.

Clif Keane and Larry Claflin, two reporters in Boston, instigated that deal. They hosted a radio show called Clif and Claf, though in our clubhouse it was better known as Syph and Clap. Both of these gentlemen, neither one of whom could find their way around a baseball field without the aid of a map and a guide, loved to sit back in the safety of the radio studio and take a lot of cheap shots at players. They tried to pass this off as incisive journalism. None of it was constructive, and a good deal of it was cruel. When George Scott reported to camp overweight, they suggested that he be melted down for hockey pucks. That sort of thing. Nothing they said broadened anyone's perception of the game or imparted any sense of the joy that baseball is about. They regularly passed on some less than complimentary remarks about me, but they never got under my skin. I always considered the source.

I thought both of these geniuses seemed anxious to get Danny Cater over here. It was as if he was the answer to everything that ailed the Sox. We kept hearing how Cater was hitting about six thousand against us in Fenway Park, and what a great first baseman he was. Clif and Claf also made it pretty clear that there would be nothing wrong in getting rid of that tobacco-chewing, Dewars-drinking left-hander, not realizing that Sparky was the reincarnation of the Babe and that dealing him to New York would spell our ruination.

I was directly affected by the deal. My role on the club in 1971 had been that of long reliever. I was the guy who would come in during the middle innings and try to keep the game close until we could take a lead and roll out Lyle. Now the Red Sox management was whispering loudly that I was going to replace Sparky as the short man. I told them what they could do with that idea. I knew I wasn't physically up to the rigors of short relief.

The ultimate reliever would be a Tibetan monk. Standing on the mound, he would raise his hand and direct the ball toward the plate simply by using mind over matter. From the moment it left his palm, it would gradually accelerate until it reached the point where the batter could make contact. Then it would disappear and rematerialize in the catcher's mitt. Even the great hitters would get jammed by that pitch. The Red Sox didn't have any apprentice monks on the roster, but they did have Sparky, and he was the next best thing. Lyle used to get a sore arm once every year. It was voluntarily self-inflicted every spring training. During his first few days in camp, he would throw as hard as he could, allowing himself to break down the adhesions in his arm. That left wing would get so sore he'd be unable to pick up an empty glass with it. After a few days of rest the soreness would disappear, and he would be ready to pitch almost every day. An ideal short man should be able to answer the bell several times a week and be used as often as three or four days in a row. I was young and my arm wasn't conditioned to throw that often. I had tried that regimen a couple of times under Dick Williams, and each time I did, my arm paid the price. It would stiffen so badly I would be unable to comb my hair for a week. I didn't feel this would be good for the club or my general appearance, so I balked.

Kasko was good enough to tell me that he understood my problem and that he had no intention of overworking me, explaining that he would work Tatum and me in tandem. We would be alternated, with an eye toward getting the maximum use out of us with the minimum amount of strain. I could go along with that. Eddie must have liked my attitude about it. Praising me in the papers, he told the press the rumors that Boston had offered me to New York were unfounded, and that he never would have permitted the Sox to trade me for Cater. I liked that. It made it seem as if Eddie was in my corner, and I think he was. Until he saw my T-shirt in spring training.

I had walked into the clubhouse in Winter Haven resplendent in the latest addition to my personal wardrobe: a T-shirt with a huge red tongue emblazoned across the front of it, along with the slogan LICK DICK IN '72. The words weren't referring to any dick in general. They were specifically aimed at Richard Nixon, who was running for reelection that year. Kasko saw it and went out of his gourd. He turned out to be more conservative than my father. Eddie loved Nixon, and he thought wearing that shirt was akin to using the American flag as toilet paper. From that day on our relationship was never the same, and I know it affected the way he used me during the season. I made forty-seven appearances, but any time I got into a crucial game it was by accident. I won seven and saved only five. Most of those wins came in games that seemed hopelessly lost when I was brought in. The team would explode for a bunch of runs, and I would luck out a win. Kasko hardly ever used me in a save situation. It was a frustrating season.

I wasn't the only player who was less than pleased with his summer. Yaz was coming off his worst year ever, and after the first few months of the '72 season, it appeared that he was still in his slump. He was really taking a lot of heat in the papers, but to his teammates, Carl was golden. He didn't let his problems at the plate affect his fielding or his relationship with his teammates. No matter how badly things were going for him, he would still come to my locker and talk baseball or fishing. Carl loved baseball, enjoyed every aspect of it. He would usually be the first one in the clubhouse, looking to get a bridge game started. I wasn't a bad card player and was often teamed up with him. He liked me because we won money together. I cherish our friendship, even though it may have shaved a few years off my career. Nightlife doesn't kill a ballplayer. What gets him is trying to keep up with the demands of running around with someone like Yaz. Not to bars or anything. He was always being asked to attend benefits or participate at openings. He rarely turned down a request, and he would often ask me to accompany him. Wherever we went, everyone was quick to buy us a drink. Carl was in animal shape and could handle anything; I never saw him drunk. But it was murder on whoever was with him. Carl would be standing in the middle of the crowd, demonstrating how he waited on the curveball, and I'd be hanging onto a bar stool, slipping into a world that was one step beyond hammered. I was amazed. I'd never seen anyone in the kind of super condition that Carl kept himself in. It was phenomenal. It didn't do my poor body any good, though.

The Player's Association, in a dispute with the owners over the size of our pension benefits, called a strike that tore out the first two weeks of the 1972 season. Gary Peters was the Red Sox player rep, and I was his assistant. I thought we were making a mistake striking when we did. Those first two weeks don't make much of an impact on attendance; the weather's too cold. We should have struck on the Fourth of July, when attendance is about to peak. Owners only believe you mean business if you hit them in the wallet. Being an assistant players' rep gave me an opportunity to observe our union leader, Marvin Miller, up close. Boy, was that impressive. He went in and beat the owners punch for punch. It wasn't because the owners were weak or disorganized, as some reports intimated. It was because Marvin was always so well prepared. He took nothing for granted. If an owner made some point, Marvin would pounce on him with twenty pounds of facts that left his poor victim mumbling to himself. The owners' propaganda machine tried to vilify him as a devil who cared more about his own glory than he did about the game. By the time they got through with him, you would have thought he had sold his firstborn to slavers. It was all bullshit. Marvin was an intelligent and compassionate man who cared about the game *and* the players.

The day we went on strike, he voluntarily gave up all claims on his salary, feeling that if we were going to be made to walk the financial plank, then it was only right that he walk with us. He did this without fanfare, and it won him a lot of respect. However, not all the players were solidly behind the walkout. Reggie Smith stood up the day we took the vote, announcing that he was voting no because every week out was going to cost him four thousand dollars, while it would cost most of the other players less than eight hundred. I looked at him and said, "Reggie, you didn't say that, did you? That didn't come out of your mouth?" But it had. Yaz and Petrocelli were also against the strike. They had been treated well by management and were close to Mr. Yawkey, so this stance was consistent with their honestly held beliefs. And Reggie would go whichever way Carl went. That was totally consistent with his nature, too. The rest of the club voted strike and the brief discussion between Smith and me was forgotten. By everybody but Reggie. From that day on I was *numero uno* on his shit list.

After the season commenced, we played as if we were still walking a picket line. God, were we bad. We were getting whipped by clubs like Milwaukee and Cleveland, teams we should have been eating up. It got so bad that Kasko took to ordering random bed checks. He assigned different coaches to stay in the lobby after curfew, in order to catch late returnees as they stumbled in. The first one, in Milwaukee, was the most successful; it nailed seven of us. Ray Culp got caught coming in five minutes past the deadline. He had been across the street buying an order of tacos to go. Upon returning to the hotel, he discovered that he was being fined a hundred dollars. He flipped out, yelling, "One hundred bucks! You have got to be kidding me! That's thirty-three dollars a taco!" No one had to tell Ray a recession was coming.

I got caught, too. They nailed me coming in the next afternoon, but still only fined me the same hundred. When Culp heard that, he was steaming. He came over to me and said, "How can this be fair? I'm five minutes late and you stay out all night, but we both got fined the same amount." I told him, "Ray, there is no justice." And there wasn't. Ray had bought only three tacos, while I had spent the evening feasting on a long-legged rack of ribs, yet we had both received identical bills. I apologized for the inequity of it all, and Ray just laughed. Culp was a tough man. He once gave up a line drive to Willie Horton that caromed off Ray's head, shooting into centerfield where Reggie Smith made a shoestring catch on it. Culp shrugged it off, got the next batter, and finished the game. When he came into the clubhouse he said, "Don't tell me I don't know where to play hitters."

Curfews and bed checks are time-honored baseball traditions, and they met with a certain amount of success with our ballclub. I can honestly say that every time a bed check was held, they found all the beds. Right where we had left them. Ballplayers get bored with the routine of life on the road, and this boredom makes it very difficult to resist the lure of the bright lights. Every city has a lot of pavement lying in it, waiting to be pounded. I recently saw a television interview with Nancy Marshall and Bobbie Bouton, the former wives of Mike Marshall and Jim Bouton, in which they discussed the extracurricular sexual activities of married ballplayers on the road. The interviewer asked then if they thought any of the ballplayers were true to their spouses. I think it was Nancy who said, "I believe Tommy John is." That was it; she couldn't think of anyone else. Out of approximately five hundred married ballplayers, she was able to come up with one name. I don't believe the odds are as bleak as all that. But they're close.

Most ballplayers subscribe to the blind frog theory of sexual awareness. The blind frog is a species in which neither gender can see. The female lets her prospective mate know she's in heat by a series of noisome movements. The male responds by jumping on anything that sends off vibrations, until he hits the jackpot. Most ballplayers are like that. They will jump the bones of anything that moves.

Baseball is a game for collectors. Teams collect wins and losses, players collect stats, and fans collect souvenirs. There was a woman in Detroit who bribed a bat boy to scrape up some of the dirt around home plate because she wanted to have some of the earth that Tiger catcher Bill Freehan squatted over every night. A souvenir of any sort allows the fan the illusion that he owns a personal share in his hero's life. In that sense the groupie is the ultimate fan. She doesn't settle for a mere autograph. She wants the hand that signs it, and everything that's connected to it. For one night. Athletes are made to feel like gladiators from the days of the Roman Empire. If you took a whole garrison of centurions into Istanbul, what are they going to do on a Friday night? You can only pillage for so long at the ballpark, then you have to search out some relaxation. Strutting into the local tavern of the newly conquered town, you go up to the bar and announce, "I just smoked the shit out of the Cincinnati Reds!" Some smitten young thing is going to immediately say, "Oh, you devil you, let's fuck!" And then it's all over. Ballplayers are suckers for free drinks and long legs who tell them anything they want to hear.

The problem with groupies—or Annies, as they are sometimes called—is that they can give you an overinflated sense of yourself. They go into orgasm if you just look at them and can really make you believe that you are the Second Coming in the sack. It's rarely true. We're just ordinary human beings with excessively greased hormones. There was a female writer in Oakland who did a study on ballplayers in bed. I remember her, because she wore short dresses and no underwear and conducted her survey by trying to screw every ballplayer she came in contact with.

When she was through, she told me that even though ball-players have great hands on the field, most of them were lousy in bed. Especially the superstars, who seemed to think that the moment they dropped their shorts the earth would start spinning off its axis. One example of this was the home run slugger who got it on with her while he spoke to his wife over the phone. When I asked what the conversation was about, the writer said, "Nothing much. He asked her how the kids were and whether or not she had gotten the car fixed. It was all very sick. As soon as his conversation was over, he reached orgasm, rolled off me, and went to sleep." She also told me that the best lovers were usually utility infielders, who, she observed, were all blessed with the ability to play a lot of positions.

Her revelations didn't surprise me. I had once attended a banquet in Washington, D.C., that was held to honor several of the nation's greatest athletes. Also in attendance was a young woman who had dated several players from Washington, Boston, and Baltimore. She covered all the sports. The highlight of this particular bash occurred when one of the honorees was introduced as "that fabulous superstar," prompting her to yell, in a voice loud enough to be heard in Guam, "Superstar, my ass. He's the worst lay in the major leagues." Everybody went into shock, and the outburst put the embarrassed ballplayer away for the rest of the evening. He crawled back to his seat and hid under a napkin.

I met the most famous of all groupies, Chicago Shirley, during my first visit to Comiskey Park. She had achieved a legendary status in baseball, and by now was something more than just another Annie. I realized that when I later met Detroit Shirley, Milwaukee Shirley, and a Shirley from Cleveland. Shirley had become a franchise, with outlets all over the country. Just like McDonald's.

Each Annie has a different approach. Some send letters with intimate photos enclosed. Others will send flowers to a player's room, accompanied by a written invitation to dinner. Then there is the direct approach. You'd be sitting in the bullpen and some hot number would lean over the stands and say, "Hey, you with the cute ass. How about it?" I had one girl do that to me. She spent fifteen minutes trying to talk me into meeting her after the game. She kept insisting that she was madly in love with me and that her life would be unfullfilled unless she took me home with her that night. Despite her declaration of undying devotion, I had to pass. She didn't shed a tear. She just asked me what my roommate was doing that night. I said, "I thought you were in love with me!" She responded, "I am in love with you. But I'm also fickle."

The most memorable Annie I had ever met was a woman who followed our club to Baltimore for a weekend series against the Orioles. Our paths crossed under unusual circumstances. I was seated in the hotel bar when one of my teammates came over and told me I had to check out the scene in his room. When we got there, I found this woman taking on what looked like half the ballclub at once. I was invited to partake, but it was one of the few times I was not interested in experiencing something exotic firsthand. I would not venture into that alley. It may not have been the voice of God that was calling us in there, it may have been millions of bacteria armed with baseball bats, waiting to bang us on the head. Or any other exposed part of our anatomy. Hours after this initial "meeting," I saw the same girl downstairs in the bar, looking to get picked up. I couldn't believe it. I just had to go over to her and ask, "Aren't you ever satisfied?" I wasn't criticizing, I was just curious. She assured me that she was easy to satisfy. She just liked to have a good time. When I asked her what she considered a good time, she said, "The Pittsburgh Penguins. All three lines."

There are dangers out there in the night, and many of them are able to hide under the cover of darkness. Two guys on our club once picked up what they thought was a very foxy lady in a dimly lit bar and took her back for an evening of ecstasy in their hotel room. The next morning one of the Rover Boys woke up and got his first look at this girl in the first light of morning. Thoroughly disconcerted, he slipped out from under the covers and sneaked into the bathroom, where he waited to observe his roomie's reaction. He was not disappointed. His buddy woke up, rolled over, took one peep, and let out a scream. It sounded as if he had suffered a heart attack. In telling us about her later that evening, they both agreed that they had felt like the producer in *The Godfather,* the one who woke up and found his horse's severed head in his bed. Both of them swore they would never fool around again. I could understand that. I've had the same thing happen. That's why I went out and bought permanent contact lenses. Before I got them, there was many a time that I would end up with a woman whose face could only be handled by an advanced form of braille. And even then, I risked ruining my hands.

Bringing home an unattractive girl isn't the only risk one takes during the relentless search for the perfect rack of ribs. I got hammered in Texas once, in a place called Friday's. At around midnight, some girl came over and started to throw all kinds of moves at me. In the midst of her come-on, she opened her purse, took out a little black pill, and said, "Take this. It will make you feel great." I'm all for feeling great, so I downed it with my beer. Within minutes I was totally wasted. I was sitting at the bar one moment, and then lying in somebody's guacamole dip the next. Then I blanked out. Upon waking up I found myself in a strange motel room, lying on a sagging waterbed to which I had not been formally introduced. I roused myself up, went outside, and found twenty-five rather obvious homosexuals prancing around the pool. I said to myself, "Oh, God! This just can't be happening to me." I started to check myself all over and kept looking out by that pool, waiting for Rod

Serling to show up dressed as Truman Capote. Fortunately, it turned out that the room belonged to that girl. She and her sister had taken me home and looked after me. That was a relief.

The worst sort of trouble can occur when a woman becomes emotionally attached to a ballplayer she knows she can't have. I saw that happen twice. Once it was with a player who treated a girl rather shabbily, telling her he was single and wanted to spend the rest of his life with her. Later she found out he was married with three kids. The next time Lothario came to town, she confronted him with the facts in a mature and sensible manner. She was great about it, even going so far as to suggest that they have one last fling for old time's sake. Midway through their lovemaking, she suggested that she assume the female superior position. He thought that was a terrific idea. A ballplayer is always looking for ways to conserve energy. She worked him over pretty good and had him just about ready to peak. He was moaning and his eyes were shut. Luckily, he opened them just in time to see the knife she was about to crash through his chest. He blocked her thrust and slung her off of him in one fluid move. Getting up from the bed, he threw her clothes at her and chucked her out of his room. That was a close shave, and he was shaking over it for days. He retained his sense of humor, though. Whenever he told the story, he finished it by saying, "There is only one thing I can't figure out. She was just as naked as I was, and that knife was like a machete. It must have been twelve inches long. What I want to know is where was she hiding it?" I guess we'll never know.

The other time I saw a girl get emotionally fired up over a ballplayer was when a lady in Anaheim fell madly in love with Lyle. She hung all over him and wouldn't let him out of her sight. When we finished our series there, she realized she wouldn't see him until next season. While saying good-bye to him, she broke down into tears. I felt badly about that, but she was with a friend who knew how to cheer her up. This friend was an older woman who was very well known around the league. As soon as this heart-broken babe started bawling, her buddy hugged her and said, "There, there, don't worry. Everything is going to be fine. The Orioles are coming in at seven o'clock to-night." That's the sort of practical partner that ballplayers pray for.

I always theorized that it was a mistake on the part of management not to take advantage of the skirt-chasing tendencies of ballplayers. On our club, for instance, we were always screwing up on the basepaths, missing signs and running past the coach's red light. If the front office was really on the ball, they would have gotten two Playboy bunnies on the coaching lines. I'm not sure how many more signs we would have remembered, but we sure would have paid more attention when they were being flashed.

A flukey piece of baserunning played a large part in our losing the division in '72. After a languid start, we began to play good ball in June. Baltimore had traded Frank Robinson—a dumb move that transformed them into just another ballclub—and none of the other teams in the di-vision had asserted themselves, so our poor start didn't kill us. By mid-season, we were involved in a four-team pen-nant race with Detroit, Baltimore, and New York. The Yan-kees were being carried by Lyle, who was easily the best relief pitcher in baseball that year. Our end of the deal wasn't holding up quite as well. Mario Guerrero, the short-stop New York included in the Lyle trade, was still in the minor leagues, and Cater was spending a lot of time on the bench. He was a mess. Danny had slumped early, just like the rest of the team, and Lyle was saving games for the Yankees from day one. The Boston media castigated the Red Sox front office for being hoodwinked by New York, and Cater had to bear the brunt of the fans' dissatisfaction with the deal. The season wasn't a month old before he had received a new nickname: "Why Me?" Danny would hit a line drive, really smoke the ball, and someone would make a great play on him for the out. He'd come back to the bench, shaking his head and mumbling, "Why me? Why is it always me?" I think the pressure of the deal got to him. That and the Wall. He saw that seductive Green Monster and tried to knock it over every time he came to the plate. That wasn't the type of hitter he was, and it hurt him. He ended up batting around .230.

Cater had the funniest way of dealing with things. He treated each at-bat as if it was a small melodrama. Once, while we were playing the Brewers, he got hit in the helmet by one of their pitchers. The shot dropped him like a sack of cement. Several of us came running out of the dugout to see how he was, and we were joined at the plate by George Scott, now playing first base for Milwaukee. Cater rolled on the ground, screaming, "I can't see! I can't see!" Everyone was frightened except George, who laughed and said, "Try opening your eyes!" That did the trick. Why me, indeed.

Danny also had a few problems in the field. He was a good first baseman, but he fouled up a lot of pick-off attempts. At first I thought he was unaware that he had been given the sign, but after talking to him I realized that he was completely unaware that a sign existed. He screwed me up on several occasions. I eventually considered hiring a Western Union man to come out to first during a game and bring him a telegram, announcing, "I AM GOING TO THROW TO FIRST STOP BE AWAKE." It's doubtful it would have made a difference. Danny was never ready for me. I think he was too busy daydreaming about how Lyle might be faring that day. Actually, I didn't blame him for messing up the play. I had a pretty good move and could pick off my own first baseman in a heartbeat.

There were several keys to our pennant drive that season. The single biggest factor was the pitching of Luis Tiant.

Tiant had been a winning pitcher with the Indians before getting traded to the Twins in 1970. He pitched well in Minnesota, but he came up with a sore arm and was released at the start of the 1971 season. Atlanta picked him up. He didn't pitch well there and before the year was half over, he was sold to Boston. It was the best deal the Sox ever made. Tiant struggled for us that season, but he ran all the time, jogging long distances in order to get back into shape. He hadn't thrown much over the last two years, and his legs were weak. As soon as they got stronger, his arm came around. Kasko did a good job with him, using him first as a mop-up man and then in long relief. Luis worked his way into the starting rotation, and once he started pitching regularly, he was awesome. He had sixty different pitches that he threw from ninety different angles. When he first came into the majors he was strictly a flame-thrower, but now he mixed his pitches up. He was like a righthanded Mike Cuellar, except he could still throw hard. Watching him pitch was the most fun I could have in baseball without being on the mound myself. He turned the pitching rubber into a stage, pirouetting and twisting into the most bizarre gyrations, so that the batters had no idea where the ball was coming from. Luis won fifteen games for us, pitching six shutouts and leading the league in ERA. He stabilized our pitching staff.

Tiant was also great to have in the clubhouse. God, I loved being around him. He was a sensitive and funny man who kept everybody in the clubhouse loose. He could criticize a player in a way that nobody found offensive. Once Harper pulled a rock in the outfield, costing us a few runs in a game we lost. When we came into the locker room, everybody was upset. Luis got up off his chair to go to the john. He took a dump, flushed the toilet, and yelled, "Goodbye, Tommy!" It broke up everyone and took the edge off a tough loss. Luis and Tommy were like brothers and were always getting on each other. Harper would make fun of

Luis' big behind and would hang pictures of orangutans with cigars drawn in their mouths over Tiant's locker. Luis was the only man I ever saw who could smoke a cigar in the shower without getting it wet. It was an amazing thing to see, like watching Houdini. He was a happy-go-lucky guy who remained the same, win or lose. But he was also a fierce competitor, and everybody on the club respected him. He used humor to make people aware that the game was important, but it was also meant to be fun. A club has to have that sort of attitude if it's going to survive a tight pennant race.

Harper was a big guy for us. Smith's knees were bothering him, and Tommy had to take over in center while Smith moved to right. He did a great job out there. He couldn't throw with Smith, but he covered a lot of ground and, with his speed, was the igniter of our offense.

Catching had always been a problem for the Red Sox, but Carlton Fisk made our club during spring training and turned the position into a plus for us. His game had changed since I had played with him in the minors. He was much improved behind the plate and was one hundred times better as a hitter. The ball jumped off his bat. Young and idealistic when he first joined us, Carlton had a utopian view of the game, viewing the majors as a large-scale version of the minors. He could not understand the clique situation on our club. The social polarization that occurs on a team is not an unusual or even necessarily a bad thing. Twenty-five guys can only stay in the same room with each other for so long. But Fisk didn't understand this. He thought everybody would be going out to eat together and be more of a group off the field. It upset him when he discovered that things weren't like that up here. He also expected Yaz and Smith, the team's two biggest stars, to be the club's leaders. When he didn't see them taking up the reins, he really let them have it in the papers. I didn't see the problem, but I never did think much of leadership talk. As far as I was concerned the best leadership is provided by a grand slam home run that overcomes a three-run lead, or by a shutout that stops a losing streak. Anyway, by the time Carlton spoke his piece to the writers—something I thought took a lot of guts, whether I agreed with him or not—we had already found our leader. And it was him.

Fisk took charge of our pitching staff and really turned it around. He had learned the importance of working a pitcher and nursing him along when he didn't have his best stuff. Fisk also demanded your total concentration during a game. If you shook him off and then threw a bad pitch that got hit out, he had a very obvious way of expressing his displeasure. After receiving a new ball from the umpire, he would bring it out to you, bouncing it on the grass like a basketball all the way to the mound. There would be an expression on his face that said, "If you throw another half-ass pitch like that, I'm going to stuff this ball down your throat."

Carlton always gave his best effort, and he demanded the same of everyone he played with. That was important. Not so much in his dealings with Tiant, Siebert, Culp, and Peters. They were veterans who knew what it took to win, and they had been around the league long enough to be aware of the weaknesses of every hitter they faced. Fisk's biggest contribution to the club was found in the way he took care of Lynn McGlothen and John Curtis and turned them into major-league pitchers. The three of them had been in the minors together.

Curtis was a lefthander with good stuff and a great curveball. McGlothen was a Bob Gibson clone. I had seen Lynn pitch in the minors and thought even then that he was impressive. But since that time he had smoothed out his motion and was throwing even harder than when I had last seen him. These two eventually pushed Culp and Peters out of the starting rotation. By July we were starting Tiant,

Pattin, Siebert, Curtis, and McGlothen. The five of them really put us on a roll. Fisk was a calming influence on Pattin. Marty had a lot of talent, but he was high-strung. He used to throw up after the first inning of every game he pitched. Carlton would make him stay within himself, getting him to take out his anxiety on the hitters. Marty still threw up with every start, but then he would come out in the second inning and look like Cy Young, Jr. He won seventeen games for us and was smoking down the stretch.

Ben Oglivie was another farm-system graduate who helped the club. He was a tall, wiry lefthanded hitter with all kinds of power and good speed in the outfield. Ben faked a lot of people out. They heard he was from Colon, Panama, and assumed he would have difficulty with English. So on first meeting they would talk to him very slowly and in a loud voice, using many hand gestures. It was a riot, because the first thing I had noticed about him was his ability to complete *The New York Times* crossword puzzle in about five minutes. He did have an accent, but he was the brightest guy on the club and had hardly any trouble understanding anybody who didn't stick his hand in Ben's face while they spoke. When we got him we were able to put him in left and play Yaz at first against righthanders. Cater played first against lefties, with Yaz moving back to the outfield. That put our lineup in great shape. Yaz came out of his year-and-a-half slump after the All-Star break, hitting the ball where it was pitched and going on a tear that lasted the rest of the season. By the final two weeks of the schedule, it was still mathematically a four-team race, but it was clear that the two best clubs were us and Detroit. In late September, we took a doubleheader from Baltimore that effectively knocked them out of the race. The Yankees followed suit, and, after the season's final weekend, we were in first place, half a game ahead of Detroit with three games left to play. All with the Tigers, and all in Detroit.

I think we were a little bit tight when we opened that final series. We had spent the first part of the season being vilified by the media for playing bad ball. Then we spent the second part hearing how, now that we were in the pennant race, we would invariably blow it. The only question it seemed was how. The pressure was getting to everybody. Luis was still wisecracking, but you could sense the edge underneath the humor. The laughter it elicited seemed forced. Even Peters, the coolest customer on the team, seemed somewhat frazzled. The night before we started that big series in Detroit, Gary and I had gone to Lindell's AC, where we ran into Larry Claflin. He came up to us at the bar and said, "You guys don't deserve to win the pennant because of the strike. Ballplayers are all alike. You're all a bunch of bastards." Normally, that was the sort of thing that Peters would have some fun with. Gary was good at using his tongue to whittle a guy down to size. This time he didn't say a word. He just started climbing over bar stools as he headed for Claflin's throat. I was able to hold him off just long enough for Claflin to make an unmolested getaway. Good thing, too. Gary was as strong as an ox, and there was no way I could have held him much longer. He would have had Claflin for dinner.

I had my own share of anxiety before that series got under way. Kasko hadn't used me in very many crucial situations throughout the season, but I was hoping to see some action in Detroit. They had a lot of lefthanded hitters—guys like Cash, Jim Northrup, and Dick McAuliffe— and I was certain Eddie would be using me against them sometime during the series. It didn't seem possible that he would risk the pennant over a T-shirt. When we headed out to the ballpark Monday night, I was antsy to get into a game of importance, and I was nervous, wondering how I would do once I got out there. I figured it could be put-up-or-shut-up time for my favorite lefthander.

We lost the first game, and our lead, when the Tigers beat us, 4–1, behind Mickey Lolich. In the third inning of that game, that funky piece of baserunning I had alluded to earlier occurred. We had Harper on third and Aparicio on first with a man out, when Carl hit what looked like a sure triple. Harper scored, and Aparicio was about to do the same, when he slipped rounding third. He completely missed the bag and was forced to reach back to touch it. Unfortunately for us, Luis' hand and Carl's foot reached for third base at exactly the same moment. Two baserunners sharing the same bag is a no-no. Yaz was called out. Instead of a big inning with Lolich on the ropes and ready to be put away, we ended up with only one run. The shock of the mishap took the wind out of our sails. What made the accident so strange—besides the fact that Aparicio was the best baserunner on the club, if not in the league—was the remembrance that the same mixup, involving the very same players, had also occurred in Detroit on the first day of the season. Lolich was the winner of that game, too. I guess the gods of baseball were trying to give us a clue that this was not to be our year.

Tiant went against Woody Fryman in the second game of the series. We scored an unearned run in the first, and for five innings it looked as though that would be enough. But Detroit tied it in the sixth. Next inning Luis was able to get only one man out. McAuliffe doubled and then scored on a single by Al Kaline, who took second on the throw home. With Duke Sims, a lefthanded hitter at the plate, Kasko came out to the mound and signaled for me to come into the ballgame. This was it.

My heart was pounding when I set myself on the pitching rubber, but I was no longer nervous. I felt like a wild animal ready to pounce on anything that moved. I liked that feeling; it usually indicated that I was going to do well. That expectation seemed justified when I was able to induce Sims to tap a slow roller back to Aparicio at short. As soon as it left his bat, I thought, That's an out. But it wasn't. Playing far back on the slow-moving Sims, Luis was unable to come in quickly enough to make a play on the ball. Sims was safe at first, and Kaline had moved over to third. The next batter, Norm Cash, tried to score Al with a suicide squeeze. Yaz, playing first, raced toward the mound, scooping the ball up in one fluid motion but bobbling it for an error as he tried unsuccessfully to get Kaline at home. The score was 3–1. We got out of the inning without suffering further damage, and I pitched a scoreless eighth, but it wasn't enough. When we made the final out in the ninth inning, that two-run deficit had remained unchanged.

After the game the clubhouse was a mortuary. There was no sound except for the whispered by-play between the writers and various players, and the sobbing of Yaz in his locker. It was an emotional experience, coming as close as we did only to lose it on the next-to-last day of the season. I felt hollow and a little insane. Trying to console myself with the thought that this had been a character-building experience didn't work. By the time we left the ballpark I was pissed. In one and two-thirds innings against Detroit, I had given up no earned runs on two base hits. I could have done that kind of job for Kasko all summer. If he had used me instead of locking me in his doghouse, the season would have turned out differently. At least, I thought it would have. Then I asked myself why I was damaging my mind with these poisonous ideas. When I got home I scooped out my brain and tossed it in the dishwasher. After a two-hour cleaning, I put it back in my head and felt as good as new. Last season was over. I was ready for next year.

5

The mound is my personal zone. I compete with myself in an attempt to place each pitch more perfectly than the one that preceded it. I could always relate to Kirk Douglas in *Young Man with a Horn*, trying to strike that note that nobody had ever hit before. I was always trying to throw the perfect sinker.

Being on the mound puts me in a relaxed state of superconsciousness. The feeling is laid back, but still intense. Everything is slowed down, yet you are able to perceive things at an incredibly fast rate. Line drives shot up the middle may look hard to the observer in the stands, but they never seemed dangerous when they were hit back to me. They floated to the mound in slow motion. When your arm, mind, and body are in sync, you are able to work at peak performance level, while your brain remains relaxed. It's Zen-like when you're going good. You are the ball and the ball is you. It can do you no harm. A common bond forms between you and this white sphere, a bond based on mutual trust. The ball promises not to fly over too many walls after you have politely served it up to enemy hitters, and you assure it that you will not allow those same batters to treat the ball in a harsh or violent manner. Out of this trust comes a power that allows the pitcher to take control of what otherwise might be an uncontrollable situation.

During those moments on the pitching rubber, when you have every pitch at your command working to its highest potential, you are your own universe. For hours after the game, this sense of completeness lingers. Then you sink back to what we humorously refer to as reality. Your body aches and your muscles cry out. You feel your mortality. That can be a difficult thing to handle. I believe pitchers come in touch with death a lot sooner than other players. We are more aware of the subtle changes taking place in our body and are unable to overlook the tell-tale hints that we are not going to last on this planet forever. Every pitcher has to be a little bit in love with death. There's a subconscious fatalism there. All baseball players attempt to suspend time, and the bitch of it is we're only partially successful.

I felt like I was about to attain a level of mastery in 1973 much like those little bald-headed kids who study Zen with their teachers in the Himalayas. But I didn't know where I would be making a practical use of my knowledge. There were heavy trade rumors surrounding me during the winter of '72, rumors that were founded in the truth that Kasko wanted to get rid of me. I asked Eddie about them on the first day of spring training. He didn't exactly give me a vote of confidence, telling me that no player should be shocked if he's traded. Hearing that, I went a step further. I asked him what my chances were of sticking with the club. Eddie gave me his most sincere look and said, "Bill, we're going to have to see. As it stands now, you'll have to beat out John Curtis and Roger Moret." Curtis and Moret! I couldn't believe this. Curtis was a starter and was already penciled into Kasko's projected rotation for '73. That meant I had to battle Moret for a spot, and that was crazy. Roger had pitched all of five innings with us the year before, having spent an entire season in the minors. Despite Eddie's erratic use of me, I did manage to turn in a winning record, and I had the second lowest ERA on the staff. Only

Tiant's was better. None of that meant anything. Eddie had made it quite clear in our discussion that I was battling for Moret's spot. I thought it should have been the other way around.

Moret and Curtis did make the club, but that wasn't enough to keep me from coming north with them. Our pitching had looked awful in exhibition games, and I was one of the few pitchers to have a decent spring, forcing Kasko to keep me on the team. All my spring-training performance did, at first, was win me a spot on the roster. It certainly didn't get me into any ballgames. Kasko didn't have me pitch an inning until an April 16 outing against the Tigers. I pitched four and two-thirds innings, giving up two hits and only one earned run. That was a pretty good performance, considering what little work I had been getting. From the day I had pitched my last game in Florida to the day I came on in relief against Detroit, I had gone eighteen days without getting into a box score. I became philosophical about it, figuring Eddie was looking out for my best interests. Pitching on two weeks' rest, I could have stayed in the majors until I was ninety. And then I would have retired only because of the difficulty I would probably encounter while fielding bunts. Pattin started that game against Detroit. He got jocked, surrendering eight runs in three and two-thirds innings. After yielding a home run to Willie Horton, Pattin charged home plate and started screaming. I freaked. I thought he was yelling at Horton, which, given the fact that Willie is built like a small condominium, was not the wisest thing to do. This was a misreading. Marty was actually yelling at Umpire Joe Brinkman, who was considerably smaller than Mr. Horton. Willie hit the home run, but Pattin took it out on the umpire. That was the day I decided that Marty was a genius.

Three days after that appearance Kasko used me against the Tigers again, this time in relief of Tiant. I pitched five and two-thirds innings, giving up only two runs. I was happy to be getting the work, but both times I had been brought into games that were lost causes. It appeared that Eddie was going to banish me for another season, to mop-up-man's limbo. That may have been his intention, but, as the season progressed, our pitching continued to get splattered, and I continued to pitch well. Eventually, I was brought into situations when the game was on the line and, when I continued to get people out, Kasko was finally convinced to give me a shot as a starter.

On May 1 I started against the Rangers and got slammed for ten hits in six innings. I gave up six runs but escaped without the loss. McGlothen was handed that when he gave up the tie-breaking run in relief. I thought I was horseshit, but Kasko said he didn't think I pitched as badly as the score indicated. I kept waiting for the punch line, but there wasn't any. Instead he told me I would get another start. As I said, our pitching was really awful. Four days after that debacle against Texas, I went seven and two-thirds innings against the Twins, winning 5–1. Another four days went by, and then I pitched my first major-league complete game, beating Cleveland, 4–3. I was 3–0 with a 2.95 ERA, prompting Eddie to announce that I was part of the regular rotation until further notice.

I had mixed emotions about starting. I enjoyed the challenge that came from knowing that the first pitch I threw in a game was an important one, and I liked the steady work. It had mopping up in 19–2 ballgames beat by a whole lot. But I hated the four days between starts. It drove me nuts. I play for the fun of the game and the sense of pure competition. But I would still get mad when I lost. I hated losing. As a reliever, if I had a bad outing I could go out and get blitzed that night, waking up the next morning ready to redeem myself. But as a starter I had that gap between games, subjecting me to too many days of penance. Ideally, I would have liked to have been Babe Ruth in his days with the Sox. I would have pitched every fourth day and played the outfield in between starts. That would have been great.

Of course, these weren't the days of Ruth. This was 1973, and I wasn't even allowed to hit anymore. I loved to swing the bat, but pitchers fell victim that season to the designated hitter. The D.H. rule was the bastard son of Bowie Kuhn and Charlie Finley. This had to be a one-night stand, because it was surely baseball's oddest coupling. They claimed it would increase offense, but what it also did was force starters to pitch more innings than they should have, thus increasing the risk of injury to their arms. It robbed the game of its strategic possibilities in the late innings and turned every pitcher in the league into half a ballplayer. Once Finley got that aberration in place, he tried to sell baseball on the idea of the three-ball walk as another way to perk up scoring. I wondered why they just didn't get rid of pitchers altogether. They could have just put the ball up on a tee and let the batters swing away to their hearts' content. Or better yet, they could have disposed of all the players. Just play out the schedule on a computer. For years I've been called a rebel. Well, I'm not. It's guys like Finley who are the rebels. I'm a baseball traditionalist.

I hated the D.H. and all the other new wrinkles that had been introduced in an attempt to corrupt the game. I wanted to go back to natural grass, pitchers who hit, Sunday double-headers, day games, and the nickel beer. And no more instant replays. I want fans paying attention out there. The instant replay used to blow my great-grandfather's mind. Every time a reprise of a great catch was shown, he'd exclaim, "I don't believe it, he did it again!" We have to drive these atrocities out of baseball. It will be doing the entire country a great service. Baseball is the belly button of America. If you straighten out the belly button, the rest of the country will follow suit.

Hitters loved the D.H. rule. Especially older players who had lost their mobility in the field but could still hit. The

Twins had Tony Oliva with his bad knees in that category, and Tommy Davis was the Orioles' most dangerous hitter, even without an ankle. Our club countered with Orlando Cepeda. He was amazing. I thought if they could ever design a wheelchair that he could hit out of, he would have hit .400 and won the MVP award. He put on the most astonishing hitting exhibition I had ever seen in Kansas City. He hit a double into the leftfield corner in the first inning. Next time up he doubled into left center. In his third trip to the plate he doubled to right center. In his last at-bat, he hit a two-bagger down the first-base line. I had never seen anybody use an entire field that way. Of course, all these shots would have been triples if he could have run at all. It was like watching a righthanded Rod Carew with power but absolutely no speed. Orlando had a great year with the bat for us, but by next season he was gone. The club couldn't afford to carry a guy who couldn't play the field. A few years after he left baseball he was picked up for possession of marijuana, as he was departing the States for his hometown in Puerto Rico. I wanted to handle his defense of the charges. I would have had him claim that the pot he was carrying was only for his own personal consumption, and that he had no intention of dealing it. Even if Orlando were carrying about six suitcases filled with the stuff, I would have argued that he expects to live to see his one hundred and twelfth birthday, and the stash only would have lasted until his eighty-second year.

Tiant used marijuana, but he never smoked it. He put it in a mixture with honey, liniment, and other herbs. He would have it rubbed into his arm a few hours before he pitched. That was the secret of his longevity. One of the trainers massaged it into Luis' wing. I don't think he knew what it was, but he was always very happy after working Luis over. He would sit on our bench while Tiant pitched, looking very content.

I pitched well during my first month as a starter and began to enjoy the responsibility of regular work. Stamina was no problem. I paced myself until I got past the sixth inning, then I pretended I was pitching in short relief. When I did get into trouble, I could turn the ball over to our bullpen. Bob Bolin was having a great year, sharing relief duties with Bob Veale. I loved Bob Veale. Six feet six inches and two hundred thirty-five pounds of pure gentleman. He was nicknamed Johnson because of his habit of calling everybody on the team Johnson. Bob wasn't much for remembering names. Also in the pen was a young pitcher named Don Newhauser. He was a righthander who would have been a star if it wasn't for his habit of hanging upside down in the bullpen. When asked why he did it, he explained that it gave him a different perspective on the ballgame. I could buy that. He had a great arm and a lot of heart, but he fell on his head while hanging upside down in the Kansas City bullpen, hurt his back, and ruined his career. That was a shame. With these guys backing up the starters, our pitching straightened itself out and we started to win ballgames. Only two things marred this happy period for me.

One was the release of Siebert. Sonny had the best arm on the staff, but Kasko had it in for him. Eddie was of the old school. If you were injured, but there wasn't any bone showing, you were supposed to play. Sonny was a great physical specimen, a former All-American in basketball, but he was a fragile commodity and could not pitch unless he was one hundred percent physically. After he hurt his ankle running on a beach in late '72, we could not get him to take his regular turn. Kasko never forgave him for that, and he got rid of him—trading him to Texas—the first chance he got. Sonny had been my roommate. He used to stand in front of a mirror at four in the morning, practicing his pitching motion. He was a good guy, but it was tough to sleep with all those lights on. Still, I didn't think it was a good idea to let him go, and I said so publicly. As luck would arrange it, the next time we faced Texas Siebert was matched against me. I beat him 10–3. I was not surprised to discover that beating him that way didn't bother me. He was my friend, but between the lines he was just another opponent.

The other incident that cast a temporary pall over the opening weeks of the season was a fistfight with my teammate and biggest admirer, Reggie Smith. Reggie and I had never gotten along. I'm still not sure why. I am sure that he was the greatest piece of baseball machinery that I had ever seen. There wasn't anything a person could do on the playing field that Reggie couldn't do better than anybody. He could hit for power and average from both sides of the plate, run like a world-class sprinter, and play centerfield as well as anybody in the league. He also came equipped with the greatest arm I had ever seen. Once, during a rain delay, Yaz and Smith were sitting in the dugout discussing their arms. They decided to pass some time by having a contest to see who could throw the ball further. Yaz had a great gun. He jumped out of the dugout, took a running start and heaved the ball from the first-base line to the base of the leftfield wall. A great throw. Reggie did not take a running start. Stepping from the dugout, he walked over to the spot Yaz had thrown from, reared back, and threw. We never saw that ball again. It cleared everything. I could not get over the power and majesty of his toss. Reggie would get off a throw like that in a ballgame, and he'd just awe the opposition. But Reggie could never hit a cut-off man, and he was constantly throwing the ball over the third baseman's head. You couldn't even back up his throws, they were so fast and high. He loved to show off his arm's strength, but he had zero accuracy.

Smith had a lot of problems in Boston. He was a black man playing for an organization that, in a scouting report written in the late fifties, had called pitcher Earl Wilson "a nice colored boy." The Red Sox had also been the last organization in major-league baseball to break the color line. The racial philosphy of the club reflected the philosophy of a very large, vocal segment of the town's population. Reggie received some hate mail, the sort that started "Dear Nigger," and then got nasty. The letters could only hurt his psyche. That wasn't enough for some crazies. They took to throwing hard objects at him in the outfield, forcing him to wear a batting helmet while playing out there. Not all these objects were tossed at him because he was black. Reggie could be less than friendly to fans, and he was not a popular figure on counts other than race. This treatment, understandably, made him insecure and might explain why Reggie took great pains to become a carbon copy of Yaz. Carl—despite the booing he heard in '69 and '71—had become an institution in Boston, a status Reggie wanted to attain but one he knew he could never reach. He tried, though. He started parroting everything Carl said. His stand on the strike was a good example. He was just going along with Yaz. After a while he earned himself a nickname: Carl Reggie Smith. Reggie did his best to act like a white man trapped in a black man's body. It was a strange and sad thing to watch.

I had been on to Reggie for a long time, but it wasn't until the club received a new double-knit uniform that I realized the extent of his insecurity. In April of 1973 a company sent us the uniform for demonstration purposes, but they sent only two sets, one home and one away. Both had the same number on the back: Carl's number eight. This was an example of an elitist mentality, using the resident superstar's number for the test run. Yaz tried on the home uniform. The company was anxious to get his opinion on it. I thought it made him look like a Shriner. I also thought that getting Carl's opinion on fashion was not the brightest idea in the world, either. I mean, hadn't these people ever seen that raincoat? Moments after Carl came out in his new threads, Reggie walked into the clubhouse. One look was all it took. He went over to where the away version of the uniform was, got undressed, and put it on. This had to be his ultimate fantasy, wearing the Boston uniform with Carl's name and number on the back. When I saw him, I nearly died. It was just too much for me to handle. I started singing, "Me and my Shadow..." Spinning around, Reggie fixed me with a glare and told me to shut my fucking mouth. He didn't like being kicked in the identity problem.

From that day on there was an undercurrent of violence whenever we were in a room together. In Cleveland I hit four home runs in batting practice, and he started yelling at me, "You couldn't hit the ball like that in a game!" He was serious, so I answered, "No shit, Sherlock. I'm not paid to hit the ball in a game. You are." That seemed to get to him. He ran over to the batting cage and came up in my face, asking, "You think I can't? Do you think I can't?" I thought he was being a bit too intense, so I kept my distance after that as best I could, but he eventually caught up to me.

It was a May 24 game against the Brewers in Boston that brought things to a head. I was pitching for the good guys, and Billy Champion was throwing for Milwaukee. In the first inning Champion nailed Doug Griffin with a slider, breaking his left hand. Reggie out of the lineup that day with a hangnail or some other crippling injury, turned to me in the dugout, yelling, "You got to hit somebody. Deck them. You got to protect your hitters." I said, "Look, Reggie, it's early in the game and there's no score. Let's get a lead or wait until we're way behind. Then I'll get them." He nodded. It was the most civil exchange we had had in months.

In the bottom of the second we scored two runs. As I took the mound for the top of the third, I figured now was the time for some retaliation. I turned to face the hitter, and guess who it was? Ellie Rodriguez. I thought, No. This is unbelievable! I drilled him on the left shoulder with my second pitch, knocking him sprawling to the ground. Jumping up, Ellie looked as though he was about to launch into his charge-the-mound routine. My catcher, Bob Montgomery, headed him off. Grabbing him around the waist, Bob held him until he cooled down. After he was released, Rodriguez walked to first and took his lead. And I tried to pick him off. The umpire called him safe on a close play, but Ellie was so pissed he screamed at me for the rest of the inning. I'm certain he wanted to mug me again, but he didn't have any relatives with him.

Later in the game, I was pitching to Brewer second baseman Pedro Garcia. A dead pull hitter. I threw him my slow curve and he hit a line shot into the visiting team's dugout. It caught Rodriguez in the ribs. I thought, You got to be kidding me! Is this fate? He who lives by the sword, dies by same. Rodriguez, a man who brought violence with him to the stadium, was getting the shit kicked out of him by this little ball. It was just extraordinary.

After retiring the Brewers in the third, I went back to our dugout and found Reggie waiting for me. I figured he was going to congratulate me for the hit. Instead he climbed all over me, saying, "So, you finally hit somebody and naturally you pick on a black guy." I explained to him that I had my own personal vendetta against Rodriguez and that he should get off my case. Reggie didn't want to hear it, so I advised him to go soak his pinky.

I should explain that throughout the game, in between appearances on the mound, I had been drinking cough syrup. I had a terrible cold that day, was sick as a dog, and needed the stuff to get through the game. By the third inning I had downed two-thirds of a bottle of Cheracol. That stuff must be pure codeine, the exact opposite of greenies. It got me hammered. Within no time I was standing on the mound having a hell of a time. I would throw the ball and think, Hey, far out. Look at that slow curve. That fucker can't hit that pitch. After the top of the eighth. I went back to the clubhouse in order to do another hit. Smith was waiting for me as I came in. He jumped out of his chair and took a swing at me. I ducked. Reggie nailed a guy who was following me, carrying my warm-up jacket. Ignoring the fact that he had almost broken the gentleman's teeth, Reggie grabbed me, picked me up, and dropped me on my head. Before he could do any more damage, a couple of stadium guards ran in and pulled him off of me. I was dazed. Between the codeine and the beating, I didn't know where I was. Somehow I managed to come out for the ninth and get the Brewers in order. When the game ended I went back into the clubhouse and found Reggie sitting in his chair with his head down. I thought he was making an act of contrition. I walked past him into the trainer's room to put some ice on my head. The next thing I know, I'm being bounced off the team bulletin board. Reggie had jumped out of his chair and nailed me again. Some players and coaches came over and grabbed him and managed to get the both of us out of there before the reporters showed up. Afterward, in the shower, Reggie came over to me and said, "Bill, you're a better man than me." Great. My head was out to Mars, and I looked like the grounds crew had used me to rake the infield. If he believed I was a better man than he was, I sure wished he could have realized it sooner.

The only satisfaction I got that day—besides nailing Rodriguez—was in picking up another win. That made me 4–1, starting a tear that had me 12–4 by the All-Star break. That mark was good enough to get me named to the All-Star team. Dick Williams, the American League manager, called me with the news on July 16, and the next day I received a letter from league president Joe Cronin, officially informing me of my selection. On the bottom of the notice, right beneath Cronin's signature, was the handwritten plea, "Play To Win!" The American League had lost nine of the last ten All-Star confrontations. That postscript was Cronin's way of letting us know that we were supposed to approach this event with our game faces on. Joe was sick of getting trounced by the National League year after year.

The game was being held in Royals Stadium, Kansas City, and when I got there I thought it was really neat. It was like being in Disneyland. I didn't think about what an honor it was to have been named to the squad. I was too busy getting off on meeting Rose, Aaron, Stargell, and all the other great players I never got to compete against. The National League lineup was awesome. Prior to the game, Williams made a fiery speech, declaring that our team was just as good as theirs and how we were going to "beat those cocksuckers." It was very rousing. He concluded his talk by announcing the starting lineups for both squads. Upon finishing, he called his pitchers together and asked, "Are any of you physically unable to throw tonight?" I raised my hand. Dick said, "But Bill, you pitched three days ago. That's plenty of rest. You should be able to go at least a couple of innings." I said, "Not against these guys." I wasn't stupid.

I never did get into the game that night. Good thing, too. Every time we sent a pitcher into the game the National League acted like his only purpose was to throw batting practice. It was raining baseballs all night long. Sitting out in the bullpen, I felt like I was watching the game from a foxhole. At one point Nolan Ryan came in to face Willie Davis. The sequence of pitches Nolan threw was fantastic. High fastball, 110 miles an hour. Ball one. High fastball, 105 miles an hour. Ball two. Low fastball down the chute, 100 miles an hour. *Vaya con dios.* Davis hit that pitch over the rightfield wall, 425 feet on a line. Turning to watch it as it shot out of the ballpark, I thought, Jesus, I guess he got all of that one. They beat us, 7–1. I think the only way we could have won would have been to erect a mechanized steel wall around the field and raise it every time their side got up.

Fisk played in that game. He was the starting catcher, going 0 for 2 and being charged with a passed ball that really wasn't his fault. He was catching Bill Singer of the Angels at the time. Singer had a spitball that could croon "God Save the Queen" in forty different languages. He uncorked a hellacious one in the fourth inning with Pete Rose at the plate. It rolled off the table, eluded Fisk, and bounced all the way back to the screen. Looking down at Fisk, Pete shook his head and said, "He surprised you more than he did me." It shouldn't have been that alarming. The entire pitching staff of the Angels—with the exception of Ryan—was throwing spitballs. If K-Y jelly went out of business, they all would have been pitching in Double-A ball.

A pitcher will use anything to hang on, and saliva provides a good medium for his survival. Ron Kline had a great spitter. He tried teaching it to me, but I couldn't get it to do very much. Many guys throw it their entire career and others only use it while their arms are sore, dropping it when they get healed. One of our pitchers, Dick Pole, tinkered with it, but he found that his sinker had a better drop. The best spitballer I ever saw was a little kid out of Dade Junior College by the name of Joe Arnold. He pitched for the Alaska Panhandlers. He could make the ball tap dance. It ended up blowing out his arm, though. That happens a lot. The spitter is very tough on the arm; it's not a cure-all, and not everyone can master it.

I've thrown two spitballs in my entire career, both to Tony Taylor in a 1973 game against the Tigers. They were thrown to protest the fining of Jim Merritt, a lefthanded pitcher with the Texas Rangers. Merritt had an arm problem similar to the one that incapacitated Tommy John, but doctors hadn't yet perfected the surgical method that would later make John as good as new. Jim had to wear a nylon sock on his left arm in order to pitch. After winning a game, he confessed to using the spitball to get some crucial outs. Joe Cronin fined Merritt a thousand dollars for the admission. That was unfair. Gaylord Perry had admitted the same thing in his autobiography. All that happened to him was that he went on to make a lot of money in book royalties. The day after the fine was announced, I admitted I had thrown spitters to Taylor. The first one broke straight down for strike three. Later I threw him another one, but it stayed up. Tony hit the dry side, and the ball ended up killing a cosmonaut. After admitting my guilt to the press, I challenged Cronin to fine me. I would have taken him to the Supreme Court for discrimination against lefthanders. He didn't do a thing. A writer later asked me why I had picked on Tony with both pitches. I don't know that I was picking on him; he went one for two with a dinger. But I suppose the reporter was right. I should have thrown at least one of them to Al Kaline.

I didn't like pitching to Kaline. Nothing against Al. He was a hell of a guy. I just hated the way umpires gave him the benefit of the doubt on almost every close pitch late in his career. I once threw him five straight strikes and walked him. He took a three-and-two slider that started on the outside corner and finished down the middle of the plate. The ump gave it to him. As Kaline made his way to first, I yelled at him, "Swing the bat, for Christ's sake. You're not a statue until you have pigeon shit on your shoulders." Al laughed at me. After the game I complained about the call to the home-plate umpire. He said, "Son, Mr. Kaline will let you know it's a strike by doubling off the wall." Umpires do make allowances for established veterans. If the pitch is close they figure if the star didn't swing, then it must have been a ball. With age come certain privileges. All things considered, it was a good thing I didn't throw Al a spitball. They probably would have deported me to Estonia.

I received more media attention as a starter than I had as a reliever. I always had something to say, and the reporters seemed to think of me as good copy. I enjoyed the by-play between us. I wasn't crazy about their calling me Spaceman. I'm not sure who first hung the nickname on me. Pete Gammons took to calling me the Ace From Space early in my career. And George Kimball referred to me as Space Cowboy. But I think it was a teammate, John Kennedy, who hung the Spaceman label on me. A reporter had mentioned something to him about one of the latest lunar launches. Kennedy pointed to me and said, "We don't need to watch that. We have our own spaceman right over there."

I was never offended by the appellation; I just thought it was off the mark. I would have preferred to be known as Earth Man. When you're out in space, you're drifting and are at the mercy of a life support system that can be cut off at any time. I had developed a way of answering questions that often had little to do with the question being asked. Early in my career, I had been misunderstood by the press. That might have been my fault; English is not my trump card. But I thought the press was at least partially to blame. So I started to lead them down a verbal primrose path. They would ask why I threw a certain pitch, and I would do five minutes on Einstein's theory of curved space. I wasn't yanking anybody around. I was trying to make a comment on the game: "Let's not take any of this too seriously. The game is supposed to be fun."

The hipper writers—Kimball, Gammons, Leigh Montville and a few others—cued into that, and we had fun with it. Others just couldn't read between the lines. They took everything I said and ran with it as if it was gospel. That didn't bother me much. What did bother me was seeing the facts of a story completely distorted. In 1973 there was a hot tale being written that Fisk and I were feuding. Montgomery had caught me a few times, and the rumor circulated that I had refused to work with Fisk, or that Fisk had refused to catch me. The truth was the Red Sox were just getting Monty some work. Since I threw easy and was always around the plate, the feeling was that Bob, who didn't have the quickest reactions in the world, would have less trouble with me than say a Roger Moret. Fisk never begged off catching me. Carlton wouldn't ask out of a game if he had both his legs cut off. And I wanted him behind the plate. He may have worked slowly, but he was a great receiver and the best clutch hitter on the club.

We did have our disagreements. I would shake him off, and that would drive him nuts. I didn't care. I believe a pitcher should never throw a pitch that he doesn't feel a commitment to. If you don't believe in a pitch, ninety-nine times out of a hundred it's going to get nailed. Then you spend the rest of the game second-guessing yourself. Whenever Carlton came out to the mound to chastise me for shaking him off, I would ask him who knew better than I what kind of stuff I had. He would answer, "Your catcher." Then we would yell at each other for five minutes. By the time we finished and he had returned to his crouch, it was forgotten.

There were other times when he would get on my case during a game in which I needed it. Once, against the Orioles, I was trying to get Aparicio to get ready for a pick-off attempt at second. Luis wouldn't go for it, yelling that I should concentrate on the hitter at the plate instead of fooling around with a trick play. That ticked me off. It showed me up, and it also told Baltimore what I was planning to do. I screamed back at him, and Fisk came running out to the mound. He jumped on me for showing emotion. He believed I should be more stoic out on the playing field. I agreed, but I had those moments when I bugged out. Carlton calmed me down. By screaming at me. He yelled, "Don't worry about these fucking guys! Cut the shit, bear down, and we'll get two." More times than not, we would.

Writers who couldn't see past their pencils took these exchanges seriously, blowing them up into a Fisk-Lee feud. Fisk was my best friend in the game. We may have argued with each other, but he could never lose my respect or friendship.

I faded after the All-Star game. I blew some ballgames and the team stopped scoring runs for me. I was weak with what turned out to be tonsillitis. When the season was over, Moret and I both underwent tonsillectomies. The surgery was performed the same day in the same hospital. I came out of the anesthetic haze before he did. Looking over at his bed, I saw that he was just lying there like a corpse. I shook him and said, "Roger, are you still alive? Speak to me." He let out a groan. A nurse came in and tried to force ginger ale and ice cream down my throat. That shit wasn't making it. I had three-quarter-inch T-bone steaks brought in. When I left the hospital, a reporter asked me if I was disappointed in my season.

We had finished second and I had won only seventeen after bagging twelve wins by mid-season. He thought I was upset that I hadn't won twenty. I didn't mind. Being a twenty-game winner wasn't something I fantasized about. I was more interested in setting obscure records, like most consecutive shutouts while allowing twelve or more hits in each game. I was disappointed that we had finished second, but I viewed my season as a personal success. Going into spring training, I would have bet one thousand dollars that I was about to be traded or shipped back to the minors. Instead, I had a good year and outlasted Kasko. He was fired on the last day of the season and was replaced by Darrell Johnson.

We knew Kasko would be gone. We were expected to win the pennant, but we didn't come close, so someone's head had to roll. I didn't think Eddie was a bad manager. He was a little too nervous and didn't understand the subtleties of handling a pitching staff. He had been a shortstop for the Reds when they won the 1961 National League Championship by pounding the rest of the league senseless. I think that made him too offense-minded. I know he didn't evaluate his personnel very well. If he was going to have me on his pitching staff at all in '72, it should have been as a starter. Not because I was God's gift to Fenway, but because of the type of pitcher I was. I was a control pitcher with good but never great velocity. I wasn't overpowering enough and did not have a resilient enough arm to pitch relief. Eddie didn't understand that. He compounded his mistake by not using me once he had me out there. He put his personal feelings about me ahead of the best interests of the team. My T-shirt may have cost us the pennant. But the following year, he put our differences aside and let me pitch. We had a lot of injuries that season, and Baltimore was better than we were. None of that was his fault. Still, I wasn't sorry to see him go.

Darrell Johnson had spent the last couple of seasons managing Boston's Triple-A farm club in Pawtucket. I knew him from his days as pitching coach under Williams. We had gotten along well. The younger guys on the club had played under him—Fisk had been his catcher in Louisville—so his hiring was a popular move with them. The veterans were leery of him. Veterans aren't always happy about managerial switches, unless the guy who was dumped is someone they couldn't bear. A veteran knows where he stands with the old manager, and when a new one is named you don't know what might go down, except possibly you. A new skipper might find that someone who was thought to be a vital cog in the club is expendable. When a change is made in the manager's office, everyone tends to step lightly for a while.

Darrell surprised everyone that first spring training. He released Cepeda and Aparicio on the same day. During the '73 season, Orlando had hit twenty home runs with eighty-six rbi's, and Luis had batted .271. Their releases sent a message to the rest of the team: "Don't get old and slow." Johnson wanted a streamlined attack that could play defense. Luis had lost a few steps in the field, and Orlando was like a giant billboard on the basepaths. I felt releasing Cepeda was a good move. As much as I liked him, I knew we couldn't carry a one-dimensional ballplayer. But I was worried about releasing Luis.

Aparicio was no longer what he once had been. But I didn't know who we had to replace him. I got very nervous when I saw Juan Beniquez in camp. Beniquez had been up briefly as a shortstop in 1971 and 1972. He was absolutely the worst infielder I had ever seen. If he could have eaten his glove, he would have died of food poisoning. Juan would make diving, backhanded stops in the hole and then throw the ball into Boston Harbor. It was brutal. I think it was after one of his tosses almost killed a peanut vendor in the twenty-sixth row that the coaches handed him an outfielder's glove. That upset him, but the pitchers were happy. I was thrilled when I discovered that the front office had told him that if he went anywhere near the infield again, they would confiscate his green card. I had hoped that Mario Guerrero would be Luis' successor. He had been kept out of the lineup by Aparicio's name and salary but, by the time of Luis' release, Mario was the better player and had earned a promotion off the bench. But our new manager had other plans.

Johnson had brought Rick Burleson with him from Pawtucket to play short. I had never met a red-ass like Rick in my life. Some guys didn't like to lose, but Rick got angry if the score was even tied. He was very intense and had the greatest arm of any infielder I had ever seen. The moment he reported to camp, he brought a fire to the club that we had been lacking.

There was one other familiar face missing when we reported to spring training: Reggie Smith. He had been traded with McGlothen and Curtis to the Cardinals for Rick Wise,

Reggie Cleveland, Diego Segui, and Bernie Carbo. That turned out to be a great deal for us. Carbo was another fire-eater, a real piece of work on the field, but a kindred spirit off of it. He came down to Winter Haven with a stuffed gorilla, given to him by Scipio Spinks. He carried it around with him wherever he went, engaging it in long discussions. I loved his innocence. The first time we talked about the Bermuda Triangle, he thought we were discussing pussy. He and I would get high together, but only during rainouts. We were the flower children of baseball.

Cepeda's dismissal allowed Johnson to get Cecil Cooper into the lineup. He was just as good a hitter as Orlando. Cecil was also ten years younger, could run, and could play first base. My favorite addition to the team, however, was Juan Marichal. I had watched Marichal when I was a kid in California and he was pitching for the San Francisco Giants. I thought he was the greatest pitcher in baseball. When we got him he was all but done. His back was giving him a lot of problems. The Red Sox finally had to put him on Clinoril, an anti-inflammatory that makes your back feel like it's twenty-five again. It helped him for only a short period of time, but during that period—about five weeks—he had the magic again. He showed us a little bit of everything, a twilight glimmer of what he had been. But it didn't last, and we had to let him go. Too bad.

Juan was a walking encyclopedia on pitching and a lot of fun to be around. He was constantly bringing people into the clubhouse. Real exotic types. Once he brought in a Rumanian midget who was billed as the world's smallest man. He was very entertaining, and everyone got a kick out of him. But he sent Juan into a panic by vanishing. We looked everywhere for him and were about to call the police, when we finally found him asleep in an old catcher's mitt.

I was inconsistent in '74. I started out pitching great, but I didn't get much hitting support. Then when our bats came alive, I became horseshit. The only reason my record stayed above .500 was because we were scoring so many runs. The strange thing about my lack of effectiveness was that I wasn't being jocked by the big-name batters. It was the Punch-and-Judy hitters like Ken Suarez and Ed Brinkman who were doing me in. I ate home-run hitters for lunch. Except for Dick Allen. He was unfair. I faced him in a game in Chicago. With a two-run lead, I had walked the lead-off hitter in the ninth. Buddy Bradford, a righthanded hitter who murdered lefties, was up, and my pitching coach came out to see how I felt. I told him I was fine and that I was going to try to get Bradford to hit into a double play. The coach pointed out that Allen was the next batter, so I said, "Well, then I *better* get Bradford to hit into a double play." First pitch, Buddy hit a one-hopper to short and we turned two. Allen got up with the bases empty, and I yelled, "Okay, Dick, let's see how far you can hit this pitch!" I threw him a terrific slider outside. Great pitch. Allen hit a shot into the upper deck that was still rising when it slammed into the facade. That ball was smoked about five hundred feet. Dick was one of the very few guys who could take your best pitches and hit them hard somewhere. He was the strongest man I had ever seen. I couldn't believe the size of the bat he swung. Stan Bahnsen had one, and he once showed it to me. I couldn't even lift the son of a bitch. When I hefted that bat, I thought, "Thank God he didn't hit the ball up the middle on me. All that would have been left of me would have been a grease spot and a pair of spikes with smoke coming out of them."

The team played well for Johnson, and I thought we were going to win the pennant. I started pitching well in late August and also managed to become a father again. Andy was born on August 24. I was pitching that evening in Fenway, and Mary Lou was watching the game from her usual seat behind home plate. Using hand signs, she was able to signal to me the length of her contractions after each inning. By the sixth, those signals ceased. She was too busy bouncing up and down. I came out of the game with a blister and went right from the field to her seat. I had her in the hospital in twelve minutes. The nurses took Mary Lou into the labor room, and she went into delivery before the doctor got there. One nurse scrubbed up to assist with the birth, while the other one tended my blister. Andy popped up not too long after we arrived. What a kid he turned out to be. I love watching him play. He runs into walls, gets his face lopsided, then gets up and runs into something else. Like father, like son.

On August 30 we were in first place, with a five-game bulge over the Yankees. The team looked unstoppable. Then we went to Minnesota and never returned. We came back in body, but our minds were left in Calvin Griffith Land. His Twins had honed our bats into fishing rods and had sent us to the Ten Thousand Lakes for the rest of the season. After losing three there, we went on to Baltimore. Tiant and I started a Monday doubleheader against Cuellar and Ross Grimsley. Unable to buy a run, we lost both ends by identical 1–0 scores. The team got five hits the entire after-noon. God, was that agonizing. That evening I lashed my hands to my bathroom sink. My hotel room was on the eighteenth floor, and I did not want to risk the temptation of walking near an open window.

We never recovered from that doubleheader shutout. The team stopped playing as a unit, and everybody tried to win games singlehandedly instead of staying within themselves and doing the little things that had gotten us our lead in the first place. We stopped bunting and began to swing at bad pitches. Guys who couldn't hit home runs were trying to hit the ball to Luxembourg. Johnson did everything he could think of to halt our slide, but it was of no use. One thing he did not do was call a team meeting. He knew it wouldn't have helped. I mean, what could he have said? "You guys better start hitting?" The Yankees finally caught us in early September, and then Baltimore overtook them. We finished third.

I pitched an unusually long game toward the end of that season. On September 21 we beat the Orioles, 6–5, in ten innings. Due to rain delays the game lasted six hours and twenty-seven minutes. I went all the way for the victory. Tiant and I pitched a lot of innings in that final month, and the toll almost killed me. On the last day of the season I went home and went straight to bed. Waking up the next day, I discovered that I could not get out of bed. My arms were completely paralyzed. I rolled around like a turtle upturned on its back and screamed for Mary Lou. I thought I had been stricken with a disease, and it scared the shit out of me. My wife packed me up and got me over to the doctor, who gave me a big shot of Benadryl. That fixed me right up. According to his diagnosis, I had taken so much of the anti-inflammatory Butazolidin over the last few months that my adrenal glands had ceased to function, and all the pitching I had done had brought me to a state of complete exhaustion. After that shot I was fine, but the stress of the episode probably took ten years off my life.

For the next couple of weeks I rested and allowed myself to reflect on the just-finished season. That led me to some severe second-guessing. Finishing third after playing so well for so long was hard to take. I blamed myself for not pitching better. Then I blamed the front office for trading Lyle. Sparky had another great season in '74, and he would have helped us. We didn't have a bullpen stopper all year. With Lyle on our side we would have won the pennant. Not just the division, the whole bag of ice. I also questioned why management brought up Fred Lynn and Jim Rice at the end of the year and then hardly played them. They might have made a difference. We weren't scoring anyway, so why not go with the kids? Knowing how our season turned out, it was an easy thing for me to say. The kind of slump we went into grabbed us by the balls without warning. In a pennant race you tend to trust the established players, the guys who have done it before, to start hitting and playing like they had in the past. I guess if Johnson had put Rice and Lynn in the lineup and they didn't hit, I could have just as easily said, "Jesus, why did he give up on the veterans?"

Now I know that we didn't win it that year because we weren't ready to win it—1974 was the turning point for our club. It gave guys like Burleson, Cooper, Beniquez, and Dwight Evans a chance to participate in a pennant race, maturing them as players. And I think the disappointment of its finish made us hungrier than we had ever been before. It made us a championship team in 1975.

he first time I smoked hash was in Cleveland in 1972. I was in a car, and I think I was driving, though I can't say for sure. I might have been tied to the roof. We used to do that to guys. Catching their hands in the car window, we would drive off with them lying across the roof like a dead moose, their pants pulled down to their knees. That was always good for a laugh.

Several of us were going to a friend's house in the rich section of town. We were smoking a joint and listening to music. Just cruising around. When we stopped for a red light, a van pulled up alongside us. There were two teenagers in it, passing a pipe back and forth. They signaled that we should pull over and join them. We got into the van, gave them a few joints, and they let us smoke the pipe. On finishing, we got back into our car and drove to our hotel. We forgot all about visiting our friend. I sauntered into the hotel lobby and said hello to a few of my teammates. Everything was fine. That's the last thing I remember. Duane Josephson, my roommate, found me about an hour later in the elevator. Actually, I was halfway in and halfway out. The doors would start to close, bang into me, and then open. Over and over again. I was just standing there, oblivious to everything. I imagine I had almost made it out of the elevator when I got nailed, and my lights went out. This taught me never to drink VO and then smoke pot and hash in the same afternoon, unless I wanted to have a deeply moving religious experience. Duane shuffled me into our room and threw me onto my bed. I wanted desperately to go to sleep and started undressing. The next morning I was still lying there as the sun came up. Completely clothed, I was still trying to unzip my boots. I had never lost consciousness and had kept thinking to myself, If I can just get these off, I'll be all right. My mind was trying to send the proper impulses to my hands that would enable them to function correctly. But it was no use. I had beaten up my body, and my brain had died.

Cleveland always did funny things to me. It was the sort of town that invited exploration, because on initial glance there didn't seem to be a whole hell of a lot to do there. On one of my first visits to the city, Sonny Siebert, who had been a star with the Indians, volunteered to take several of us to the best bar in Cleveland. We went on a Thursday night, arriving there at ten o'clock. The place was closed. Everybody was mystified. We kept asking Sonny, "Are you sure this is the place? Jesus, if it's closed at ten p.m., when is it opened?" After other experiences similiar to this one, it was understandable that many players wrote off the city as a place where nothing was happening. How little they knew. They hadn't discovered the Cleveland Public Library.

I had gone there the day after I first smoked that hash. Feeling totally alive, I realized I had never felt so good. The hash had been cleansing, pushing out the alcohol that had been stored in my system and accelerating my metabolism. That afternoon, I walked all over Cleveland until I felt a tug at my sleeve that pulled me into the Cleveland Library. I had been there previously, having spent hours in its reference library on the ground floor. I had never ventured into any other section, but that day, the invisible force led me to the shelves marked philosophy and religion.

They were on the third floor. A higher level. Once there, the force directed my attention to a book by an Indian mystic, Paramahansa Yogananda. His close friends called him Yogi. The book was a chronicle of his life and times. One story told of his disciple, a man police mistook for a bandit. They cut off his hand. Gazing at the wound, the disciple stemmed the flow of blood by the sheer force of his will and walked off. He left his hand with the police, giving them something to practice using their cuffs on. The parable was used to illustrate how the disciple had achieved complete mastery over forces previously thought to be uncontrollable. I liked that. After putting Yogananda's book aside, I found other books by men like Gurdjieff and Ouspensky.

Their writings turned me on to self-determinism. They convinced me that everything we needed to live a successful life was locked away in our minds, and that unless we understood that, we were sleeping our lives away. I didn't grab any of these books from their resting places; it was more like they grabbed me. It was as if each volume had stood up on the shelf, jumped into my hands, and said, "Well, thank you for coming up and visiting us. We've been stuck on this shelf for years, gathering dust and waiting for someone to look us over. Have we got a deal for you. We will paint your brain any color for only $39.95."

Those books marked the beginning of my quest for knowledge. I began with Gurdjieff. Reading other mystics and philosophers, I worked my way up to Buckminster Fuller. And he led me back to Gurdjieff. It was wild. Seemingly, all these philosophers—Fuller, Ouspensky, Gurdjieff, and the rest—were disciples of the same school of thought. Each one added something else to the previous master's work, but in the end you were returned to the original form. Therefore, the end was merely another way of reaching the beginning. That seemed far fucking out. I didn't understand all of it, but I got the basic idea. We come out of the world, not into it. We are an extension of the planet and if we care for it, we are caring for ourselves. That made me realize that, although I loved the way I made a living and had no wish to stop, playing ball satisfied only my own needs. It did not contribute to the earth's well-being. I decided to change what had been a selfish existence by donating my free time to other people and their worth-while causes.

I got involved with Fair Share, a group that labored to help consumers gain more control over the public utilities, and I worked for almost anyone else who bothered to give me a call. I jumped on the zero-earth-population band-wagon, a good cause but a source of some embarrassment for me. Shortly after joining them, Mary Lou became preg-nant with our daughter, Caitlin. Feminists asked me to support the ERA in Massachusetts. At first, I told them I couldn't support any ERA unless it was under 3.50, but they talked me into campaigning for them. The amend-ment made sense to me. We are all extensions of the planet, therefore we are all equal. I didn't see any reason why that shouldn't be part of the Constitution.

My voicing of these views in public, I discovered, earned me a lot of enemies in the media. Especially among the older writers. They wanted to know how I had the nerve to offer opinions on issues outside the provinces of sport. I was told to shut up and play ball. I paid no attention to them, feeling that all of us, even ballplayers, had an obli-gation to work for the good of humankind. My critics count-ered that I was being irresponsible, claiming that people would follow me blindly simply because I was a celebrity. I felt if that was the case, it was a sad thing. I didn't believe my views would, or should, carry more weight with the public just because I made my living playing baseball. If that *was* the case, however, it was due to society's faulty view, not mine. I also knew one other thing. If instead of working against, say, the nuclear arms buildup, I had joined the "America, Love It or Leave It" crowd, those same writers who criticized me would have made me out to be a pitching patriot. It wasn't the sight of a ballplayer who voiced his opinions that bothered them. It was the fact that those opinions were so drastically opposed to their own beliefs.

My teammates paid little attention to anything I said. As professional ballplayers, all they cared about was performance on the field. Once the 1975 season got into full swing, nobody could complain about our work between the lines. We were cooking.

It never fails to knock me out when people come up and talk about the year we won the pennant. Everyone tries to pinpoint a certain game as the most critical one, and they want to know what I was thinking on such and such a pitch. The answer to the latter question was always the same: "Everything but the game." My mind spins off on tangents all the time. When pitching, the game becomes an adjunct to some current fantasy. My mind drifts away and comes back only if I'm hit hard. But if I'm getting people out, I lock into a flow, allowing me to coast through my random thoughts. For example, it may appear to the casual observer that I'm pitching to Reggie Jackson with the bases loaded. But in my head I'm having an audience with a guru in the Himalayas. That keeps pressure off of me. Of course, a line drive off my kneecap will bring me back in a hurry, but I didn't get hit by many of those. This mental state contributed greatly to my success. Hitters couldn't guess what I was going to throw, because I never had a clue. That gave me an advantage over them that I wouldn't have had if I had been a slave to an orthodox thinking pattern. It was hell on my catchers, though.

I also don't recall any crucial games that season. The whole year flew by in a rapid blur, with one game running into another. What I do remember is Wise, Tiant, Moret, and Willoughby pitching their nuts off, and Lynn and Rice playing as if they were on a mission from God. And a whole team pulling together, whipping ass on an entire league. We were awesome.

That was Freddy Lynn's golden year, but Burleson might have been our least expendable player. Shortstop was the one position our depth couldn't cover. We had no one to replace Rick if he had gotten hurt. Luckily, he only missed four games that year. He was a scrapper. I would load the bases, and he would trot over to the mound, saying, "Get the ball down and make them hit it to me. I'll turn two on the sons of bitches." The way he said it, I felt that if I failed, I would have been in physical danger. The Rooster had a menacing air about him.

I had seen him lose control of himself once in Minnesota. A fan in the lobby of our hotel had made an obscene remark about our club. It was something quaint, like, "The Red Sox eat my dick." Rick tore into him, yelling at the guy as he crumbled to the ground in fear. It was devastating. I thought the guy was going to shit all over himself. I finally pulled Burleson off, saying, "Rick, I don't think the guy can hear you," and I'm sure I was right. You could have blown a trumpet in the guy's ear and he wouldn't have noticed. He was too busy watching his life flash in front of his eyes. Rick turned to me, and said, "Jesus, Bill. I'm sorry. I just winked out on him." Thank God Burleson filtered most of his aggression through his play on the field. I remember thinking years later, when the Iranians were holding our embassy people captive, that instead of the Marines we should have sent Burleson and Petrocelli over there. They would have come back in forty-eight hours with the hostages, the Ayatollah, and a couple of million barrels of oil.

Those people who disliked my speaking out on issues had a field day when I took a stand on busing in Boston. None of them realized that that was precisely what I wanted them to do.

The Red Sox had been playing well up until mid-June, when we hit a bad streak just as the Yankees were making their move. New York had been favored by the odds-makers to win the pennant, and when they started to come on, many reporters took the opportunity to write their "How Will Boston Blow It This Time?" columns. On June 23 we got whipped by the Indians, 11–3. The fans were all over us that evening, booing the club as if it had just lost the pennant. Yaz had a particularly bad game. After striking out in the eighth inning, he slammed his bat into the bat rack and bruised his left hand. Minutes after the game ended the writers were on us like vultures, lighting down in our locker room and asking whether or not we thought we could ever recover from such a terrible beating. After asking these and other equally dumb questions, they tried to get to Yaz. Carl had ducked into the trainer's room— which was off-limits to the press—and wouldn't come out. He just refused to deal with the bullshit.

I could understand that, so I created a diversion. Determined to give an insane response to an insane situation, I picked up a trash can and heaved it across the clubhouse. I yelled, "Boston is a horseshit city, a racist city with horseshit fans and horseshit writers. The fans boo Yaz when he's playing his heart out, and they boo Fisk who always gives his all. They are all afraid we're going to lose their precious little pennant! If the writers and fans in this city want to quit on us, fine. Then they're quitters. But what can you expect? The only guy with guts in this town is Judge Arthur Garrity!"

Garrity was the federal judge who had ruled in favor of the compulsory busing of schoolchildren in order to achieve racial integration in the Boston public school system. That was not a popular decision. Minutes after he delivered it, Garrity was being burned in effigy throughout the city. I thought he had done the right thing. But I also knew that by making an issue out of it at this precise moment, I would take the media spotlight off whatever was temporarily ailing us and goad most of the writers into forgetting about Yaz so they could take out after me.

It worked. For the next couple of days, no one remembered we had even played a game against Cleveland. Instead of reading how we were blowing the pennant, fans were treated to articles about Bill Lee and his big mouth. I got a lot of hate mail over that incident. One of the nicer pieces said, "I thought you were an asshole before, but now I know it." My favorite letter came from City Councillor Albert "Dapper" O'Neil, a leader of the antibusing movement. The letter was typed on paper bearing his official letterhead. It was the funniest thing I ever read. The typing ran all over the page, the punctuation marks were misplaced, and an easy word like serious was spelled s-e-r-i-l-u-s. The letter accused me of being ignorant, cast severe doubts on my ability as a pitcher, and questioned my manhood. It ended with a postscript asking me if I had the guts to write a reply. I did. I wrote, "Dear Mr. O'Neil, I think you should know that some moron has stolen your stationery and is writing letters to me on it."

I had known this was going to be our year when Fisk got hurt and the team didn't fold. Carlton had been injured for a good part of 1974, and the team collapsed without him. I was partially to blame for his getting hurt in '75. During an exhibition game against the Mets, I threw a sinker to Joe Torre that was supposed to go down and away, but instead headed down and in. Joe had a funky stroke, and, when he fouled the pitch off, the ball shot off his bat at an odd angle. Fisk, reaching down to get the ball, had his right leg stretched out. From the mound, I could see that one of his nuts was hanging out, pinched between his thigh and his cup. The ball nailed it. Oh, did that make me wince. Carlton went down as if he'd been shot. He would be unable to play for the first two months of the season. I felt awful about it, but I rationalized that this was my temporary contribution to zero population growth. That accident only fortified my feelings about cups. I didn't believe in them. I always wore a jock strap, but I never wore a cup. It was one of the reasons I developed such quick hands; I was always able to protect my private parts. The only reason I even wore a jockstrap was to keep my balls in place. I never worried about them getting hit, but I did not, under any circumstances, want them bouncing around while I was trying to pitch.

With Fisk on the disabled list, Tim McCarver, Bob Montgomery, and Tim Blackwell handled the catching duties. They helped keep us from going under by contributing heavily on defense and holding their own on offense. I saw their performances as evidence that we finally had the bench strength we had always needed.

McCarver was great. I called him "Old Second Inning," due to his habit of having to take a dump in the john between the first and second inning of every game. He had the most reliable body clock in the world; we used to set our watches by him. Timmy had been on three pennant winners—and two world champions—with the Cardinals. He was a tremendous addition to our club. He had no arm left, but he possessed an invaluable knowledge of the game and the art of setting hitters up. He was our morale-booster, possessed of an incisive wit that allowed him to put the game in its proper perspective and to pass along constructive criticism in a manner that was well received. He was also a gentleman. You could make the rounds with him at night, secure in the knowledge that the moment you passed out, Timmy would be there to catch you and load you into a cab, sending you safely home.

McCarver was released after Fisk returned to action. Timmy was hitting .381 when they let him go, but even if he had been hitting .081 it was a bad move. Contenders need veterans like him who accept their role, have the best interests of the club at heart, and can deliver in the pinch.

Management figured, "Well, he can't throw any more, and we've got two backup catchers who are younger than he is." They failed to see the intangible virtues he brought to the team. It wouldn't be the last time they would make that mistake.

Lynn and Rice bugged my eyes out the first time I saw them play on a regular basis. I think Freddy had one slump all year. Before it got too severe, several of us took him out for an evening of mayhem and got him ripped. He was yelling and singing, and I ended up carrying him back to our hotel in midtown New York. I opened the door of his room, threw him on the bed, and left him there. The next day, he went four for five. End of slump.

Freddy was an ebullient kid with an infectious enthusiasm for the game. Rice was his opposite. He was very quiet and a bit surly when he first came up. But that was just a defense. He turned out to be a warm guy who was harboring an unspoken resentment toward the Red Sox front office. He let it out later, accusing the Boston management of not bringing him up sooner because of his color. The Red Sox were something of a racist organization, but I don't believe color had anything to do with his not being brought up sooner. I think it was a tailoring problem. When he was ready to play in the majors, the club didn't have a uniform big enough to fit him. Jim was one big, solid piece of muscle. Once, Evans and Carbo were going at each other in rightfield during batting practice. Evans had said something about Bernie, so Bernie got pissed and tagged him. Bernardo was like that. He was pure oxygen looking for a flame to test the theory of spontaneous combustion. Evans came back with a right hand, and the two of them started wrestling each other. Rice broke it up. He did this by first separating them, picking them up off the ground, and holding them aloft. One in each hand. He then politely asked them to calm down. Instant serenity.

When Dick Allen retired, Jim inherited his title as the

strongest man in the game. I once saw him snap a bat in two. On a checked swing. The head of the bat nearly decapitated the third-base coach. Seeing this, the umpire was quick to rule, "No swing. Ball one. Okay, Jim?" He wasn't about to risk getting Rice mad because Jim is not of this earth. I think he was raised near a landfill containing nuclear waste and was slowly exposed to radiation. It's the only possible explanation for his superhuman strength.

The Yanks caught us briefly in late June, but then we passed them and were never headed. Baltimore started to make their move in the final weeks of the season. In early September we could feel their crab breath on our necks. A Baltimore disk jockey traveled to Kenya, seeking a witch doctor who would cast a spell on us on behalf of the Orioles. The doc did cast the spell, but warned that it would be useless unless the Orioles refrained from consuming meat, candy, and alcohol for the rest of the season. They also had to vow that they would refrain from having sex for twelve hours prior to each game. No wonder they couldn't catch us. We held them off and clinched the division with a September 27 win over New York. I didn't have much to do with our stretch drive. My elbow had almost expired, a victim of the designated-hitter rule.

On August 24, I beat the White Sox for my seventeenth win of the season. I didn't get another victory the rest of the year. Obviously, I wasn't destined to win twenty. If I had been, I would have done it that year. Shortly after that win, our pitchers started taking batting practice in preparation for the World Series. There was no d.h. in the Series back then, and Johnson wanted us to be ready to face live pitching. I loved it. The first time out in the cage, I hit a few home runs and really started hot-dogging it, trying to hit each successive shot a little bit farther. After being held out of the batter's box for so long, I did not want to leave. The next day my muscles were sore from overswinging, but I paid no attention. I took batting practice again, got jammed by a pitch, and swung too hard. I had hyperextended my arm, tearing a small tendon in my elbow. I was useless for the next six weeks and didn't completely heal until the World Series started. The injury kept me out of the playoffs against Oakland.

We took the A's in three straight, clinching the pennant in Oakland with a 5–3 win. As soon as that game's final out was made, we went berserk. Mr. Yawkey made his way into our jammed clubhouse and invited all of us to a victory celebration he had already scheduled for that evening. I attended, but I don't remember very much of it. I got blitzed forty-five minutes after it started and stayed in that condition until we met Cincinnati.

I was up for the Series. I liked the idea of competing against the best in a forum that allowed small margin for error. That Cincinnati team was the Big Red Machine. The scouting report on them was amazing: "Pitch around Rose, pitch around Morgan, pitch around Perez, etc." According to our scouts, the best strategy to use against the Reds was to start the game with the bases loaded, five runs in, and their pitcher at the plate. Then you had a chance.

The Reds should have had Jack Webb as a manager. I had never seen a team so well-schooled in basics as they were. They were the third most fundamentally sound team I had ever seen. Only the USC Trojans of 1968 and any one of the Taiwanese Little League champions would rate higher. The Reds were a club that took its personality from one individual: Pete Rose. Pete and his club were always battling you. Rose is extremely carnivorous, an obvious flesh-eater. Meat diets tend to bring out man's competitive nature, while robbing him of the ability to show compassion for his fellow human beings. Carnivores are not concerned with problems outside of baseball. All they care about is scoring the winning run and having the opposing shortstop placed on the dinner menu.

I had no anxiety before the American League playoffs. I knew I wouldn't be pitching, and, like the rest of the club, I figured Oakland was ready to be taken. I did experience some anxious moments before the Series started. I was afraid we'd be swept out of the Series without winning a game. I was fearful not because a sweep would have been embarrassing; I didn't want to beat the Reds four in a row, either. I knew that these games would be our last chances to play ball for the rest of the year, and I was afraid it would be over too quickly. I wanted to string out the fun and excitement for as long as it could last.

Tiant's seventy-year-old father, a former pitching star in Cuba, threw out the ball for the first game in Boston. The Red Sox and the State Department had been able to bring Luis' mother and father over from Cuba, allowing them the privilege of watching their son pitch in a World Series. During the pre-game festivities, the elder El Tiante walked out to the mound and threw the ceremonial first ball to Fisk. He threw a strike. Then he threw another strike, followed by still another. I'll tell you something, he was in great shape. Every pitch he threw had mustard on it and he probably would have kept throwing if someone hadn't led him off the mound. I swear, he could have gone nine.

His son pitched the opener for us against Don Gullett. It was a close duel for a while, but then we blew them away. Tiant threw a five-hit shutout. I started Game Two. While warming up, I noticed the Reds watching me from their dugout. They couldn't believe what they were seeing, I was throwing so much junk. Most of them were laughing, and I thought they were going to knock each other over, racing to the plate to hit against me. Pete Rose was their lead-off hitter, and I struck him out. I didn't hear too many peeps out of them for the rest of the afternoon.

It was a weird game. The day was drizzly and the base-paths were sloppy. We put six men on in the first two innings, but scored only one run. The Reds tied the score in the fourth, and then we got a run in the sixth to take the lead, 2–1. That's where matters stood when the sky opened up and the umpires called a rain delay. As we waited in our clubhouse for the game's resumption, we were joined by Mr. and Mrs. Henry Kissinger and about three hundred Secret Service men. Kissinger sat on a table, signing autographs for the writers and players. At one point he informed one of his agents that he had to go to the bathroom. The Secret Service men had to check out our john before he used it, making sure that no revolutionaries were coming up through the plumbing. All they found was the Tidy Bowl Man. They frisked him for hidden weapons, but he was clean.

During that delay, unbeknownst to yours truly, Johnny Bench was being interviewed for television in the Reds clubhouse. When asked what he'd be looking to do against me when play resumed, John replied that he was going to try to hit me to the opposite field. He had been trying to pull me all afternoon, and I had gotten him out by pitching him away. Bench was now telling sixty-five million Americans that he was going to take the ball to right, and not one of them thought to call me with a warning. Did that piss me off later! I don't watch much TV, and when Bench and I faced each other after the rains let up, I was unaware of his strategy. John led off the ninth with the score still 2–1. My first pitch to him was a sinker low and away that he hammered to right for a double. Johnson came out to yank me, replacing me with Dick Drago. Dick retired the next two hitters and needed only one more out to give us the win. Davey Concepcion was the next batter. He broke our hearts with a seeing-eye single up the middle that knotted the game up. Then he stole second and scored what proved to be the winning run on a double by Ken Griffey. At the press conference afterward, a writer asked me to sum up the Series so far. I told him it was tied.

We lost Game Three in Cincinnati, 6–5. That was the Armbrister Game. With the score tied 5–5 in the bottom of the tenth, Ed Armbrister, a backup outfielder, was pinch-hitting for the Reds with Cesar Geronimo on first. While attempting to sacrifice, he bounced the ball high in the air in front of home plate. Armbrister, batting from the right side, was very slow getting out of the batter's box. Though clean-shaven when the pitch had first been delivered, he had grown a beard by the time he took his initial step in the direction of first base. Fisk crashed into him as he was in the process of fielding the ball. Pushing Armbrister out of the way, Carlton gunned a throw to second in an attempt to get Geronimo. The ball sailed past the second baseman and out to Lynn in centerfield. Geronimo tried to take an extra base, but Freddy came up with the ball and fired it to third. Catching the ball on one clean bounce, Petrocelli made a perfect tag to nail Cesar for the out. But the umpire blew the call. Geronimo was ruled safe, and the game was as good as over. In looking back on that game, everybody focuses on that brief collision at the plate, not realizing that it was the blown call at third that would eventually kill us. Geronimo scored the winning run on a base hit by Joe Morgan, and yet that's the play that nobody talks about. Instead, everybody chooses to argue whether or not Armbrister should have been called out for blocking Fisk at the plate. He wasn't, but he sure should have been. His interference was blatant. Larry Barnett, the home-plate umpire, made the wrong call, and Darrell Johnson didn't negotiate properly in an attempt to get him to reverse it. He didn't argue vociferously enough. An energetic display won't get an umpire to change his call, but it might lend you some protection for the next close play. Many umpires will tread lightly if you intimidate them with enough bluster. Darrell didn't give it his all. If it had been me, I would have climbed up Barnett's back and bit his ear off. I would have Van Goghed him.

A loss like that could have hung us, but, if anything, it only made us play harder in Game Four. An exhausted Tiant had just enough to win that game, 5–4. Luis could hardly lift his arm over his head, and the Reds hit rockets off of him, but it didn't matter. He had guts, brains, and Fred Lynn in centerfield. Freddy made more great catches in that one game than I had seen in my entire career. The Reds won the fifth game, 6–2, taking a 3–2 lead in games won. We went back to Fenway, needing to win two.

Game Six was delayed by three days of rain. When the Series was resumed, Darrell made his fatal error. For the last two years, I had been unhappy with the way Johnson had handled our pitching staff. He left starters in too long and never really established any sort of order in the bull-pen. Nobody out there knew what their job was supposed to be. There was no official short man, because Darrell just went with whoever had the hot hand at the moment. When he managed us to the pennant, I attributed it to his talent for falling out of trees, but landing on his feet. He still managed to land on his feet in this game, but he also stubbed all his toes.

The mistake he made was in starting Tiant in Game Six, instead of me. That's not my conceit talking, it's just common sense. Those rains had been a godsend, giving our tired pitching staff some much needed rest. Luis found it especially beneficial, but he still needed one more day. On the other hand, too much rest was hazardous to me. I was primed and ready to go on what would have been my normal starting day. But Darrell passed over me to go with his best.

The choice, wrong as it was, did result in setting up the dramatic events of the magic sixth game. Unable to stay in one place, I divided my time that evening between the bullpen and the dugout. We scored three runs in the first inning, but the Reds got to Luis for three in the fifth and two in the seventh. By the bottom of the eighth, the Reds had a 6–3 lead. Lynn led off with a walk, Petrocelli singled. Cincinnati's relief ace Rawley Eastwick was brought in, and he struck out Evans and then got Burleson on a fly ball. Carbo was sent up as a pinch hitter. As he walked to the plate, I knew he was going to hit a home run. Eastwick was a fastball pitcher, facing a dead fastball hitter with a strong wind blowing out. It was a scene written for Bernie. I stood up in the dugout and tried to get his attention, pointing to the wall and imploring him to hit it out. Bernie jolted Eastwick's second pitch, hitting it into the center-field bleachers. When he made contact, everyone in our dugout went crazy; we all knew the ball was gone when he hit it, and that it was now just a matter of time before we would win this game.

I was in the trainer's room when Fisk hit his famous twelfth-inning homer off Pat Darcy that ended the game and gave us the victory. It was getting late, and I knew I was going to be starting the next day, so I was stretching out, trying to get some rest. I saw the shot on TV. Carlton golfed the crap out of a fastball. He used a six iron, drawing from right to left and putting a shade of English on the ball. It landed on the left digit of a local green. The drive almost went foul, but Fisk used his body language, ordering it to stay fair, and it obeyed.

I felt I would pitch well in the seventh game. I had crazy rushes of energy surging through my body, but my mind was mellow and in complete control of the rest of me. I would be starting against Don Gullett. Prior to the game, Sparky Anderson, the Reds' manager, had announced, "I don't know about that fellah for the Red Sox, but, some-time after this game, my boy's going to the Hall of Fame." Upon hearing that remark, I replied, "I don't care where Gullett's going, because after this game, I'm going to the Eliot Lounge."

Scoring three runs in the third, we had Sparky's Hall-of-Famer out of there by the sixth inning. When we scored those three runs, the crowd went wild. But, after we failed to score again, I could feel the paranoia creeping through the stands. It was as if everyone was thinking, Okay, how are we going to fuck this one up?

We carried that 3–0 lead into the sixth. Rose led off that inning with a base hit. I got the next hitter on a pop-up and then faced Johnny Bench. Swinging at a fastball low and away, John hit a nice two-hopper to Burleson. It was a sure double play. But before I had thrown the pitch, the coaches had moved our second baseman, Denny Doyle, over to the hole, away from second. Rick was ready with the throw, but Denny had to come a long way to get to the bag. Flying across second, Doyle took the toss and fired the ball to first before he had a chance to get set. The throw went sailing into the stands. Instead of being out of the inning, I had Bench on second with two men out. And Tony Perez at the plate.

I had been having good success with Tony, throwing him my slow, arching curveball, so I thought it would be a good idea to throw it to him again. Unfortunately, so did Tony, who timed it beautifully. He counted the seams of the ball as it floated up to the plate, checked to see if Lee MacPhail's signature was on it, signed his own name to it, and then jumped all over it. He hit the ball over the left field screen and several small buildings. The score was 3–2. Pitching with a broken blister in the top of the seventh, I put the potential tying run on. When I walked that lead-off hitter, I was sick with myself. I did not want to come out of that ballgame, but Darrell was right in bringing in Roger Moret. That busted blister had made it impossible for me to get the ball over the plate. The moment it popped, I knew I was finished for the season. Now, all I could do was watch. When Roger allowed that tying run to score, I wanted to dash out and buy some razor blades. For my wrists.

Jim Willoughby relieved Moret and got us out of the seventh. He pitched great through the eighth, but in the bottom of that inning, we were done in by the d.h. rule. Since there was no designated hitter for this Series, Johnson felt forced to lift Willoughby in favor of a pinch hitter. It was a tough decision to make. We either had to take our best shot for a possible run or leave in a guy who had been our best pitcher over the last two months. I thought we should have left Jim in. Willoughby was a good-hitting pitcher, and, by taking him out, we were forced to insert a rookie, Jim Burton, who hadn't been used much all year. Willoughby was a veteran who had possessed great karma since August. We should have gone with the hot hand.

Jim Burton, though, came on in the ninth and pitched well. He just had bad luck. After walking Griffey, who was sacrificed to second, he retired Driessen, and then walked Rose. Joe Morgan was the next batter. Burton threw him a hell of a pitch—a slider down and away—but Morgan was just able to fight it off, blooping it into short centerfield in front of Lynn. Griffey scored the tie-breaking run. We went down in order in the bottom of the ninth, and the Series was over.

I was upset, at first, about the loss. I was even more upset that I hadn't started Game Six, allowing Luis his rest. Luis would have won that seventh game; I'm certain he would have blown them away. But I eventually realized that, if it had gone that way, the Series wouldn't have been as great as it was. That sixth game was something else. I wish I had been in it, but if I had been, I might have gotten jocked worse than Luis—or I might have pitched a shutout. Then we wouldn't have had Carbo's and Fisk's home runs to remember. We didn't win the Series, but we didn't lose it either. Baseball won. We were part of an event that we could tell our grandchildren about. I want to win as much as anybody. I felt our loss deep in my guts. But, if we had to lose, we couldn't have picked a better way. We gave it everything we had from the first pitch to the last.

* * *

Shortly after the World Series, I was invited to tour Red
China with a group of U.S. athletes and writers who were
going over to study Chinese physical culture. Phil Shinnick,
the broad jumper, Dr. Harry Edwards, the man who led
the black boycott of the 1968 Olympics, and George Starke,
a lineman with the Washington Redskins, were among those
going. There were about twenty of us. I had my first re-
servations about the trip when I discovered how our jour-
ney was being routed. We were going from Boston to New
York, from New York to Montreal, from Montreal to Vancouver, from Vancouver to Tokyo, and, finally, from Tokyo
to Canton. When I inquired why we were taking such a
circuitous route, I was told that we could not fly over directly from the States, because our State Department would
not give any of us visa clearance. They were not interested
in helping what was apparently a radical group of sports
activists gain access to a Communist country.

We were supposed to visit for twenty-one days; I only
lasted fourteen. I still have no idea who organized this
shindig. We were supposed to be a group of people involved
with sports, interested in exploring alternative life-styles
that might enhance our approach to our games. The trip
was going to allow us to interact with the Chinese and
absorb mass quantities of Eastern consciousness.

This was a liberal group going over there. Most of the
members were long-distance runners, who naturally tend
to lean toward the left. Conservatives don't like marathons,
realizing that, though they may add five years to your life,
the pain is unbearable. Also, they realize that it's much
easier to climb into a Rolls-Royce and go someplace where
your legs can be exercised for you. Liberals, however, know
that while physical exertion is sometimes painful, it is also
able to cleanse the mind and body. A forty-five-minute run

is a gift from God that so exhausts you, you see stars and feel as if you have just spent a month in Tibet as soon as it's over.

The Chinese had an amazing sports program. Everybody participates in it; this is not a country of spectators. Every morning at six a.m. the entire Shanghai community would get out in front of their homes and take part in a communal exercise program. These sessions were organized, but participation seemed to be a spontaneous thing. Chinese children seemed able to accomplish more at an earlier age than children in the States. In Canton, I saw kids, seven and eight years old, vaulting over sidehorses. And it was not uncommon to catch sight of a four-year-old running the half-mile before going to school.

There was little emphasis placed on winning in China, and no one associates disgrace with failure after an honest effort. Fear of failure is not encouraged. In America, if you're the scrawny kid in the group, you're usually picked last for any games, and, the moment you screw up you're usually mocked. I didn't see any of that over there. On the contrary, quite often it was the untalented kid who got picked for a team first. The Chinese placed friendship ahead of competition. They were not concerned with final scores.

I wish I could say the same for Harry Edwards. He seemed to be keeping a running tally on points scored in a game whose only participants were he and I. Harry resented the fact that I was the only one on the trip making money from sports who wouldn't apologize for it. To him, I was the bourgeois baseball player, representing everything that was corrupt in American athletics. He told me this, though never in a hostile manner. Harry played the part of the benign uncle who was trying to convert me. But I didn't need conversion. I had already been down this road and had passed where he was.

Harry thought it was significant that I came down with the Vancouver flu in Hong Kong. He claimed, "The reason you have come down with this virus is because of your compromised social consciousness. You are now in Utopia and have been forced to deal with the fact that you are a product of the Western world, whose values have been confused." I disagreed, explaining that I had gotten sick because I had gone jogging. Being six-foot-three, I guess all the coal dust had settled on my head and in my lungs before it had a chance to reach the much-shorter Chinese. Harry said that reply was just another example of my pinnacle-oriented, capitalistic view. Jesus, I can't stand a guy who can't take a joke. One evening, at the dinner table, Harry again discussed my need for a higher consciousness, advising me to free myself from my dependence on the almighty dollar and to become one with the masses. I told him, "Harry, you don't have to go to Chattanooga to see Rock City." Upon hearing that, Allan Silber and Phil Shinnick spontaneously blew their chicken soup all over the table and laughed so hard that Harry got up and left. And the next day Mr. Edwards came down with the flu.

Harry had been the one who told Tommy Smith and John Carlos to give the black power sign at the 1968 Olympics in Mexico City. He was a complex man. He spoke social revolution fluently, but he never did get around to telling me what he was going to do with the three Cadillacs I heard he owned back in L.A. Surely, when the new order took over, those extravagances were going to present him with a dilemma. Harry may have been all for the poor masses, but he sure did have a passion for big cars.

The worst part of our trip came whenever we held a self-criticism session that featured lots of empty breast-beating. It was the most useless thing I had ever seen in my life. One time the group assembled to discuss the heavy use of marijuana by some members of our entourage. It was felt that this, along with the constant playing of rock 'n' roll on our cassette recorders, might pose a danger to the spiritual nature of our trip. I didn't make that meeting.

I was asleep when it was held, exhausted from listening to rock 'n' roll after having smoked too much reefer.

I did attend one of these sessions in Canton. It was a cold day, below freezing outside. Twenty of us sat in a hotel room with all the windows shut. Before one *mea culpa* was uttered, I said, "Gee, we keep talking about raising our consciousness, yet, here we are, breathing in each other's germs instead of having a window open. Let's get some air in this joint."

I opened all the windows and the group immediately started to split up. The people who, like me, had realized that they were of Western descent and that there was no way we could be Easterners, headed back for the warmth of their beds. The ones who stayed and froze were the ones who insisted on repenting for their sins while saying, "God, I wish I was Chinese." That was a crock. I realized that the Chinese had their virtues, but, like all human beings, they also had their faults.

I liked their holistic approach to the treatment of disease. Doctors in China are paid to keep the populace well. Their system is founded on the theories of preventive medicine. I also noticed that none of the homes in Canton had any locks on the doors. There is no fear of theft. The towns-people police themselves and they have committees that make sure the city is kept clean. They really jump on you for littering. You see very little arguing or fighting over there. One argument I did see took place when a cabbie opened his door too fast and knocked over a passing pedestrian. A crowd gathered around the driver and chastised him for being too concerned with getting where he was going to notice who he might bump into on the way there. They are a patient people with a high regard for each other.

But they were not perfect. They carried their emphasis on communal welfare over the happiness of the individual to an extreme that denied a lot of the freedoms we take for granted in the United States. I didn't meet very many freethinkers over there. Everyone just sort of drifted along with the program for better or for worse. I don't know if a person as outspoken as I am could function there. I also found an interesting set of contradictions existing in their so-called highly developed physical consciousness. Though they were sticklers for intense exercise, almost all of them get hammered daily on gallons of caffeine. And they smoke severe nails for cigarettes. God, the Chinese pull away like chimneys. They have a cigarette over there called Phoenix. Smoking one is comparable to sucking on an exhaust pipe. The advertising for it should read, "Phoenix, the cigarettes that killed Chou En Lai."

China's economic system seems to be a failure. Their plumbing is awful. In order to go to the bathroom you had to use what they called a honey bucket. It wasn't filled with honey. You took a dump in it and left it outside your door every night. While you slept, it was picked up and brought to the compost heap. That's the bad job in their society. It's what happens to you when you can't hit .300 anymore. I never heard anybody complain about it, though. In fact, I think the hit song in Shanghai was, "I Carry Shit Up the Side of the Hill for the Commune." Last on my list of complaints are their beer and their baseball program. Chinese beer tastes like crankcase oil, and their baseball program is prehistoric.

The game is still in the embryonic stage over there. I saw a contest that the Canton team played against a club from Japan. The Japanese team scored twenty-six runs in the first three innings, while shutting the Chinese team out without a hit. In the fourth inning, the Canton club took the field, claimed they had lost the baseball, and the game was called. I could appreciate that bit of chicanery. It's something I had been tempted to do many times back in the States.

I had a conversation with a Cantonese truckdriver, who was supposed to be the best pitcher in the province. He asked me, "What do you do for a living?" I said, "Play baseball." And he said, "Yes, I know. But what do you do for a job?" He could not understand that playing baseball was my job. To the Chinese, baseball is just a nice exercise, like calisthenics. One gentleman laughed when the truckdriver told him what I did for a living and asked me what I got paid. I told him in nice, round Chinese figures. His eyes bulged out of his head and he said, most earnestly, "Tell me, how do you play this baseball?"

Harry Edwards thought the Chinese would dominate every sport in world-wide competition within ten years of our trip. He based this belief on the Chinese collective consciousness, their political ideology, and their emphasis on conditioning. Well, it doesn't look like that will happen anytime soon. Their system hasn't allowed them to straighten out their economic woes, making it impossible for them to afford the modern training facilities found in other nations. They also lack a competitive edge, and I think that will hurt them. They are going to run into a lot of athletes on the world-class level with honed killer instincts, Roberto Duran—types whose only interest in consciousness is in seeing how quickly they can separate you from yours. It may not be an attractive quality, but I think it's a necessary asset in any high level of competition. Harry also ignored the fact that, while the lack of a fear of failure may make for a healthier head, it is a basic tenet that one travels fastest when one is being chased, especially when the chasers are the demons he carries inside him. The Chinese are not win-oriented. We played basketball against a team of Chinese athletes. We cleaned their clocks and it never bothered them. Some of the women on the trip were upset over this, claiming we had taken advantage of those poor, uncompetitive Chinese, and that we wanted to win too badly. I said, "Winning is better than the next worst thing." I can't digest losing. The Chinese seem to swallow it easily, and I think it will prevent them from becoming a world sports power.

After recovering from my flu, I decided to split while the trip still had a week to run. I was tired of the rhetorical bullshit that was going down on a daily basis. Catching a freighter out of Shanghai, I started my trip home. I did stop in at the Shanghai Library before leaving and received a tremendous shock. After coming out of the seventh game of the World Series, I had comforted myself with the knowledge that one billion Chinese didn't know or care about my giving up that home run to Tony Perez. I didn't know that the Shanghai Library had a foreign newspaper section. When I visited it, the first thing I saw, hanging from a rack, was a copy of *The New York Times*, dated October 23. On the front page was a photo of Perez taking me deep. Wrong again.

7

1 should have known that 1976 was going to be a bad year, when I spit over the Great Wall of China, and the wind blew it back in my face. Another tip-off should have been provided by Tiant's wig. Luis had bought a rug over the winter. In the past, with his shiny bald head, he had resembled a cuddly Buddha, but, when he reported to spring training, that wig made him look more like a two-toned Mercedes.

Darrell Johnson had done his best to trade me during the off-season. Failing to do that, he instead traded Moret to the Atlanta Braves for lefthanded relief pitcher Tom House. When the deal was announced, Johnson told a reporter, "Lee's lucky he's still here. He's like a cat. He's been falling out of trees all year and landing on his feet." When that quote was relayed to me, I said that was a pretty witty line for Darrell, and I wondered who had been writing his material for him.

The Moret trade was no surprise. Roger was a good pitcher, but he was uncomfortable in the Boston organization. He felt misunderstood and mistreated. The players called him Wrong Way. I don't know why. He was usually headed the right way, but he did have a habit of falling asleep while going there. He did that once while driving his car. He was doing eighty when he nodded out. The car slipped under a rock, tearing off part of his roof and almost killing Roger in the process. Only the fact that he was so completely relaxed saved his life. He did miss that evening's game, spending most of the night in a local hospital. The next day, the front office read the riot act to him. I'll never forget how that stunned him. He sat in front of his locker, shaking his head, saying, "They keep talking about fining me, or suspending me, or trading me to another club. But nobody has asked me how I am or what the X-rays showed." That really blew him away.

I could never figure out how the collective brain of the Red Sox front office worked. If it worked at all. It was one of the great unsolved mysteries of my life. Immediately after coming within one run of the world championship, management started taking the team apart. Moret went to Atlanta, Beniquez, who had played sensationally in '75, went to Texas for Fergie Jenkins. And Carbo was traded in mid-season to Milwaukee for Bobby Darwin. We had been the deepest team in the majors—that's one of the reasons we came so close to winning it all—and the first thing they did was get rid of our depth. Petrocelli was fazed out at third and eventually replaced by Butch Hobson. Hobson, a rookie who had graduated from our farm system, made some great plays when he first came up, but his arm was terrible. Not weak, it just lacked accuracy. He certainly was an aggressive player, sometimes too aggressive. The first game he played for us, he rounded third and creamed Oriole catcher Rick Dempsey on a close play at the plate. Rick was out cold for fifteen minutes. Butch didn't play baseball; he played roller derby on spikes. On pop flys near the dugout, he would dive headfirst into the bat rack. He was never concerned with making the catch. For Butch it was the crash that was more important. From the dugout, you could see him thinking, "Hmm, let's see how badly bruised I can get on this play. How far can I dive into the ground without killing myself?" I never saw him come out of a game wearing a clean uniform.

Despite the changes, I thought we would win the pennant if we could get past Baltimore again. I was always fearful of the Orioles. Yaz saw our chief challenge coming from another direction. After our first spring training game against the Yankees, Carl warned us that they were a better club than last year. Much better. There wasn't any one thing he could put his finger on, but it had something to do with the way all of them ran to first base. There was an intensity there he hadn't noticed the year before. It was only an exhibition game but already Carl knew.

The people of Boston live in silent dread of the Yankees. When I first joined the Red Sox, our games against them weren't the crowd-drawers they became later, but the Boston press wrote them up as if they were the first skirmishes on the road to Armageddon. Clif Keane was in awe of the Yankees even when they were a bad ballclub. Every Red Sox fan knows how New York stole all their stars—Babe Ruth, Herb Pennock, Waite Hoyt, Sparky Lyle, and others—and left Boston with a bucket of ice and a broken Louisville slugger as payment. To be a Red Sox fan was to have a definite aversion to pinstripes.

I always pitched well against the Yankees. Due to the dimensions of their stadium, their teams were built around lefthanded power. When facing their lefty hitters in New York, I would throw a lot of soft stuff in their kitchens. They would try to pull it over the rightfield fence, and the result would be a lot of two-hoppers to my second baseman. When they came to Fenway, they'd shoot for the Wall. I'd nail them with hard sinkers inside. They never were able to adapt, and after a few wins against them, I felt like I owned them.

Another reason for my success against them was my flat-out dislike for their organization. They were an elitist corporation with a self-promoted public image of cold arrogance that went against my grain. The Yankees represented the political right in baseball, while the Red Sox were their opposite number. We were composed of the stuff that had made this country great. We were like a bunch of modern-day pilgrims.

Whenever the Red Sox prepared to play the Yankees, it was as if they were dressing up for battle. You play against other clubs, and it's as if they were all Cleveland. Against the Yankees we would button up differently, taking a little bit longer then usual to put on the uniform. We knew we were getting ready to take the field and uphold our values. It was as though we were knights in armor. That's how I felt. And I wasn't alone.

Petrocelli hated the Yankees. He had been involved in that Pier-Sixer with them in 1967 and had managed to drop about half a dozen of them. I was there in 1973, when Fisk and Gene Michael went at each other. That wasn't much of a fight. Fisk emerged from it with two scratch marks on his right cheek. They looked like two hookers fighting it out over a John. Michael was supposed to be feisty, but I never saw him throw an actual punch. He was probably afraid he would crack his freshly polished nails.

The Fisk-Thurman Munson rivalry was hyped up in the papers, and there was some truth to it. They never actually fought each other; they were both swinging pretty big purses at the time. But I know they were aware of each other's presence. Munson was always checking Fisk's stats, and Carlton would go nuts any time a reporter mentioned Munson's name.

We got off to a slow start in '76, and the Yankees broke out of the gate fast. I couldn't buy a victory, but I wasn't worried. When we made our way into Yankee Stadium on the evening of May 20 for our first confrontation of the season, I figured now was just as good a time as any for us to start getting our record healthy, and for me to pick up my first win. Instead, it turned out to be the night I left my shoulder in New York City.

Billy Martin was managing the Yankees. He and I did not get along. I don't know why. I had a lot to do with Billy getting his job in New York. Shortly after Moret and I shut out the Yankees in a 1975 doubleheader, Bill Virdon was dumped as their skipper. That opened the post for Martin. Billy was available because he had recently been canned by the Texas Rangers. I also played a role in that firing.

Mike Hargrove, the Texas first baseman, was a hitter who drove me nuts. Known as the Human Rain Delay, it takes him about ten minutes to get set at the plate. He goes through a ritual before and after each swing. He pounds his spikes, adjusts something on his leg, twists his thumb, reads a chapter of Fitzgerald, and then he's ready. The pitch is delivered, and, unless he gets a hit or makes an out, he goes through the whole routine again. One afternoon, he really got to me, and I wasn't even pitching. I decided to retaliate. Every time he stepped out of the batter's box, I would count to twenty. If he hadn't stepped back up to the plate by then, I would pick up a bat, pound it on the steps, and yell, "Time's up. Strike one!" Hargrove took it in stride, and the home-plate umpire, Nestor Chylack, loved it. But it drove Billy off the wall. He yelled at me, and I ignored him, which only got him angrier. He started swinging from his dugout roof, pointing at me and scratching under his arms like a chimpanzee. A few days later, the Rangers' owner, Brad Corbett, told him to pack his bags. I like to think I had something to do with that. After all, you're an owner with a large investment in a team, and here's a guy who is supposed to lead your ballplayers, providing them with a role model. And he's swinging from the dugout, impersonating a chimp during a major-league ballgame. That's bound to cause you to have some severe doubts about him.

I wasn't worried about Billy Martin on the evening of May 20. I was just interested in getting myself and the Red Sox back on track. For the first five innings, I did exactly that. I had a 1–0 lead in the sixth when Otto Velez, New York's righthanded d.h., came up with Graig Nettles on first, Lou Piniella on second, and two men out. With the count two and one, I thought Otto would be pulling the ball, so I fed him the sinker, low and away. But Velez went with it, hitting a scorching line drive over my second baseman's head. The rightfielder, Dwight Evans, came tearing in and grabbed the ball on one hop. Now, with an arm like Evans out there, God could have been rounding third, and he would have been out. And this was Piniella. Lou runs as if he's got high-heeled shoes on. Tight high-heeled shoes. Lou should have been out gracefully; there was no need for any contact. But since there was a big crowd there, and he wanted to show them and Billy that he was a Martin-type ballplayer, he decided to crash into Fisk at the plate. Lou had forgotten a cardinal rule: "Never ram into a catcher. It will make him wink out." Fisk, being as stubborn and tenacious as he is, decided to stand in front of Piniella and take his best shot. Flipping Lou over, Carlton tagged him with the ball and his fist, not necessarily in that order. Piniella is not the best guy in the world to pull this maneuver on. Lou is not a disciple of Gandhi; he wakes up in the morning pissed off. Now we had two guys winking out on each other. This was a twin wink-out, better known as a twinkie. The whole thing took me by surprise. I was backing up the throw to home plate—just doing my job—when the next thing I knew, I was in the midst of a brawl. Velez came charging in, trying to get at Fisk, and I tried to stop him. Otto was not exactly a dwarf. I tried to tackle him high in order to lessen the risk of injury to my shoulder. Wrong. I should have tackled him low and just taken my chances. Actually, I should have just kicked him in the cubes and gotten my face out of there.

Somehow, in the midst of this melee, I got spun around while grabbing Velez and was hit from behind. A picture later showed that Mickey Rivers had hit me in the back of the head with a sucker punch. That dazed me. He packed a pretty good wallop for a skinny, little guy. As I tried to clear my head, Nettles came over, picked me up, and dropped me on my shoulder. He later claimed that he was only trying to keep me out of the fight. He did do that. I guess Graig's idea of keeping the peace was to arrange for me to get a lot of bed rest in a quiet hospital.

Immediately after he had ground me into the Stadium turf, I got up, went to pick up my glove with my left hand, and discovered my arm was dead. There was no pain; it was just numb. My first thought was, "I don't think I can finish this game." Then, realizing how badly I was hurt, my brain screamed, "I have no fucking feeling in my arm!" Turning to Nettles, I yelled, "You son of a bitch! How could you do this to me? I played ball with your brother Jimmy in Alaska, you no-good prick! How could you be such an asshole!"

I believe it was the use of the word asshole that set him off again. He came at me, and I tried to swing at him. Nothing moved. It was like trying to swing a piece of dead meat. Ducking under a punch I never threw, Nettles came up and hit me again. He gave me a shiner and knocked me down. He hit me so good that I just sort of slid halfway into our dugout. I felt like Popeye after being stomped by Bluto. I wanted to yell, "Where's my spinach!" Before I had the chance, a fan came out of the stands and tried to kill me. I held him off with my feet. The entire episode became a Fellini movie. As the reel unwound, I saw the trainer examining my arm while I'm lying on the floor and I've got some poor son of a bitch nailed to the dugout wall with my spikes perforating his chest. And 45,000 Yankee fans are screaming for the lions to devour the Christians. It was insane. When the dust had settled, and order had been restored, the umpires decided to throw Nettles and me out of the game. As it turned out, I really had no choice in the matter. My arm was totally screwed up.

I didn't know how badly I was hurt. I was rushed to the hospital for a preliminary examination and X-rays. I heard one doctor say that he thought I might never pitch again. That certainly did wonders for my spirits. That night, I lay in my hotel room after having consumed four Demerols and seven shots of VO. I was out of my brain. I swear to God, I started hallucinating. I imagined seeing George Steinbrenner coming in through my window, leading helmeted troops of Yankees into my room. George took out a magic marker and drew lines across my body, telling an aide, "Okay, you can start cutting here." The next morning, after the demons had vanished, I met with the press. I told them what I thought of Steinbrenner and his goons, criticizing him and Martin for their Brown Shirt mentality. That fight was a product of the Martin influence. There is a lot of fascist in Billy's approach to the game. I'm sure he thinks Mussolini was just a nice guy whom Hitler led astray.

After I made those statements comparing Martin and Steinbrenner to the Nazis, Billy really had it in for me. He once paid a clubhouse boy to stick a dead fish in my trousers. The clubhouse boy was mature enough to bring it over to me while it was still in the bag. He asked, "You don't need this in your pants, do you?" I told him I didn't and we both got a laugh out of it. I understand that there was a note attached to the fish, but I never got a chance to read it. Supposedly the message said, "Stick this in your pussy." I doubt that. I don't believe Billy could spell pussy.

When my X-rays came back, they revealed a torn ligament in my left shoulder. After five weeks of complete rest I started to work out. I ran long distances with my left arm strapped to my side, which allowed me to run without harming my shoulder. I also started weightlifting. Nothing too intense. I started with a rubber hose tied up in knots. Seriously, that's all my shoulder could tolerate. At first, I got depressed, thinking my career was shot. But then, I figured, "Hell, I never threw that hard to begin with. I can come back from this." I did worry about being able to water the lawn, though. I mean, damn, that hose was heavy.

With each therapy session, the arm came around a little bit more. I had good days and bad days, but the good were on the heavier side of the scales. When I reached the point where I could throw again, I found that my elbow couldn't handle the stress of throwing the sinker, and that I couldn't get any snap on my breaking ball. I had made the mistake of favoring my shoulder and using too much elbow with my tosses. Now the elbow was hyperextended. The Red Sox physician wanted to grease me up with cortisone, but I wouldn't let him. I opted instead for acupuncture. It got me back in harness in no time, though I did come out of it looking like a salt shaker. I was pitching again by mid-July, throwing in relief. I got hit hard at first, but I gradually started to pitch well, working my way back into the rotation.

My first start after the injury came against New York on July 24, in Yankee Stadium. I got mashed. Prior to the game, my father, who thinks Billy Martin is the best manager in baseball, called me and said, "If you have any guts at all, you'll knock Nettles on his ass his first time up. You'll really hurt him." I was all for that. The problem was that, after the injury, I couldn't throw hard enough to hurt anybody. So, I just tried to get him out. Tried too hard, really. He hit a home run off me the first time I faced him. So did his tag-team partner, Rivers. I left the game after four innings. That was depressing. Not because I had given up the home runs or had been knocked out of the ballgame. I was upset because I realized that I didn't have the velocity to pitch the Yankees inside like I used to. That brawl and the resultant injury had robbed me of that. Instead of going right at guys, I now had to go to the slow curve and pitch to spots even more than I had in the past. I would make that adjustment, and I would still win. It just wouldn't be as much fun as it had been.

I did start to pitch well in August. It was too late to help my teammates, though. We were going nowhere, on our way to finishing light years behind Steinbrenner's Storm Troopers. My injury contributed to our fall from grace. The club never did make up those seventeen wins I had been giving them every year. We were also hurting in the bullpen. Tom House, supposedly our ace short man, could not do the job. I recall one game against the Yankees, in which he was brought in specificially to get Chambliss out, and Chris took him deep for the ballgame. That loss killed us. We were still in the pennant race, but, when the Yankees won that game in extra innings, they soared and we packed it in. I'm certain that was the game that convinced the Yankees that they were going to do it that year. Just as it convinced us that we weren't. I know I was pretty convinced when that ball left the park.

House was hurting when we got him from the Braves. He had to do a certain number of exercises and stretches every day before a game. He was a bionic man with torn cartilage in both knees. Once Johnson saw that Tom wasn't going to be effective for us, he started playing Reliever's Roulette, using a different short man every other game. None of them panned out. The Red Sox got so desperate that they finally made that big deal with Oakland, sending the A's Fort Knox in exchange for Joe Rudi and Rollie Fingers. Bowie Kuhn nixed the deal, saying it was not in the best interests of baseball. I seem to recall Rudi reporting and suiting up with us, though he never got to get into a game. I never did see Fingers. You can bet I wouldn't have forgotten if I had. Putting that sucker in our bullpen might have given us another pennant, if we only could have fixed one other chink in our armor.

The year 1976 was the first year a player could play out his option and become a free agent. All he had to do was go through an entire season without a contract. When the season was over, he could entertain bids from as many as thirteen major-league clubs. There were three potential free agents on our club: Freddy Lynn, Carlton Fisk, and Rick Burleson. Jerry Kapstein was their agent. They were like an oil cartel. I have no use for agents, who come in and turn baseball into a game of corporate musical chairs. A baseball player should be like the ancient samurai. A samurai warrior had integrity when he defended the underdog, but, if he took his act down the block to some other dynasty for bigger bucks, then he was no longer being true to himself or the game he played. He was not going to hit .300 that year.

When Fisk, Lynn, and Burleson got entwined in the economic machinations of free agency, it seemed to take something away from their game. They had lost that spark that had come out of the youthful dive-for-every-ball enthusiasm that all three of them had. They still played hard; you can't just shut their kind of intensity off. But they had lost their edge. Free agency seemed a burden for them. It was tearing at their brains. Over the course of the full season, I could see it playing havoc with the concentration, impairing their ability to give one hundred percent. That doesn't mean they dogged it. They were giving everything they had, but they didn't have one hundred percent to give. The game itself, left on its own, is demanding enough. They didn't need the albatross of unsigned contracts and front-office mind-games wrapped around their necks. The press compounded the pressure. Fisk's locker was near mine, and, after every loss, I knew I would be hearing at least one writer asking him if his contract squabbles were hindering his performance. Freddy and Rick were going through the same thing. There was no place for them to hide. When they finally did sign, late in the season, you could sense their relief.

Two events occurred in '76 that would directly affect my future with the club. Three, actually, if you count the injury. The first occurred in mid-season. Mr. Yawkey died.

Mr. Yawkey and I weren't particularly close, but whatever relationship we did have was a good one. We had a common bond, solidified by our mutual interest in the *National Geographic*. I had a subscription to the magazine, and I would bring it into the clubhouse, leaving it at my locker while I did my running. One afternoon I returned to the clubhouse to find that my latest issue was missing. I didn't think anything of it. I figured someone had taken it to read in the can and had forgotten to return it. But, the same thing happened again the following week, and the week after that. I was puzzled and determined to catch the culprit. Before I had a chance to enlist the aid of the CIA, however, the Mystery of the Missing Magazines was solved. The break in the case came one afternoon while I was meeting with Dick O'Connell in his office. I had only been there a few moments when Mr. Yawkey popped in and handed me a brown paper bag, saying, "I think these are yours." Inside the sack were the purloined magazines.

After making a positive ID, I nodded that they were. He sat down, and we got into a discussion on the subject of ecology. Mr. Yawkey told me how he used to watch the ivory-billed woodpeckers as they flew along the coast of South Carolina. He lamented that they had become extinct. Then he told me how he used pesticides on his property down there, explaining, "We spray the Carolina coast with pesticides because we have had problems with the soft pine beetle." I tried to tell him that the ivory-billed woodpecker was the natural predator of the soft pine beetle, and that by using pesticides he was breaking up the natural order and depriving the birds of food. That's why his precious woodpeckers had died off. He admitted he had never thought of that. He should have.

On the last day of the 1976 season, a pigeon flew into the bleachers and crashed into a seat, killing himself. I knew it was the late Mr. Yawkey. He had been sent back as a pigeon with instructions to get a firsthand knowledge of the dangers of pesticides. Having done that, he was now simply shedding his skin so that he could assume another form. I wish they had let him come back as our owner again. After he died, the Red Sox ceased to be the one big happy family we had been. That point would be driven home to me later.

Not long after Mr. Yawkey passed on, the second event that would eventually pave my road out of Boston occurred. Darrell Johnson was fired and replaced by Don Zimmer. Zim had been our third-base coach, and I thought he had done a hell of a job. But making him manager was an admission by the front office that the team was being run on the Peter Principle. They were raising Zimmer to a position in which he could operate at his highest level of incompetence. He had some strange ideas about pitching. He constantly encouraged his pitchers to loosen batters up with a brushback. One pitcher turned to me and asked, "How bright can this guy be? Here he is walking about with a plate in his head, the souvenir of a serious beaning, and he's talking about knocking guys down."

I couldn't understand it either. I believed in drilling guys only as a form of reprisal. If an opposing pitcher hit one of my teammates, then I was obligated to hit one of his. An eye for an eye. Usually the reason for a knockdown is that the pitcher made a bad pitch on somebody and got jocked. Angry at himself, he knocks down the next hitter. This is supposed to make the pitcher feel better, while also making up for the horseshit pitch he had thrown to the previous batter. It does not work that way. All the beanball does is reinforce your conviction that you are throwing bad pitches. The more intensely you believe that, the more bad pitches you will throw. This is the power of negative thinking.

Of course, there were some guys you couldn't avoid hitting. Jerry Terrell of the Twins was one of them. He would do anything to get on base or drive in a run. Jerry was always willing to take one on the elbow for the team. Maybe that's why he did so much praying in the on-deck circle. He also liked to try to get pitchers to balk. I saw him do it once to Diego Segui. Diego had a 3–2 count on him with two men out and the bases loaded. As Segui went into his wind up, Terrell reached down and grabbed a handful of dirt. Diego was so distracted by the move he balked in a run. Afterwards, Terrell said, "God made me reach down and grab for that dirt." My ass, it wasn't God. It was fear, fear that he wouldn't hit the ball, and fear that it would be strike three. Segui was pissed off when he heard that explanation, but he shrugged it off quickly. Diego was a Latin Catholic and he could understand Terrell's belief. But he also knew that his God and Terrell's God would never meet. Terrell's was born again. Diego's had been here from the get-go.

I worked hard during the winter to get ready for the '77 season. I stuck to my own program of running and lifting light weights. By spring training, I felt great. The Yankees had picked up Reggie Jackson and Don Gullett in the free-agent market during the off-season. We countered by getting Bill Campbell, the relief pitcher from Minnesota. I liked that. He was a great pitcher, and I figured he would be all the cure our bullpen needed. I didn't care what we were paying him. I wasn't crazy about free agency, but I knew there was no way we could pass on a pitcher of his ability. I did wonder how he would respond to the pressure of having everybody in Boston expecting him to save every game, pitch us to the pennant, help us sweep the Series, and end the Middle East crisis, all without breaking a sweat. I also wasn't sure how wise it was to sign a pitcher to any kind of a long-term deal. You never knew when someone might drop him on his shoulder.

Campbell had no problem handling the pressure. He was one cool customer. One evening he and I went to an all-night diner in Cleveland where the counterman makes great corned beef sandwiches. Well, they may not be great, but at two in the morning, who knew? We walked down the middle of the street to get there. You tend to walk down the middle of streets in this particular section of Cleveland, away from parked cars and alleys. You're negotiating for a little bit more reaction time. When it's late at night, you want the chance to be able to ascertain whether that guy coming towards you is carrying a machete or a dog leash. Campbell and I were about to cross the avenue in front of the diner when all hell broke loose. A car was giving off a nasty backfire. Except it wasn't a car backfiring at all. Some cop had gone into the diner with his wife just as two hoods were sticking up the place. The cop laid his wife across a table, used her as an armrest, and blew both guys away. One crook died in the diner's doorway. His partner barely made it to the street before buying the farm. The owner of the place got shot in the leg.

I was paralyzed with fear, but Campbell was stepping over bodies, saying, "Yeah, that one's gone, but the other one's still twitching." Bill had been in Viet Nam a long time and it helped him develop the intestinal fortitude that all relief pitchers need. I don't know what he did wrong while he was over there, but he must have pissed off someone because they made him carry the radio pack. The radio pack is a big, shiny object with long antennae. Campbell was six-foot-three to begin with, so he must have made a hell of a target. It's a miracle he survived to pitch in the American League. He threw great that first season with us, but Zimmer pitched him too often and he threw his arm out. Bill had a hell of a time coming back. His arm healed just as his contract with Boston reached its final year. I thought that was nice. It was as though he was being rewarded for surviving Nam.

Bernie Carbo and George Scott returned from exile in Milwaukee before the season started. We got them in a trade for Cecil Cooper. I also came back in 1977. Of course,

I hadn't been aware that I had been gone, but everybody who looked at my 9–5 record said, "What a great comeback!" At the end of the season, I went over the team's stats and it seemed as if every hitter in our lineup had hit ninety home runs and had three hundred runs batted in. Looking over the numbers, I thought, "Gee, you mean we didn't win the pennant?" No sports fans, we didn't. We finished third, one and a half games behind the Yankees.

Zimmer hurt us that year. He didn't have a clue on how to handle a pitching staff. I noticed right away that the biggest difference between him and Johnson as managers was that Johnson was taller. Zimmer worked Campbell to a state of collapse, and he never settled on a starting rotation. At one point, he had eight guys moving in and out as starters. He also held out pitchers so they could face certain teams. Wise wouldn't pitch for a week and a half because Don wanted to save him for Baltimore. He would do the same thing with me, keeping me on ice until we faced New York. It was a half-assed way to run things. None of us could establish a good working rhythm pitching under those conditions. Laboring in the bullpen for him wasn't a treat either. Unless you were Bill Campbell, you never had any idea when or how he was going to use you.

Don let his personal feelings get in the way of his decisions. Fergie Jenkins didn't think Zimmer knew diddly about pitching, and he let him know it. Don responded by jerking Fergie around all season. This was one of the best pitchers in baseball. Instead of letting Jenkins do his thing and help the club win, Zimmer did everything he could to bring out the worst in him.

Don also alienated Wise. Rick had gone through a few bad outings, and Zimmer tried to bury him in the bullpen. When Wise complained about it, he was immediately consigned to the manager's shit list. Zimmer took to jumping on Wise for little bullshit things such as growing a beard, even though other players had been allowed to grow one.

He would even hold pitchers' meetings and not bother to invite Rick. It was weird. Zimmer made no attempt to set up lines for communication with either Jenkins or Wise, despite their being two of the best pitchers we had. I took it upon myself to let Don know that I thought his treatment of them was hurting the ballclub. That landed me on the list with them. And Willoughby eventually pissed him off by hanging out with us. By mid-season, the manager had stopped talking to half his pitching staff.

Zimmer thought we were a danger to his ballclub. He was of the old school, and we were part of the counter-culture. He and the front office thought that we were going to corrupt the morals of the rest of the team. One executive warned one of the younger pitchers, Allen Ripley, not to socialize with us if he knew what was good for him. He didn't listen, and, the next thing he knew, he was back in the minors.

Jenkins, Wise, Willoughby, Carbo, and I banded together to form the Loyal Order of the Buffalo Heads. Jenkins had nicknamed Zimmer Buffalo Head, pointing out that the buffalo was generally considered to be the dumbest animal in creation. It was also Fergie who had summed up Zimmer's problems with us by saying, "The man knows nothing about pitching or pitchers. He's a lifetime .230 hitter who's been beaned three times. He hates pitchers. We will never see eye-to-eye."

If Jenkins was the Order's president, then Willoughby was its resident mystic. Carlos Castenada had Don Juan as a mentor. I think pitchers should also have a guru. We should go into the desert during the off-season and try to live off the land while looking for Don Juan the philosopher. When we find him, he'll probably look like Tom Landry, and he'll say things like, "Take whatever they give you," and "Throw strikes.'"

The first mystic sage I ever encountered was a shopping-bag lady I met in Detroit. She told me not to walk in that city carrying any more money than I could afford to get rolled for. Willoughby seemed to have that same gift of the all-knowing. He was a complex person. Jim would be serene and earth-oriented before a game. But, after a game, he would pound six beers into himself and become a different guy, hellbent for leather. He would get loud for a few hours, totally exhaust himself, and then retreat into a state of calm that was awesome to behold.

Once, the Buffalo Heads were sitting in a hotel room at two o'clock in the morning. There were beer cans stacked to the ceiling, lending a certain ambience to the occasion. Willow was holding court. Speaking in a quiet, almost meditative tone, he told us about an experience he had had in Phoenix. He was with the Giants in spring training and had gotten ripped with several of his teammates. They went driving up and around the mountains just outside the city. They drove onto a point, got out and watched as the sun came up over a mountain ridge. Just beyond the sunrise, a group of clouds appeared in the sky. The first cloud was shaped like the letter G. The second was shaped like an O, and the third took the form of a D. GOD. Willoughby was moved by this recollection; I thought he was on the verge of tears. Wise couldn't figure out why Jim was getting so carried away. He looked at Jim and said, "Big fucking deal! Some clown on the other side of the mountain saw DOG." That blew Willoughby away. Wise never opened his mouth much, but when he did a pearl was sure to drop out.

I was with Willoughby hours before pitching my first major league game under the influence of a controlled substance. Actually, that's not true. If THC is fat-soluble, then I have pitched my entire major league career under its influence. We were playing Seattle in Boston, and I had stopped off to pick Willoughby up at his room in the Fenway Motor Inn, not far from the ballpark. It was too early to head for the clubhouse, so we sat in his room and I smoked three bowls of hash. THC is a short-term depressant. It acts on you like heavy gravity, pulling you closer to the earth. Your lights go out right away. The metabolism is slowed to the extent that you are no longer burning anything up inside. Your organs come to a halt, and you're put in a yoga-like trance. You emerge from that state with a tremendous surge of energy. I hadn't expected to pitch that day. Wise started and got hammered early. I was sitting in the bullpen, just starting to rush out of my trance when...*boom!* I was in the ballgame.

It was quite an experience. I could see every play in my mind moments before it actually occurred. My concentration was centered only on home plate and the catcher's glove. The whole game became a cardiovascular dance. The faster I pitched, the more perfect my pitches became as each strike fed off the preceding one. I felt no pain in my shoulder or elbow, and my concentration was so intense that there were no fans present and no hitters at the plate. It was just me, my catcher, and his signs. Fisk was using Greek signals that day. Two omega was a slider low and away. I pitched five and two-thirds innings that day and gave up only two runs. I was still recovering from my shoulder problems, but the THC relaxed my muscles so they couldn't bite me. It also relieved whatever fear I had that throwing might cause me pain. When you're healthy, you're in a pure state without worry. But when your shoulder is hurt, you'll do anything to anesthetize yourself. You can only take so much Butazolidin before your blood thins out. Then you have to reach into your metaphysical grab bag.

Zimmer was intent on breaking up the Loyal Order. He took after me, sticking me in the bullpen and telling me it was for my own good. Don claimed that pitching in relief would give me a chance to build my arm back up. Then he did his best to make sure that I couldn't get into a ballgame.

When I finally did make an appearance, it was completely against his wishes. Ramon Hernandez, a lefthanded reliever, had been told to warm up because Zimmer was about to bring him into a ballgame. He tried, but he couldn't get loose. He kept throwing, shrugging after each pitch and saying, "I'm not ready, I'm not ready." Zimmer came to the mound and signaled for the lefthander, but Ramon just could not answer the bell. Champing at the bit for some action, I jumped up, threw two pitches, and raced out to the mound. Zimmer went nuts, yelling, "I didn't call for you. I want it to be known that I did not want you out there. If you hurt yourself, it's not my fault!" I told him, "Relax, I'm just coming out to help Ramon. He can't make it today. You need a lefthander, and I'm going to prove to you that my arm is sound." He stormed off into the dugout. I had good stuff that day. I threw the batter three deuces and said, "See you later." A few more appearances like that, and I was able to get back into Zimmer's twelve-man rotation. I pitched well during the last six weeks of the season.

The fate of the Loyal Order of the Buffalo Heads was sealed on September 18, 1977—Brooks Robinson Day in Baltimore. Its members had done some heavy-duty partying the evening before. Fergie and I had polished off the last bottle of wine at five in the morning. By the time we got to the park that afternoon, we all looked as if we had rolled out of the same trash can. I felt terrible. I went outside the ballpark and jogged five miles around a nearby lake. Upon returning to the clubhouse, I found Bernie asleep behind an ultrasound machine. Willow and Wise were in the trainer's room, tending to their shattered skulls. I could not find Fergie. It wasn't until the game started that I finally found him out in the bullpen, asleep in the cart used to haul relievers out to the mound. Our starting pitcher was getting mauled that day, and, by the third inning, the call came down to warm up Jenkins. Walt Hrinak, the bullpen coach, told Zimmer that Fergie wasn't around. Walt was five-foot-eleven, and he was not about to try to wake up this six-foot-six giant who was growling in his sleep. He did his best to cover for him, but he finally had to admit that Fergie was visiting the Land of Nod.

Jenkins caught hell for that. He was reprimanded and fined. Zimmer was so angry he told the front office that he wanted our whole group shipped out. All of us except for Bernie. I guess Zimmer figured that Carbo was an innocent whom we had led astray. Or maybe Jenkins was right about him. Maybe he just didn't like pitchers. On the last day of the season, Zimmer asked individual players into his office in order to thank them for their contribution to the team. None of the Buffalo Heads were invited. That was a bush move, designed to show us up. On that same afternoon Fergie, Wise, Willow, Bernie, and I posed together for a photo. No one had to tell us anything. We knew it would be the last time the five musketeers would be together in a Red Sox uniform.

8

I n the months leading up to the 1978 season, I had felt like I was starring in *Invasion of the Body Snatchers*. Every morning, I would wake up and another friend had vanished. Fergie was traded to Texas for a couple of used baseballs and an autographed picture of Roy Rogers and Dale Evans. Willoughby was sold to the White Sox. We didn't get anybody for him. All we got was money, and a dollar bill never struck out anyone. I led a silent protest when that deal was announced, leaving a lit candle on Zimmer's desk as part of a novena for a departed friend. I thought Wise would survive the purge. He was our best pitcher in Winter Haven, and the front office was worried about Tiant's arm. No chance. Rick was shipped to Cleveland in a deal for Dennis Eckersley. After that trade, every time I came into the clubhouse, the first thing I would do was to check to see if Bernie was still with us. We'd look at each other, smile, and shake our heads without saying a word. We were the only Buffalo Heads left, and we knew it wouldn't last for long.

Eckersley had the world's greatest vernacular. He knew more words that weren't in the dictionary than ones that were. If he threw a "yakker for your coolu," it meant you were going to get nailed in the ass with a fastball. "Cheese for your kitchen" was a fastball up and in. We never went out partying. Instead, we went out to "get oiled." The first time we went to a bar together, I asked him what he drank. He said, "I oil on eighty weight." That meant he preferred Jack Daniels. Dennis called me Sherwin Williams, claiming that I was the greatest painter of home plate that had ever lived. I said, "Well, then why don't you call me Picasso or Renoir?" But, no, Sherwin Williams was his idea of a great painter. I guess it was because Sherwin had made more money than the other two. Eckersley also named me Salad Master, as in "Bill, you sure do throw a lot of salad up there." He called himself either Cheese Master or Style Master.

Dennis and I had a brotherly relationship. He told me the story about losing his wife to his best friend, Rick Manning, the Cleveland centerfielder. It was sad. He would turn to me and ask, "What went wrong? Why did this happen?"

I told him that his life had been passing him by too quickly and that he wasn't prepared for everything that was coming down. I told him that eventually, when he stopped looking for it, he would find the answer. The first time we faced Cleveland, he talked about his broken marriage intensely. He spent an entire evening getting angry at his wife, Manning, and himself. I thought to myself, Uh-oh, he's going to decapitate Manning tomorrow."

The next afternoon, he threw Rick nothing but fastballs down the chute, and Manning got two base hits. After the game, I asked Dennis, "Why didn't you hit him? I was sure you were going to nail him today." He just shook his head and got a faraway look in his eyes while telling me, "No, that's all in the past."

I realized at that moment that we now had a real pitcher on our hands. That afternoon, he proved to himself that he was above his personal problems. He had acquired the maturity he needed to become a big winner. The bust-up of his marriage did not hurt him any more, although being separated from his daughter still ripped him up. He dedicated his twentieth win of that season to her. I'll tell you something, he was great for us. Dennis just blew people away. He handled lefthanded hitters well and, with his kick and delivery and the way he came around from third base, no righthanded hitter claiming sanity was happy about facing him.

I tried to be a technician on the mound; Eckersley was more of a manic dancing master. He was a pitching Reggie Jackson, putting pressure on himself and then coming through. He would go nuts between the lines, yelling at hitters and challenging them to hit his fastball. He'd tell batters on their way up to the plate that there was no way they were going to hit him, and then he'd strike them out. It was as if Dizzy Dean had been reincarnated. Dennis lived on a diet of prime steaks and Jack Daniels, and he threw severe heat. While he was still an Indian, he pitched a no-hitter against the California Angels. He had two men out in the ninth and the last hitter was taking his time getting to the batter's box. Eck came halfway in from the mound and shouted, "Stalling won't help. There's one more out to go, and you're it." Then he reared back and blew the sucker away. I loved that confidence of his.

We pounded a lot of pavement together. Once, we went into a late-night place in Texas. It featured a beautiful strobe light that flickered through a prism onto the dance floor, and it had a great band. We were there with about six of our teammates, and none of us realized when we first walked in that it was a gay bar. Gays drove Eckersley crazy. We hadn't been in the place five minutes before a guy came over to Dennis and lisped, "Hi, can I help you? I haven't seen you here before." Eckersley was paralyzed. His drink dropped from his hand as if he'd been jolted by an electric current. Falling to the floor, it landed straight up without spilling a drop. Most amazing thing I ever saw. I thought to myself, "Wow, that's what I call shock!" Eckersley started screaming, "Get me out of here!" Dick Drago walked over to him and said, "Calm down. They're just fags." Drago never passed judgments on anybody, and he was totally fearless. A couple of clubhouse boys who were doing the town with us were petrified, though. One of them grabbed me and said, "Lee, don't get out of my sight. If you leave me here, I swear I'll get you. If it takes me the rest of my life, and if I have to hunt you down halfway across the universe, I will. I'll find you and then I'll kill you."

The places you end up in on the road can be unbelievable. During one trip to New York, everybody on the team was trying to decide which places we were going to check out. We came up with a small list, but some people in our hotel said, "Those places ain't nothin'. If you want to see New York, you have got to go to Xenon." We went there, and the moment we walked in, I said, "God damn, this is outrageous! I mean this is *really* outrageous! And people think I'm bizarre?" There was a girl there walking around with giant paper clips stuck through her nipples. She was dressed in velvet and chains and she was talking to a guy who had emblazoned on his shirt a big dick that glowed in the dark. Dancing nearby were two coneheads. Their bodies had been painted sterling silver, and that was all they wore. That evening, I came in touch with religion, thinking, "It really would be easier for the camel to pass through the eye of the needle than for a rich man to pass through the gates of heaven. But, let's see how they stack up when they both try to get into Studio 54!"

In Milwaukee, we always made it a point to visit The Safe House. There, walking into what appeared to be an old bookstore, you were greeted by a receptionist sitting at a desk. She would ask you what you were looking for, and you were supposed to reply, "I'm looking for a safe house." She would push a lever, and one of the bookshelves would slide open, permitting you to walk into a huge bar that had tables surrounded by bullet-proof glass, and a separate room with a see-through mirror that permitted you to watch out for enemy agents without being seen yourself. Some of the ballplayers especially liked the phone booth located in the rear of the bar. Dialing 876 on the phone would cause the back of the booth to slide open, exposing a stairway that served as an exit to the street. It was convenient to know about that little trick if you were stuck with a woman you wanted to get rid of. You just sent her to the phone and told her to dial the number. *Adios!*

I loved Kansas City. It had the best steaks in the league and the best beer. Yaz used to smuggle ten cases of Coors beer out of K.C. every time we played there, sneaking it onto the team flight. I thought eventually he would get caught and that we would all be arrested for transporting alcohol across state lines for immoral purposes. But he never got nabbed. Yaz is blessed. I believe that is one of the reasons he was able to play so well for so long. The other reason is his uniform number. Yaz wore number eight. I had noticed that, starting in 1975, Carl was taking catnaps in the trainer's room. With his uniform on. When laid on its side the number 8 resembles the symbol for infinity. That symbol was recharging Yaz's batteries. If he had just worn his uniform while he slept at night, I am convinced he could have played forever.

We stayed at a hotel in Kansas City that had a giant leather baseball glove in its lobby. I loved that glove. You could crawl up inside its pocket and cuddle up in it. The glove would cradle you as if you were a caught fly ball. It was a very secure place to be during a hangover.

There was a woman in Kansas City whose ex-husband was a member of the local symphony orchestra. She had a thing for ballplayers. She once went on a date with one of our outfielders, taking him, me, and one of her girl friends out to dinner. It was not a romantic evening. After finishing his meal, the outfielder said to her, "Let's go." It was as if he figured, "Okay, I've been fed. What's next?" She suggested they go to her apartment, adding that she first had to call her ex to make sure he wouldn't be dropping in. When her former husband found out who she was bringing over there, he asked if he could come by anyway. He wanted to get an autograph. It was unbelievable! I was surprised he didn't offer to watch their lovemaking while accompanying them on the vibes.

There are some rambunctious ladies in Kansas City. I recall one in particular who got hammered during a game and somehow made her way into our clubhouse. Tiant and I were the only players in there. Luis was sitting at his locker, bare-assed. She took one look at him and her little eyes nearly popped out of her head. It was love at first sight. Luis, you see, is a giant both on and off the field. She started sputtering, but before she could get anything out, our traveling secretary came in and chased her out of there. Luis just sat back with a big grin on his face, watching the whole episode.

Every time we came in to play against the Royals, I looked forward to seeing George Brett. I could not get over how much like me he was, always taking care of business on the field, but also always having a good time while doing it. He would throw the greatest parties at his house. Eckersley, Carbo, and I got invited to one of his bashes, but by the time we got there, George was nowhere to be found. Someone suggested that he might be unconscious under the couch, but no one bothered to lift it to find out. Andy Hassler, a lefthanded pitcher who had just come over to Boston from the Royals, was there, and he kept telling us that we couldn't stay. But, we had just gotten there and hadn't had a drink yet. We were, therefore, in no hurry to leave. Hassler and his fellow revelers had to throw us out bodily. That pissed off Bernie and Dennis, and they decided to turn over a Corvette that was parked in the driveway. I thought that was a good idea, but we realized that the car was made out of fiberglass, and none of us wanted to risk cracking it. We turned our attention to a giant Lincoln

Continental parked nearby, with its windows all fogged up. With mayhem dancing in his eyes, Bernie opened up its door and found a member of the Royals getting it on with some lady. Bernie didn't miss a beat. He just stuck out a cigarette and said, "Oh, excuse me. I was looking for a match."

The Red Sox started spring training with a new second baseman, Jerry Remy, who had come over from the Angels in a winter trade. That was a good pickup for us. Remy had more range than Doyle, and he gave us speed at the top of our lineup. He fit in right away. The first time we played the Yankees he said, "I hate every one of those pinstriped sons of bitches." We had also gotten Mike Torrez away from New York in the free-agent draft. He had been the Yankees' best pitcher in September and I figured that losing him was bound to hurt them. They had picked up Goose Gossage. That scared me. I don't usually think much of one-pitch relievers. Their use and success is another step forward for the age of the specialist. But Gossage's one pitch was a fastball that could only be heard, never seen. I knew he would make the Yankees tough.

Sometimes, getting new guys on a club, despite their talent, can present problems. It can take a while to click as a team. The new people have to get used to new surroundings and establish new loyalties. But in '78, we gelled right away, jumping out of the chute like we were the 1927 Yankees. We had all the usual hitting we had become famous for, and we matched it up with good pitching. Eckersley, Torrez, Tiant, rookie Jim Wright, and I gave the Red Sox their best starting rotation in years. I had won my first six decisions and was feeling great, when my arm began to tire. The muscles weren't properly built up yet; they were still hurting from the Nettles fight. My left arm was dropping lower with each start, making it difficult for me to get anything on the ball. I tried lifting Nautilus, but found that my pitching arm could barely lift ten pounds.

This forced me to throw even more junk than I had before, and it reduced my effectiveness. But it didn't stop us from winning ballgames.

Our entire lineup was a squad of assassins. And Rice was its leader. There didn't seem any way to consistently get him out. Early in the year, some pitchers tried backing him off the plate by throwing at him. Jim Colborn was one of the last to try that. He threw a pitch close to Jim's chin, and Jim trotted out to the mound to have some words with him. I thought Colborn was going to commit suicide. Rice told him, "If you come close to me with one more pitch, I'm going to tear your head off." When the other pitchers throughout the league heard about this, the brushback pitches became fewer in number. A pitcher doesn't like to give up the inside of the plate, but he also values his life and limbs. There wasn't anyone in the league who wanted to mess with Big Jim. As Colborn put it after their confrontation, "When he came out to the mound, I thought it was all over. I figured he was going to turn me into Rice-a-roni."

We were kicking the crap out of everybody; when we played the Yankees, we made them look like a pickup team. By mid-June we were so far out in front that fans were already inquiring when we would start printing playoff tickets. There was an atmosphere on our club, a sort of "no way we can lose" cockiness that all great clubs have to have. We had everything going our way, and then June 15 rolled around and we blew it.

The Red Sox trainer had been a fellow named Buddy Leroux. Everybody on the club used to call him Popping Fresh because he looked like the Pillsbury Dough Boy. He got his revenge. After Mr. Yawkey died, he and Haywood Sullivan raised the money to buy a controlling interest in the club. After that sale was negotiated, Zimmer told us that we had nothing to worry about. He swore the Red Sox were not going to change and that we would still be a family.

Bernie and I were sure we were going to be dealt from the team, and we both had a lot of anxiety as the June 15 midnight trading deadline approached. When it passed, we were still on the club. We went out celebrating that night. The next day, I woke up and got the paper. Bernie had been sold to Cleveland for $15,000. Pocket change. I couldn't believe it. It was the dumbest thing management could have done. The front office was angry with him because he was unsigned, and had, in their view, taken too much time recovering from an ankle injury he had suffered in late May. Instead of fussing with bullshit like that they should have realized what Bernie meant to our club. Carbo would spend days honing his bats down with a bottle, staying ready for that moment he would be needed. He had that Wally Moon inside-out stroke that was magic in Fenway. All he wanted from management was a fair contract. Carbo didn't care about making big money; he cared about helping his team win ballgames. The front office didn't see that. All they saw was an unsigned player who liked to take catnaps all the time, and who hung out with that left-handed troublemaker.

After reading about the deal I went to our clubhouse, ready to kill. I cleared out my locker, tearing my nameplate off the front of it. Then, grabbing my bags, I walked out of the clubhouse and off the team. Returning home, I tore the telephone off the wall. My kids got into bed with me, and we spent the rest of the day crying. It was pretty shitty. I missed that evening's game. The next morning, my front porch was crowded with reporters and cameramen. All of the local papers the following day had my picture splashed across their front pages. Beneath each of them was the caption BILL LEE WAVES GOOD-BYE TO THE PRESS IN THE BOSTON CLUBHOUSE. Someone's sense of location must have been severely off. Those shots had been taken in front of my house, and I wasn't waving good-bye to anyone. I was telling the media to get the fuck away from my home. I was usually available to the press, but this was one of the few moments when I felt they were intruding on my personal life.

Haywood Sullivan tried to get through to me by phone, but obviously, it was out of order. He finally reached me via telegram and requested a meeting in his office. When we met, on June 17, the first thing I noticed was that there were ashes all over his desk. Wiping them off, I told him, "This was Mr. Yawkey's desk, and I don't think you're taking very good care of it."

That remark precipitated a shouting match. Haywood yelled that I had to answer for walking off the club. I shot back, "You sold Bernie, the guy who got us there in '75. The best tenth man in baseball and one of the best individuals on the team. You sold him to Cleveland for fifteen thousand pieces of silver, all because you didn't want to pay him what he was worth."

Sullivan said that was history and then wanted to know if I was ready to come back to the club. I had already decided I would. Bernie had talked me into it, saying, "Bill, I love what you did, but you have to go back. You can't jeopardize your career over me, and you have to think of the kids coming up in the organization. You have to be around to protect them from all this bullshit." When I told Haywood I would return, he said fine, but added, "You have to face the music some time, you might as well face it now. We're docking you a day's pay." I asked how much that would come to, and he said it would be about five hundred dollars. I told him to make it fifteen hundred, and to let me take the weekend off. He didn't appreciate that idea.

During this battle of wits, Sullivan had left the door to the office adjoining his slightly ajar. It was opened just enough to afford me a view of Mrs. Yawkey sitting in her rocker, rocking back and forth. It was as though her rocking gave Haywood strength. As long as she rocked, he yelled at me. As soon as she stopped, he calmed down. It was like a scene with Tony Perkins in *Psycho*. She emitted no sound; the chair did all her talking for her. It said, "All right, Norman. You can slip him into the shower now." Buddy Leroux was standing beside her. I could tell by the look in his eyes that he was on my side, but he couldn't say anything. He was the silent partner.

When he finished with me, Haywood went inside to confer with Mrs. Yawkey. Then he came back and sent me down to the clubhouse to see Zimmer. Zimmer was angry. The moment he saw me, he lit into me, calling me a quitter. I didn't back up a step. I asked, "How could you do that to Bernie?" Zimmer answered by claiming that we no longer needed him on the team. That made me mad. I shouted, "But you said we were a family here, and you also said that Bernie was as close to you as your son. Well, I have news for you, pal. You don't sell your son to Cleveland!" I finished up with a prediction, telling Zimmer, "You are going to rue the day you got rid of Carbo. The day will come when you are going to need him. There will be a crucial spot in a crucial game when only his bat can save us. Only he won't be here."

Zimmer waved me off and went back into his office, seething. By then, the media had started coming in, gathering around me to find out why I had returned. It was a circus. Bob Bailey watched and shook his head in disbelief, saying, "Do you realize that this country gave away the fucking Panama Canal yesterday, but Bill Lee is on the front pages!" Bob had a way of putting events into perspective.

I didn't receive any flack from my teammates over my one-day strike. Fisk stood by me, taking the Voltaire stand. He didn't necessarily agree with my action, but he would defend my right to take it. He said he thought it was a bit selfish on my part to walk out the way I did, but he respected me for standing up for my convictions. I'll never forget him for that.

Getting rid of Carbo killed us. The Lord of Baseball turned his back to us, saying, "That's it. You have spent your karma. Abner Doubleday will no longer look after you. You are disregarding the family unit and have treated your veterans unfairly. Therefore, you are going to get negative results for the rest of the season, tigers."

It didn't hit us immediately, but little things started happening to our club, little things that would gnaw away at our lead. Burleson got hurt and his replacement Frank Duffy was unable to do the job at shortstop. Hobson racked up his elbow so badly, he had to run halfway across the field to get off a throw from third. Zimmer tried replacing him with Jack Brohamer. Jack was good with the glove, but, when he played in place of Butch, we were giving up a lot of hitting power. That injury tore Hobson up. He would come into the clubhouse after a costly misplay with his head hanging down. Butch had a rigid code of personal honor and he felt like he was letting the team down. Dwight Evans, having a great year, got beaned and started suffering dizzy spells in the outfield. We could have used Bernie as his replacement. Instead, we were forced to go with Gary Hancock, a rookie who wasn't ready. The team's casualty list eventually got so lengthy that Zimmer felt forced to use Fisk in leftfield. I'll never forget that game. Fisk was in left, and Rice was in center. I sat on the bench that afternoon, wearing a cap six sizes too big for my head; the extra inches made it easier to pull the cap down over my eyes every time a ball was hit into the air. When asked why I obviously didn't want to watch my battery mate set up under a fly ball, I replied, "For the same reason I don't stand around to watch people jump off bridges."

George Scott went into a terrible slump at the plate and in the field. He had lost his mobility, leaving it in a rib franchise. George had always had a problem with his weight, but never like this. He'd sit at his locker, stare at his stomach and say, "I got Dunlop Disease. My belly done lopped over my belt."

When Harvey Haddix had been a coach with the club, he had always been after Scott to trim down, telling him that, if he didn't, pitchers would be able to throw fastballs by him on the inside part of the plate. Scott didn't believe him, so Harvey challenged him to a test. He told George, "I'm going to throw you ten fastballs up and in, and you aren't going to touch one of them." Harvey was about forty-six years old at the time, and hadn't pitched professional ball in almost ten years, but when he put George to the test, Scott couldn't touch him. He threw the ball by George nine consecutive times. George fouled off the tenth pitch and considered that a victory. By the middle of 1978, even George had to admit he was too heavy, so he decided to lose weight. It was a big mistake. As his belly shrank, so did his batting average and power totals. He had created the George Scott Diet. After one month, you were guaranteed to lose numbers everywhere.

I couldn't worry about the size of George's stomach; I had my own physical woes to think about. By late August, my shoulder had gotten so unraveled that Zimmer took me out of the starting rotation, claiming he was giving me a short rest. It lasted about twelve years. Once again, Don buried me in the bullpen.

During the enforced vacation, my shoulder received some help from an unexpected source. I had belonged to a booking agency that occasionally sent me out on speaking engagements to various college campuses. The same people who handled me also handled Dick Gregory. Dick had lost over one hundred pounds after giving up all junk foods and adhering to a strict regimen built around macrobiotics, fasting, and physical exercise. He had been traveling across the country, lecturing on nutrition and had developed power-packed food pills. These pills enabled him to run fifty miles at a clip, while subsisting only on the pills, vitamins, and water. I had never met him, but someone at the agency had told me that he was trying to get in touch with me and had asked that I be given his number. When I got him on the phone, I introduced myself, and he didn't even say hello. All he said was, "Where are you?" I told him I was at home and gave him my address.

Fifteen minutes later, a brown Rolls-Royce pulled into my driveway. He popped out of it, walked up to me and said, "Hi, I'm Dick Gregory. You may not know this, but these pills are going to bring your arm back. From what I've read about your injury, I know that your problem is lactic acid. Too much of it has been stored in your system, and it's centering around the injured area. It's as though you had washed your clothes with too much detergent. You've got all this excess soap in you, and your system can't get clean due to the build-up. He took some comfrey root out of a bag and explained, "This is what you need. Take two hambones, put them in a pot of boiling water, and then throw in some comfrey root. Those two hambones will join together. Comfrey root is your key; it makes thing whole." Then, he laid everything on me, a variety of herbs in capsule form: ginseng, sarsaparilla root, goldenseal, ginger root, and others. He also gave me plastic packets filled with his food tablets. It would take me two handfuls to get it all down; I'd do thirty capsules and pills in one shot. Dick claimed they would neutralize the acid in my body. I took them first thing in the morning and, boy, did I get a buzz on. They gave me a tremendous power surge. I realize now that it was a form of megavitamin therapy, and that Dick was way ahead of his time. He couldn't have been with me more than ten minutes. Once he delivered his gospel, he was gone. I never saw him again, but we ve spoken over the phone. What an amazing piece of work! He cares about his fellow human beings and the planet. I like that program. And his pills really helped me. My arm came back as good as new.

I was happy that I was finally healthy enough to help the ballclub. On July 19, we had been fourteen games ahead of the Yankees and, to be honest, we had figured they were history. No longer worried about them, we were going to turn our attention to knocking off Milwaukee and Baltimore. During one series against New York, we had blasted one of their pitchers, Jim Beattie, into the minors. He was demoted immediately after we drove him out of a game. That same evening we almost ended Catfish Hunter's career. He pitched an inning in relief of Beattie and had nothing. Our club knocked him all over Fenway. It was pathetic. He was a Yankee, and we wanted to beat him. But nobody wanted to beat him that badly. Watching him get tagged was like watching a fighter get battered into pulp. You kept hoping the referee would stop the carnage. Guys on our bench were saying, "Christ, why don't they get him out of there." It was that brutal. Everytime Catfish served up a fastball, one of our batters would hit it an awfully long way.

Ron Guidry and the Yankee bench kept New York from drawing its last breath. Guidry was ridiculous; he awed me. Everything he threw was hard and down. He was very tough to evaluate, and it was hard to hit the long ball off of him. Come to think of it, it was hard to hit any kind of ball off of him. Guidry never walked anybody in crucial situations, and he struck out almost a man an inning. The most impressive thing about him, though, was the way he would sustain his velocity throughout nine innings, throwing hard from pitch one to pitch one hundred. I also couldn't get over the fact that he didn't hit a slump. A lot of pitchers have tremendous two-thirds or three-fourths of a season.

But they always have those two or three week stretches when they can't buy a win. Even the twenty-game winners go through these periods. It's one of the mysteries of pitching. You throw the ball to the same spot, with the same velocity, and, for months, the hitters can't smell you. Then you have a stretch when you're throwing the same pitches to the same batters, but now they're kicking the crap out of you. If we could figure out the reason for that, there would be no baseball. Pitchers would throw nothing but shutouts, and attendance would fall to zero. For one summer Guidry must have found the secret. He didn't have anything but great stretches. He lost only three games that year, and it seemed as if the teams that beat him should have apologized for it.

When the Yankees got hit by injuries, they had the bench strength to keep them above .500. We didn't have their depth. As soon as our regulars got hurt, we were in big trouble. We started to lose game after game. Meanwhile, New York got healthy, and Hunter's arm came back from nowhere. Suddenly our lead over them was down to four games, and it was time to sing "Dum-dum-dum-dum, here come the Yankees!"

They roared into Fenway on September 7 for the start of a four-game series. No team ever looked more intense than they did. Getting on the field with them was akin to stepping into a wading pool with Jaws. Every time we made a move, they would bite off another limb. It was terrifying to watch. We had expected at least to split with them in our own ballpark. That's what everyone said and wrote, "All we need is a split and we're in good shape." That was the wrong attitude to have. The Yankees weren't thinking split. You could see that in their eyes. They came in thinking sweep.

By the fourth inning of the first game, we had to regroup but couldn't. We were playing scared. Guys on our club kept looking into their dugout and shaking their head in disbelief, as if to ask, "Who are those guys? That's not the same team that played us in June." That was an understandable reaction. I mean, Jesus, we had beaten Beattie into shellshock the last time we had seen him. In that game, he looked as if he didn't belong in the majors. He kept looking around at the stands, obviously thinking, "Where did all these people come from?" But when he came back against us in September, he had undergone a complete personality change, transforming himself from Major Catastrophe to Sergeant Rock. Everything he threw was a hand grenade, and the expression on his face said, "Hit that, asshole!" We didn't score off him until the ninth, and by then, we were behind by a couple of touchdowns and a field goal.

After they beat us the first two games, we were finished. We spent the final two games waiting for something to go wrong, and it invariably did. By the time the Yankees left Fenway, we were walking around in a daze. It was as if the entire team had just returned from Cambodia.

I was fit to be tied. I was ready to pitch in that series, but Zimmer wouldn't give me a start. Despite the great record I had against New York, Don wouldn't start me because he hated my guts. I understand he told someone, "There's no way that California fag is ever going to pitch for me." He did end up using me in relief against them, in the second game, when things were hopelessly out of hand. I pitched seven innings against them and gave up one earned run. Everytime I got up in the bullpen, I received a standing ovation from the Fenway faithful. They stood whenever I warmed up, came into the game, or got a man out. I even got an ovation when I went into the dugout to take a piss. The fans knew. There was no way I shouldn't have started one of those games. Maybe I would have gotten jocked, but my record against New York was worth taking a gamble on. But Zimmer couldn't be persuaded. Despite my pitching well in relief, he still refused to use me the following weekend in New York, when we lost two out of three.

There were two great comebacks that year. The Yankees came back from a fourteen-game deficit to catch us, and then we came back to tie them for first on the final day of the season. Give Zimmer some credit for that. He didn't panic and neither did the club.

Zimmer still managed to screw up our playoff game against the Yankees, though. He named Torrez to start. Nothing against Mike. He was a good pitcher and had given us a good year. But he had pitched badly in the second half of the season, and the Yankees always had eaten his lunch. That was my game to win. I had the Yankees' number, and my arm was sound. On the morning of October 2, hours before the game, I grabbed our pitching coach Al Jackson and said, "Al, I can go today. I can give you at least five good innings." Realizing that he wasn't convinced, I picked up a ball and offered to throw a line drive, from the mound, over the centerfield wall. Al laughed and told me not to bother. He liked me and he had said he wanted to get me into the game. But he knew there was no chance. Zimmer's dislike of me was so large, he would rather lose the pennant than let me pitch.

That playoff game flashed before my eyes. Yaz hit the home run to give us a lead against Guidry, and the fans shook Fenway with their celebration. But I knew we needed more than just that one run. I didn't change that assessment when we scored another run in the sixth. I knew Mike wouldn't pitch a shutout, and I knew he couldn't go nine. He had pitched so many innings in the final weeks of the season that it was bound to take its toll. I could see he was tiring in the fifth. I wanted to run in and give him a rest. When Bucky Dent hit the three-run homer in the seventh, I flew into a rage. Not at Mike, who had pitched a gutsy game. My anger was directed at my favorite manager for not getting Torrez out of there when he was obviously spent.

With one out in the bottom of the eighth, New York led, 5–4, but we had men on first and third. Gossage was pitching, and all I could think was, "Jesus, there's a Carbo wind blowing out of here. Bernie could wrap this game up for us right now." But Bernie was in Cleveland, watching the game on television. That crucial situation when he could win the pennant for us had made its appearance, just as I had predicted it would. The curse of Carbo was upon us. Gossage struck out Hobson and Scott; they never had a chance. Bob Bailey had pinch-hit against the Goose earlier and had taken three strikes. He claimed at least one of them sounded low. Bernie was having the last laugh. Gossage was a righthanded fastball pitcher, and Bernie was a lefthanded fastball hitter. All three of those at-bats were tailor-made for him. Hobson, Scott, and Bailey were right-handed hitters, overmatched by the Goose. As the three of them struck out, I sat in the bullpen wondering if Zimmer and the front office finally realized what Carbo had meant to this team.

We came close to tying it in the ninth, but in the end, Gossage got Yaz to pop up to Nettles with the tying run ninety feet from home plate. I sat in the bullpen in a state of shock. I wanted to run over to the Yankees and say, "Come on, let's play another game. You guys won the division, that's all taken care of. Let's just play one more for fun." I didn't want the season to be over. I wanted more baseball. More Fenway.

I knew there was no way I would be back there next year. I walked out onto the field after everybody had left, and I said good-bye to the foul poles and the bleachers. And I thought about the good times.

I didn't think about the games I had won there. I thought about the friends I had made. Most of them were team-mates. How could I say good-bye to Yaz, or Fisk, or Luis? They had become a part of me. I thought of some of the writers—George Kimball and Leigh Montville, to name two—who had written nice things about me over the years. And I stopped to remember other friends, some of whom I hadn't thought of in years.

Bob Veale. I could never get over how much he looked like Willie Stargell. He and I would go bass fishing in Winter Haven. All those Southern good old boys would be out on the lake, whistling "Dixie" and wearing Confederate Army caps, when I would come rounding a corner, rowing this six-foot-four, 260-pound black gentleman. Bob would smile at them and say, "Good morning, how are you doing on this fine day?" Suddenly, there would be a wide circle between our boat and theirs. Didn't bother us. We always caught a lot of bass. When Bob joined the Red Sox, he didn't have control of his breaking ball, but he could throw just as hard as he ever did with the Pirates in his heyday. Oh, was he strong! He used to build up his arm by throwing an eight-pound shot from left field to right field. He threw it like a baseball. I tried to catch it once. That should prove how dumb I am. That sucker pulled me down to the ground, and buried my glove hand two feet under Fenway sod. Thank God, I caught it in the webbing or it would have taken off my right arm.

Mike Garman had been a relief pitcher with us. I loved to be around him; he was so unpredictable. Once, after he got beat in a ball game, he decided it would lift his spirits if we stopped into a local tavern. On arriving, he announced that he wanted a shot from every bottle of liquor on the bar shelves. And he wanted the shots to be doubles. After about eight drinks, he became Hopalong Cassidy, yelling, "Yee-hah! Let's go and party." We went out and got into his car. Since there was no way I was going to let him drive, he insisted that he at least be allowed to give directions. He barked, "Turn left. Now, turn right. Make another left, and then turn right again." After half an hour of this we were still in the bar's parking lot. Mike, having tired of playing navigator, rolled down his window, hung his body outside the car, and threw up for forty-five minutes. Then he passed out.

Randy Miller never got an opportunity to pass out in the major leagues, and that was too bad. He was a pitcher who bounced around the Boston farm system for a couple of years. He once told me that curveballs did not curve. It was space that was curving. The ball was going straight, but if you threw it slower than the speed of the earth's rotation, the earth would curve up into it. I wasn't quite sure what to make of that, but I sure kept hoping Randy would make the team. It would have given me someone to talk to.

How could I ever forget Dick Pole? He had gone through a bad stretch in 1976, pitching worse with each successive game. The word was he was going to be traded, released, or sent back to the minors. After a bad outing in Chicago, he sat in the back of the bus, drinking out of a flask and singing, "I'm gone, yes I'm gone."

Ballplayers do drink on the team bus. Why do you think so many of them carry attaché cases? It's to store their stash. Dick had consumed five or six beers immediately after the ballgame, and had a few more drinks on the bus, so he was fried, but remorseful. Carlton and I decided to cheer him up by taking him out for a night on the town. After having dinner at the Four Torches, we decided to have a drink in every bar we passed on the way back to our hotel. I discovered an amazing thing that evening: there sure are a lot of bars in the Windy City. By the time we got to a place called Faces, we were hammered. While we were there, someone grabbed a microphone, and revealed that there was a celebrity from the baseball world in the audience. Fisk thought this was a reference to him. He stood up just as the announcer concluded his introduction by saying, "...so let's hear a warm welcome for the Voice of the Chicago White Sox, Mr. Harry Carey." Carlton responded by yelling, "Big fucking deal!" Not a good thing to say in a room filled with Chicagoans. They love Carey more than life. They almost had to call the National Guard to get us out of there in one piece.

I thought about the Yankees. I hated what they stood for, but I enjoyed playing against them, especially when I beat them. Everytime we played them it was always a great ballgame. Except once.

Thinking about them brought to mind Lou Piniella. He was my favorite Yankee. It amazed me how he could take all of Steinbrenner's bullshit and still go out and do the job at the plate. It was as though he fed off all the crap. I loved his insights. He would say you can be hitting .300 at the end of June, and you can be hitting .300 at the end of August, but, if you're a .250 hitter, you'll be hitting .250 when the season ends. He once hit a home run off me after I had thrown him one too many fastballs inside. After the game, he saw me and said, "Bill, you can come into my kitchen, but don't you dare sit down to eat."

I also liked Mickey Rivers, even if he did punch me in the back of the head. I enjoyed watching him walk; his heels never touched the ground. And he always had an expression on his face that made it appear as if he had spent a lifetime staring into the Great Gorge. Listening to him talk was a wonder; it was as though he wasn't on speaking terms with the English language. He was once quoted as saying, "I don't get upset over things I can control, because if I can control them there's no sense in getting upset. And I don't get upset over things I can't control, because if I can't control them there's no sense in getting upset." Out of the mouths of babes....After hearing that, I could never again think of him as Mick the Quick. I thought it would be far more apropos to call him Altered States.

I fixed on a mental image of Zimmer. A reporter had once asked me, "If Billy Martin is a rat, what is Don Zimmer?" I answered, "Don is a gerbil. A cute, puffy-cheeked creature."

Zimmer didn't appreciate that, and I guess I should have apologized. To the gerbils. No sense insulting defenseless animals. I think my problems with Don stemmed from the fact that I always had an answer for him. For example, when the Red Sox had visited Puerto Rico for some exhibition games, he had told us that sports jackets were required apparel for the trip. I wore my jogging top. When he tried to reprimand me for it, I said, "You said we were to wear sports jackets, right? Well, this is a jacket, and jogging's a sport." Zimmer didn't like that; he thought ballplayers should be seen and not heard, so we never got along. That was still no reason for him to put personal feelings ahead of what was best for the team. When we were taking our swan dive, he turned me into the Boston version of the Maytag repairman, making it impossible for me to help the club.

I put him out of my mind. I wanted to concentrate on only the best things. Over the last few years, as baseball in America had escaped the clutches of the Industrial Revolution, the game had enjoyed a rebirth. Stadiums encouraged a laid-back form of active participation. Fans could come in, watch the game, drink a beer, and talk about current events. They could do all this without missing the beat of what was happening on the field. The ballparks had become like those coffeehouses in Austria, where Freud and Jung used to drink coffee and bullshit with each other. My thoughts turned to the fans. I loved Boston's fans. They were baseball purists who lived for the game. They had supported us through the best and worst of times, demanding only that we give our best and that everyone have a good time.

Reverend Smith and his wife were two of those fans. They used to sit out in the bleachers and root for us. I enjoyed entertaining them and the rest of the people out there. During batting practice, I would go out to the outfield and put on a show, hitting fungoes straight up into the air and catching them as they came back down. Once, while doing this, I slipped and fell. The ball smoked me in the chest, but I still caught it, lying prone. I got a standing ovation for that maneuver. Everybody thought it was part of my act. I was hurting. I ran off the field hyperventilating, and had to crawl around the clubhouse for an hour, trying to catch my breath.

Mike Mulkern was a bleacher bum. I would kick bubble gum into the bleachers, and he would stand up and act as a goal post. My first couple of kicks were wide, but I soon found the range and would put the gum through his outstretched arms regularly. After a couple of weeks of that, he came down near the field and invited me to play football with him and his friends at Harvard Stadium. I became a regular member of their crew, and he became my best friend. With the help of him and our little group, I once played three games in one day. I pitched a shutout for the Boston *Phoenix* in an early morning softball game, beat the Orioles at Fenway that afternoon, and played on the winning side in a touch football game with Mulkern that night. It was one of the great days in sports history.

I knew I was going to miss all my friends at the Eliot Lounge. I want Sparky Anderson to know that being able to go there is better than going to the Hall of Fame.

I knew in my heart that I did not want to leave Boston, but I also knew that what I wanted no longer mattered. I had always said that, due to my outspoken manner, the Red Sox front office would get rid of me the moment I became a mediocre pitcher. I had gone 10–10 in 1978, and that was as mediocre as a record could get. Any day now, my body would be floating through Boston Harbor, drifting out toward the far reaches of the Atlantic.

On December 7, 1978, Zimmer called me with the word. I had been traded to the Montreal Expos for infielder Stan Papi. It was the thirty-seventh anniversary of Pearl Harbor. The battleships and I had been kamikazed on the same date. My first reaction was to wait to hear who else the Red Sox got. But Stan was all that Montreal gave up. I couldn't believe it. He was a lifetime .230 hitter. I thanked Zimmer for calling and hung up. A few days later, an official notice came from the Red Sox. It said, "Dear Bill, you have been (check one):——Sold——Traded—— Released." I liked that. The personal touch.

The initial shock of the news wore off quickly. I had been prepared for it. I comforted myself with the thought that I wasn't leaving the Red Sox; the Red Sox were Mr. Yawkey and Dick O'Connell. This team was just a front for a finance company in Cincinnati. They were so anxious to get rid of me, they had practically given me away. Zimmer and Sullivan didn't like my mouth and had convinced themselves that I was washed up. Well, no matter what they thought, I had a little surprise for them. I knew my arm had completely healed, and I was determined to win so many games with the Expos that everytime Zimmer or Sullivan looked at my stats, they would kick themselves. Right in the balls.

9

Being traded to Montreal and the National League gave me a chance to be a complete player again. I would be allowed to go up to the plate with a bat in my hands. For that reason alone, the move saved me from the onset of terminal brain damage.

I was excited about playing in a new league and being reunited with Expo manager Dick Williams. I was a pioneer, ready to explore a vast, uncharted area of the baseball universe. Shortly after the transaction was announced, Mary Lou and I were flown up to Montreal for a press conference. We were met at the airport by Sidney Maislin, a part-owner of the club, and his limo. He drove us to the Queen Elizabeth Hotel, telling us along the way how happy he was to have me with the Expos. The day was surrealistic. There was a lightly falling snow, but the climate was warm and sunny. Later that evening, the team held a dinner reception in my honor. I was getting turned on by the way the press and the city were reacting to me. The energy generated by an organization can make or break a player. This exhibition was a revelation, causing me to think, God, the people who run this game really know how to drag you down, but they also know how to throw a party. I had forgotten that.

The Expos obviously wanted to make it clear that they

didn't care about what had gone on between me and management in the past. It was as if they were saying, "Okay, Lee. We're going to treat you right and see what happens." During the dinner I was presented with a bat. Attached to it was a note which read, "Hope you still remember how to use this." One of the executives apologized for not having time to get my name inscribed on it. Examining the bat barrel, I discovered that they had given me a Bob Bailey model. I told them, "Oh, don't worry. This will be fine. This sucker ought to have a lot of wood left in it. Bob never got it off his shoulder last October in Fenway."

In spring training, I found that Dick hadn't changed. He was still the same man and manager. Williams runs a very professional camp. Coaches and players know exactly what is expected of them, and there's never any time wasted. Dick told me he was glad to see me and that he had been trying to get me for the last year and a half. The first Expo player to greet me was Warren Cromartie. I had come tipping into the Montreal clubhouse in Daytona Beach carrying my knapsack and wearing my beard and my Bermuda shorts. The clubhouse guards tried to run me out of there, yelling, "No, no. The mission is on the other side of the canal." Cromartie called them off me, informing them that I was the Expos' new ace lefthander. Then he turned to me and said, "Well, Willie Lee, my man! How are you doing, Space?" I asked him who he was, and he said, "I'm Cro. Warren Cromartie. And I know all about you. I could not wait for you to get here." I said, "Warren who?" I wasn't being unfriendly; I just didn't know anybody in the National League. I did see a familiar face in the clubhouse, though. Tony Perez came over to my locker, stuck out his hand, and said, "By the way, thank you very much." God damned power hitters. They never forget a friendly arm.

The Red Sox came in to play us an exhibition game, and when I showed up, the Boston writers were standing three deep around my locker, waiting to ask me whether or not there was life after the American League. After fifteen minutes of questioning, one of the writers said, "Bill, there's one question we have been dying to ask you for a long time. Was there any sort of drug problem on the Red Sox?"

I answered, "There sure was. I think the entire team abused nicotine, caffeine, and alcohol far too much."

I explained that coffee and amphetamines weren't being used for kicks, they were being used to sober up. A player did not gulp down greenies with the expectation that it would enhance his performance. He did it to get his pulse going on the morning after the night before. The reporter wasn't satisfied that his question had been answered, so he said, "No, I don't mean coffee or greenies. I was wondering if the club had a problem with marijuana?"

I said, "Hell, no. How could they. I've been using that stuff since 1968, and I've never had a problem with it." Twenty pencils hit the floor simultaneously.

You could see the news flashes shooting through the writers' heads: DATELINE, DAYTONA BEACH—SPACEMAN IS GONE. HAS BEEN GONE SINCE '68. They got very excited. One of them asked if I had used it lately, and I replied that I had, explaining that all pot did was make you more aware of the environment and allowed your life to revolve around a peaceful lunar cycle, something that was preferable to living within the confines of the more aggressive sun cycle. Noticing that they were feverishly writing my words down, I launched into a soliloquy on marijuana, pointing out its use in alleviating the nausea experienced by cancer patients after chemotherapy and how it enabled a smoker to reach a sublime state of meditation. My purpose was to prove to them that marijuana could blend in with our culture and be a productive force. I also figured that this would take their minds off any other questions they had about drug-taking on the Red Sox.

The next day, the headlines across North America read LEE ADMITS SMOKING MARIJUANA.

Commissioner Kuhn did not like that. Bowie sent three guys in a late-model Ford to see me. When they arrived at our camp, our general manager, John McHale, came into the clubhouse, pale as death, and said, "God, Bill. There are some people here from the commissioner's office, and they want to talk to you. Use this back room. When they get here, just keep your head. Relax and cooperate with them, and everything will be fine."

I could see McHale was upset. He must have thought, Jesus, we got this guy, and he looks as if he might be able to win for us, and now this. I knew we shouldn't have taken Lee. God damn Dick Williams. How could I let him talk me into getting this guy? Despite what had to be going through his mind, John didn't come down on me, which was more than decent of him.

I went into the back room, and one of the three agents introduced himself, saying, "Hello, I'm Art Fuss. We are with the Commissioner's office, and we'd like to hear more about your smoking marijuana."

I told him, "Look, if you check that story with the writers who were present, I believe you'll find that I never claimed to have smoked anything. I only said I had used it."

Art wanted me to clarify that statement, wondering, "How do you actually use it, if you don't smoke it? We know there are various other ways it can get into the body."

I answered, "Well, Art, every morning I run five miles to the ballpark. After first waking up, I prepare myself for this arduous task by eating a big plate of organic buckwheat pancakes for breakfast. I sprinkle the marijuana on the pancakes while they are cooking. The moisture of the batter soaks down the pot, enabling the THC to be absorbed by the pancakes during the frying process. That THC makes me impervious to all the toxic bus fumes and other forms of air pollution I may encounter while running."

Fuss's assistant was writing all this down, and Art was nodding his head yes, saying, "Sure. I can see that. I think Bowie will buy this."

I thought, "God, ask him if he wants to buy a bridge, too."

That was the last I saw of Mr. Fuss. I later learned that he had been an FBI drug enforcement officer and had worked closely with the Nixon administration. Good thing I wasn't wearing my "Lick Dick" T-shirt during the interrogation. Art would have left the clubhouse with my ass in his briefcase.

A couple of weeks after his visit I got a letter from Bowie. It read, "We have seen your statements and consider them to be contrary to the best interests of baseball. This is to inform you that you are never to make statements like that again. It is also to inform you that you are being fined two hundred fifty dollars. Make the check payable to my office, and we will donate it to charity."

I knew if I sent it to his office it would probably end up in a "Let's bring back Richard Nixon" fund. So I sent him a check made out to St. Mary's Mission in Alaska, knowing that two-fifty would keep the missionaries in moose meat all winter. When news of the fine was made public, members of the ACLU called me, informing me that my first amendment rights of free speech had been violated. They threatened Kuhn with a grievance hearing on my behalf. A few weeks later I received another notice from his office, telling me that the fine had been rescinded, and that they were letting me off with a reprimand.

If asked today, I would honestly have to answer that there is a drug problem in baseball. For people who allow it to get in the way of their work. I believe fifteen percent of major league ballplayers have a serious drug addiction, forty-five percent are occasional heavy partyers, and the remaining forty percent play golf. The addicts are into some deep shit, but the occasional user is in such good shape, he just burns the chemicals up and they have no lasting effect. A guy who guzzles a bottle of VO in an evening is much worse off than a guy who does a few joints. Drugs are less of a problem in baseball than alcohol. THC never did anything but good things for me. It gave my body another voice, one that would remind me, "Bill, you're hungry. Let's eat," or "Bill, it's time to take a shit." The first few times I smoked reefer in college, I would be carrying on a conversation with a beer in my hand, and the brew would actually get warm before I had a chance to consume a drop. My thoughts would be racing at me so quickly, that I couldn't take time for a sip. The drug had postponed my ingestion of alochol.

The difference between alcohol and marijuana is that alcohol is an aggressive drug that hampers the raising of consciousness. Initially alcohol stimulates you, but then it becomes a depressant. Drink becomes dangerous when used in conjunction with amphetamines or coke. Often an athlete will get hammered at night, filling his body with poisonous spirits. He wakes up a near corpse the next day. Nothing on him works; he is unofficially brain-dead. But he has a game that afternoon and has to get out of bed. So, he hits a little speed or a little coke to get his pump going. Coke sprinkled over hot cereal in the morning is rapidly becoming the breakfast of champions. This leads to a dangerous cycle. Later on in the evening, after speeding the day away, your brain is buzzing. You want to put it to sleep. Enter Jack Daniel's, ready to play the part of the Sandman. When you wake up in the morning you're hung over again, and the cycle starts once more.

There are no specific pushers dealing to ballplayers. When you're a famous athlete, everybody is a pusher: doctors, lawyers, accountants, stockbrokers, agents, and ex-jocks. People who get their thrills being with ballplayers will come up to them and say, "That was a great play you made today. I've got some good shit here. Let me lay some on you." They don't charge the player a nickel. They do it only to be part of what they perceive to be the athlete's special world.

Drugs also serve as tokens of appreciation. While coming off the field in Montreal after throwing a good game, I would often find my path littered with small packets of hash. The stuff would come flying out of the stands as if they were the ears and tail of a just-killed bull. People would approach me as I left the ballpark, saying, "Great game," while slipping something into my hand. It was widely believed that whenever I tipped my hat to the crowd as I came walking in off the mound I was acknowledging their applause. Hell, no. I was using my cap to catch their gifts. You do have to be careful when you accept something, though; you can't always be sure what someone might be giving you. You may think you're laying down lines of coke, but it might be Drano. If it is, *hasta la vista*.

I didn't care much for coke. Pepsi was as far as I wanted to go. I've tried it, though. I'll try almost anything. The problem with coke is that it gets out of hand economically. Also, it's not much of a high. All it does it keep you awake and chattering. I'm already like that naturally. It does have a way of energizing you, and that's its main attraction. Baseball is trying to solve its drug problems, but it's going about it the wrong way. As long as there is night baseball, 162-game schedules, and long, boring road trips, there are going to be drugs in the game. Players need something to keep them going. If we all go to Chicago and play the ultimate baseball game in the sunshine of Wrigley Field, we will be able to be home by five, have a small barbecue, eat tofuburgers, and live in a perpetual state of grace. But, until that time, there will always be that girl at the bar who will entice you with the pipe she has in her bag, and the lungs she's carrying on her chest. And, after six VOs, you will not want to go home. If it's not an exotic creature murmuring in your ear, then it's the song of Mescalito that will lead you astray.

Mescaline was the cause of my first truly psychedelic experience. I did some in Minnesota and spent the rest of the afternoon running around the drops of a raging rainstorm. When I reached my destination I was bone dry. Not a drop had touched my body. My mind was brought to its most finite level of understanding. I thought, We should tie Zimmer to a chair and drop about four tabs of this stuff down his gullet. Then we'll talk to him for sixteen hours. That will straighten him out. But then I decided, No, why share it with him. He'll only want to talk about baseball or horse racing. He'll drive us nuts.

Many people have made a fortune selling drugs. Ewing Kauffman was able to buy the Kansas City Royals with part of the profits earned by his pharmaceutical company. I can think of a lot worse things in baseball than marijuana or peyote, if used in moderation. Things such as walks, designated hitters, and astro-turf.

I tried to balance out any drugs I put into my system with a rigorous training program. I started running in 1973, shortly after I had my tonsils out. It induced me to quit smoking cigarettes and to radically change my eating habits. I became very scrupulous when it came to food, reading books like *Diet for a Small Planet*. I cut down my intake of animal protein. When I did eat meat, I wanted to know as much about it as I could. For instance, if I was planning to have duck, I wanted to meet the bird several weeks before it was served to me. I wanted an opportunity to take it out to dinner, and to find out what *it* ate. I needed to know if he smoked or if he drank. If he did, did he do it in moderation? I felt it was important that we get to know our meal.

I also learned the value of not wasting any potential foodstuffs. That's a lesson I carry with me to this day. While driving the back roads outside of Montreal, I have, on occasion, had the misfortune of hitting a flying grouse with my van. He would die instantly. Rather than leave him for the worms, I would take him home, pluck him, and cook him up for dinner. Some may be grossed out by that, but I would ask them to remember that one man's accident is often another man's meal.

In perfecting my own training program, I came to realize that there are a lot of questions about conditioning in baseball that must be answered. Maybe a few priorities have to be more closely examined, also. Ballplayers, especially pitchers, are constantly playing in pain, and most drugs do little to repair the cause of it. They only deaden the hurt. The season is much too long. There should be fewer games spread out over a longer period of time. The brand of baseball played would improve, and careers would last longer. But the owners won't touch that proposition, fearing the loss of gate receipts. That is short-term thinking on their part.

Attitudes toward sports medicine, however, are changing for the better. Denny McLain tore up his arm pitching for the Tigers in 1969. The doctors kept pumping him up with cortisone. After a while the arm didn't hurt any more, but it hadn't been helped, either. The day came when Denny tried to throw a slider, but his shoulder arrived at home plate before the ball did. He was out of baseball within three years, and now I understand he weighs over three hundred pounds. That's another problem with cortisone. Like pot, it can give you a severe case of the munchies.

Baseball has cut back on the use of this type of drug, but it must still develop more of a Chinese mentality in dealing with the body. It must examine the issue of preventive medicine. Montreal has concentrated on flexibility exercises as a safety measure against the occurrence of muscle pulls. They've done this with much success, and the rest of baseball should follow their lead. I think the next steps taken should involve diet (there's still too much junk food in the clubhouse), mental approach, and the use of yoga as a relaxant. The game will get there. Baseball has made quantum leaps in the area of conditioning since 1969. The collective consciousness has been raised.

Playing in Montreal was a trip. The National League seems to favor a more dangerous brand of ball than I was used to seeing. Everybody in the league runs, and the NL team rosters are made up of a greater number of carnivores than the rosters in the AL. It is a very aggressive brand of ball; second basemen have a hard time buying life insurance because all their opponents know how to break up the double play, and they do so with a vengeance.

Gary Carter is a typical National Leaguer. The first time I saw him was in an exhibition game against the Red Sox in 1976. He wasn't catching that day; he was playing left field. Watching him, I was reminded of a giant Pete Rose. Carter was like a Greenie Master, naturally wired without the use of amphetamines. It was as though he drank three cups of coffee before each pitch. He kept running into things that day, and finally got knocked unconscious trying to break through a stone wall while chasing a fly ball. Holding the gate open as they carried him off the field, I thought, "Gee, those walls sure can slow a guy up."

I'm positive that Gary's the only man in baseball history who was put behind the plate so he wouldn't get hurt. He was amazing to pitch to. Carter is always in the game and never gives less than one hundred percent of his concentration whenever he's behind the plate. He was a good hitter when I joined the club, but he wasn't much in the clutch. His intensity kicked back on him, and he tried too hard. Gary became a much better hitter with men on base as he matured. Tony Perez was the clutch hitter on that '79 team. I hated his hitting that home run off me in the Series, but I loved having him on my side. He was a super guy in the clubhouse. Always even-tempered, he never got too high or too low. Tony was always ready to give advice when asked, and he was the best hitter with men on base that I had ever seen.

I won sixteen games my first year with the Expos, and I thought I had never pitched better. My best game of the season was a 3–0 shutout of the Dodgers. Since I was no longer in the American League, I had decided that the Dodgers would become my NL version of the Yankees. There were a lot of similarities. Like New York, they were an elitist organization that assumed the baseball sun rose and set solely on them. As an added incentive, one of their big honchos was Al Campanis, the scout who told me I would never make it in the big leagues. Somebody should have told him that no matter how many brain cells an Irishman burns out with his drinking, he never forgets. I had a fire in my belly when I first faced them, a sure sign that I was going to pitch well.

But I surprised even myself with the shutout. Normally, everything I throw—when I'm going good—is down, and I get a lot of groundballs. That day everything was up, but the Dodgers could hit only harmless fly balls and pop-ups. I discovered the reason for this unusual occurrence after the game. I had jogged to the ballpark, wearing a heavy back pack that pulled down on me with each step. By the time I had reached the stadium, I was four inches shorter than usual. That's why my ball was up. I was too short to get on top of it. By the late innings, I had attained my normal height and started getting groundballs again. That shocked the Dodgers. They thought a relief pitcher had been brought in without their realizing it. After that game, they were so baffled, I owned them.

Steve Garvey epitomized the Dodgers for me. Clean-cut and laid back, he's a man with his future laid out for him. In a magazine interview, I was once quoted as saying, "Steve Garvey is called Mr. America, but he's pushing sugar down the throats of this nation's children by promoting the cause of Coca-Cola."

The first time we played the Dodgers, Steve came into our locker room and said, "Bill, I read that interview in which you said that I was promoting Coca-Cola and that it was bad for kids? Well, you have it all wrong. I don't do any advertising for Coca-Cola. I work for *Pepsi* Cola."

He was serious. He said it as if he thought Pepsi was some sort of wonderful new foodstuff that would end the problems of world malnutrition. It just blew me away. Another conversation I had with him took place during a ballgame. I had singled off Sutton and was leading off first, when I caught Garvey looking at me in the most bizarre way. I asked him if anything was wrong, and he said, "Gee, Bill. I've been thinking about this the whole game, and I still can't make up my mind. I can't decide if you look better with the beard or without the beard."

I just nodded at him and thought, "This guy is either shitting me, or he's Alex in Wonderland." Based on later discussions, I would have to say he is for real, and I respect that.

His manager, Tommy LaSorda, once made a statement to the effect that the Expos didn't belong on the same field with a club like the Dodgers. The next time we played them, I retaliated. I came out for infield practice with my zipper undone, my pants halfway down to my knees, my socks askew, and my shirt unbuttoned. I went to the shortstop's position and dived for balls for fifteen minutes, getting as filthy as I could. When I had finished, I strolled over to Tommy and asked, "Why can't we play on the same field as the Dodgers? Is it because of the way we dress?"

LaSorda stared at me as if I had just flown over the cuckoo's nest and had landed in his lap. Before I could say another word, somebody rescued him, handing him a baby from the stands. Tommy walked over to the cameramen assembled near the dugout. He wanted to make sure they got a shot of him kissing the child. I thought that was a good move on his part. It was good public relations and it got him away from me. Sometimes, the best way to deal with me is to ignore me completely.

My jogging program suffered a slight setback in the middle of the 1979 season. Nothing too serious. While running to the ballpark, I got hit by a cab. It happened on a rainy Saturday morning in Montreal. Sunday is usually a good day to run because there is very little traffic. I was moving along the highway, and the only vehicle I noticed was a florist's truck traveling in the slow lane. What I couldn't see was the taxi following behind him. It came around the truck on the inside. Hearing him make his move, I put one foot on the sidewalk curb in an attempt to get out of his way. That's as far as I got. The cab clipped me on the left leg, knocking me to the side.

When I came to, I discovered my entire left side was numb. X-rays later showed that I had almost cracked my upper leg, but that my overdeveloped leg muscles had provided my bones with protection. I only missed my next two starts, but I think that collision cost me a shot at twenty wins; it took me several starts to reestablish my pitching rhythm. I suppose the accident could have been Fate once again telling me that I was not destined to win twenty. But, I'm not so sure. That cab driver's face bore an uncanny resemblance to Zimmer.

I went through a four-year stretch of pennant races and second place finishes that was remarkable: one and a half games out of first in 1977; one game out in 1978; two games behind in 1979, and one game out in 1980. In four years, the teams I had played on had finished a total of six and a half games out of first place. It was frustrating in one sense, but rewarding in another. Coming close to the top year after year without winning is a character builder. Of course, by the third consecutive year of this nonsense, I was thinking, "Fuck character, let's get into the Series."

I have no idea why we couldn't finish first. The Expos had so much talent. Maybe our stadium was built on top of an Indian graveyard, and we were paying the price for desecrating it. If I had to put my finger on one reason for our inability to win the pennant, I couldn't. There were twenty-five reasons. They were called the Pittsburgh Pirates, and we could not beat them. Our club was in awe of the Pirates; half the team idolized Willie Stargell. Everytime we played against them, I thought they were going to run over and ask Willie for his autograph.

In Pittsburgh, late in the baseball season, the football Steelers' cheerleaders would work out in a room next to the visiting baseball team's clubhouse. One enterprising Expo found a hole in the wall, an imperceptible one that allowed us a view of their shower. Twenty-five of us would line up to check out the action. This activity was not without its risks. Occasionally someone would yell a warning that the writers were coming in, and a player would get spiked while running out to his locker with the rest of the mob. I was always certain that the peephole had been drilled by someone in the Pittsburgh organization. It was one of the major reasons why we could never beat the Pirates in their own ballpark. Every time we took the field there, we were leaving our minds back in the clubhouse.

We did have a great lineup, and the Expo outfield was phenomenal: Andre Dawson, Warren Cromartie, and Ellis Valentine. Dawson is going to win the Triple Crown some day, and Cro is an excellent line drive hitter, but Valentine was the guy I thought would end up in the Hall of Fame. He looked like the second coming of Willie Mays when I played with him. He had great speed, power, and an arm that was as strong as Reggie Smith's, only more accurate. But he seemed haunted by a fear of failure, despite projecting a loosey-goosey image that was false. Ellis was sensitive. I had the feeling he was carrying around a lot of stuff from his childhood. He spoke with his mother quite often, and I got the impression that he never felt he could please her completely.

His career fell apart after he got hit in the face with a fastball. Ellis had tried to block the pitch with his hand, but it slipped through his shield of invulnerability. That freaked Ellis out. He started questioning himself. When he came off the disabled list, he tried to come back wearing a helmet to the plate. It made him look like a helicopter pilot. Ellis hit well while wearing it, but then he slumped, took it off, and was gun-shy again. His teammates got upset with him because we felt he was becoming a malingerer. Ellis became paranoid, accusing people of talking about him behind his back. He got into many heated arguments, especially with Cromartie. Ellis and Warren had been the best of friends, but they gradually became arch-enemies.

Unlike the Red Sox, the Expos had a knack for developing impressive young pitchers. Boston wasn't good at doing that; the Monster chewed up too many psyches before they had a chance to develop. Montreal didn't have any obstacles such as that to overcome. I had never seen so many good young arms. They brought up Scott Sarderson, Bill Gullickson, David Palmer, Dan Schatzaeder, and Charlie Lea. When I got a good look at that group, I wanted to give all of them a good stiff bite on the elbow. Palmer had the best stuff of that bunch, but I thought Charlie Lea would become the best pitcher.

Charlie joined the club on the road, pitched one game in relief, and flew back with us to Montreal. During the flight Charlie, celebrating his promotion to the big time, had a couple of drinks and they went right to his head. Walking behind him as we disembarked from the plane and walked through the airport terminal, I watched as he jabbered away about how great it was to be in the majors. Charlie was so busy talking, he didn't notice an I beam that was standing in the middle of the corridor, minding its own business. Walking into it, Charlie managed to split himself wide open. I caught him before he hit the ground. I said, "Welcome to Montreal. I will take you to see the historic Queen Elizabeth Hospital." I felt that we Lees had to stick together, even if he did spell his last name the wrong way.

Ross Grimsley was supposed to be the ace of our ballclub; he had won twenty games in 1978. But he had lost his velocity. That was not good. There had previously been a line of demarcation between his fastball and his change. One was slow; the other was slower. But in '79, everything he threw came up to the plate at a steady fifty miles an hour. Those weren't baseballs; they were meatballs. He had been throwing a very moist sinker, but the opposing batters were hitting the dry side. Our ace in hiding was Steve Rogers. Steve had great stuff, but he didn't win a lot of games for us, despite having a low ERA. He didn't get much support from his teammates, at the plate or in the field. I blamed that on his nickname.

Steve answers to Cy, as in Cy Young. That was a mistake. If you go around calling yourself that, pretty soon your teammates believe you don't need any help from them. They assume that if you're Cy Young, you can win ballgames all by yourself. That was my theory. One of our relievers had another. He once said, "Steve doesn't have any balls." Despite the anatomical location, he was questioning Rogers' heart. I disagree. It wasn't that Steve didn't have any heart. It was that he was too inside himself. If he made a good pitch, one that got the job done, he would still be unsatisfied. He always felt he could have made an even better pitch. Steve was never really pleased with himself. He was also too much of a primper out on the mound, taking too much time and disturbing his fielders' ebb and flow. Some of his mannerisms on the pitching rubber are those of an asshole.

Elias Sosa was in our bullpen, and he was a totally open and honest man. He would question things like the mysteries of electricity, speculating on where it came from.

Elias was curious about the things lesser minds took for granted. He was also an easy mark. Guys would leave messages for him at our hotel, asking him to get in touch with G. Raff or Elly Fant. He would always return the call. Rogers thought he was odd, so he named him Lights as in "the lights are on but nobody's home." That was funny because if anybody was Lights it was Steve. I recall a game in which he had a 1–0 lead. Rogers was hitting with the bases loaded, nobody out, and a count of three balls and no strikes. He looked down to the third base coach for a sign, and naturally the coach signaled that he should be taking. So what does our resident genius do? He bunts the ball to the pitcher who starts a home to first double play. After the game, Steve said, "I thought the coach gave me the bunt sign."

Oh, I see, Steve. And you think Sosa's not all there? Rogers did start winning big after Williams left the club. That's not surprising. I don't think his ego was strong enough to thrive under a manager who could be as acerbic in his criticism as Dick is.

Rodney Scott was the key to our infield. He would mess up a play, and the rest of the team would start to piss and moan about how he couldn't throw. But with two men out and runners on second and third, he'd go into the hole, backhand the ball, and throw the runner out by a step and a half. A play like that would save us two runs. Rodney was the Tony Perez of fielders. Real clutch. He was a hard worker and he eventually became excellent at making the double play. At bat, he only hit .230, but he walked a lot and stole a ton of bases. He could bunt and hit the ball the other way, talents that made him the perfect man to bat behind Ron LeFlore and, later, Tim Raines. I loved the way Rodney played behind me. As a groundball pitcher, I thought he was indispensable on a club that never emphasized the importance of defense.

LeFlore hooked up with the Expos and Rodney in 1980. They batted at the top of the lineup and were awesome, stealing 160 bases between them. The three of us ran around together. I got along well with Ron. He kept coming over to talk to me when he first joined the club. I couldn't figure out why, but I think he felt an affinity between us. We both had defiant natures.

Ron had been in prison; the Detroit Tigers had discovered him playing on a penitentiary baseball team. He told me about his life, explaining that he had learned about heroin and hookers before he had even heard about reading, writing, and arithmetic. During his incarceration, nothing could break him down. He was like a Steve McQueen character, sitting in solitary, bouncing a ball off the door and doing thousands of push-ups, hoping to reach a point of exhaustion so he could fall asleep. He dealt with the prison experience on a totally physical level and came out in animal condition. Some of the players were wary of him. They assumed he might be dangerous. Ron was very sensitive, and I think he came to me because he instinctively knew that I had no prejudices. I didn't give a shit about his past, and I admired the way he dealt with it. He would kid that he had gotten his diploma from Jackson State, and that, while it was a different kind of institution, it was just as tough as USC in its own way.

Ron was one tough piece of work, but he was not the toughest person I met in baseball. The toughest person I ever met in the game wasn't even a player; it was a player's wife. She would come into whatever town we happened to be in on the road, completely without warning. Then she would wait in front of her husband's hotel room with a gun. She would just sit in the hall, waiting to make sure he was coming in alone. I have no idea why she brought the gun; she sure didn't need it. This woman had one of the best right uppercuts in North America. She put it on display one evening in a Montreal watering hole. She was in there with her husband when a woman, unaware that Mrs. was at the table, came over, put her arms around the startled star, and told him, "It's been so long since we've seen you here. We really missed you." Pecking him on the cheek, she started to leave when the player's spouse grabbed her gently by the elbow and asked, "Excuse me, do you know this man?" The woman said, "Oh, yes. I know him very well." That was all the Mrs. needed to hear. She grabbed the lady by the back of the head and pulled her face down into a right hand, and then said, "Well, now you know his wife!" I don't think that woman regained full consciousness for ten minutes. I mean, she was smoked. After hearing about that exhibition, I thought, "God damn, I hope Mary Lou never learns to throw a punch that well."

The fans in Montreal were marvelous, very much like the fans in Boston. They really turned us on during the pennant races, coming out in large numbers, screaming themselves hoarse. The team used them as an extra source of energy and strength. They deserve a big winner because they place so little emphasis on winning. All they care about is watching a good effort and having fun. I loved playing for them.

They were also protective of their heroes. Once, an Expo outfielder had played a particularly great game—a home run and a couple of circus catches to preserve a win—and he had decided to celebrate. Nothing heavy, he just went out to have a good time. During the course of the evening, he wound up in a local tavern where he met a young lady. He was smitten. After a few drinks and some light conversation, they both agreed it would be an excellent idea if they were to continue the celebration in the privacy of her apartment. The bar was not well lit, and when they got outside it was pitch black, so he had no idea what she looked like. Some fan who had watched them leave, came tearing out of the bar. Blocking the path to the outfielder's car, he got down on his hands and knees and begged the player not to take her home without first looking at her. He pleaded, "I know this woman. She is a dog! If you take her home, you will embarrass yourself, the team, the city, and the entire country!" But the outfielder would not be dissuaded. It was three a.m., and Miss Canada wasn't coming in that morning.

My contract would have been up at the end of the 1979 season, but there was no way I would even consider becoming a free agent. I didn't believe in peddling my services to the highest bidder. I had fallen in love with Montreal and did not want to play anywhere else. I had never had a contract hassle; money didn't mean very much to me. I thought I had tons of money. There was twenty thousand dollars in my savings account, and that seemed like a lot. I had always figured that when I was through as a major-leaguer I would go to work on my grandfather's walnut ranch. I wasn't concerned about the future. The future might not get here. I viewed free agency as a corruption of the game, putting too much emphasis on things monetary. That view was verified by the number of under-the-table offers I received from parties who wanted me to leave Montreal.

One of these offers came from Atlanta. It did not come from Ted Turner or anyone in his organization; that would have been blatant tampering. The offer was made over dinner in an Atlanta restaurant by a group of local businessmen. They had come over to my table, uninvited, and had bought me a drink. We started talking baseball, and they asked me where I thought I would be playing the following season. After telling them I hoped to stay in Montreal, they got all whispery, and one of them said, "We have a lot of pull around here. We're all interested in Atlanta; we all do a lot of business in the city. We are quite certain that if you declared for free agency, the Braves would make you a substantial offer. Much better than the one you'll get from the Expos. And, of course, with endorsements and commercials, we could see to it that you do very well off the field, also. The money is there."

I thanked them and forgot about it. That sort of thing happens to free agents all the time. Organizations are forbidden to talk to you because of tampering, so some highly influential member of the community extols the virtues of playing in their city. They always choose their words carefully.

There are some forms of tampering that are blatant. I know of a shortstop who was going to declare free agency, but didn't. He signed with his old ballclub. But before he did, he went to a dinner where a rival team's front office representative made it quite clear that his club would beat any offer his current team made to him.

I never got involved in that crap. It went in one ear and out the other. At the end of the 1979 season, John McHale asked me what I wanted. I said, "Give me a three-year, no-cut contract at $300,000 a year with $200,000 of the total package deferred over the next ten years." John said, "Done." Nothing to it. I didn't have an agent or a lawyer. I wanted to stay in Montreal, and we made what I thought was a fair deal. It was the only thing I could do. My principles told me that when you tied yourself to the economic god of free-agent greed, the spirit of Abner Doubleday was bound to turn his back on you. So, why—since I hadn't fallen victim to the lure of the dollar—did 1980 see me slide into the toilet?

I wasn't throwing well when the season started, but I was getting untracked and had pitched eight great innings against St. Louis when I decided to celebrate. I dragged myself home that night and made the mistake of pushing myself out of the door the next morning in order to get my running in. It was 8 a.m. when I passed a friend's house and decided to see if she was in. Rather than risk waking her by ringing the doorbell, I thought it best to climb up the facade of the house's outer gate, grab onto its awning, and gently tap on her window. It was an older building, and when I pushed up to grab the awning, a brick broke and I began to fall. I grabbed a piece of wrought-iron trim to support myself, but it snapped. Falling over ten feet, I caught my left hip on a small iron fence below. I lay on the floor, curled in a little ball, unable to breathe.

When I finally rose, I found I was bleeding like a stuck pig. I sat down, allowed myself time to hyperventilate, and got my act together. There were no cabs in sight, so I walked three-quarters of a mile to the nearest hospital. I was examined there, and the diagnosis was that I had chipped the crest of my pelvis and had completely ruptured my hip muscles. The nurses had to drain eight hundred cc. of blood off my hip on three separate occasions. My body was black and blue from the crack of my behind to an area just below my navel. That was scary; the color camouflaged my dick. It appeared as if it had been cut off. The following morning I was sore all over. I felt like I had been hit by a giant fungo bat. The nurses packed me in ice for three days, and I couldn't rejoin the club for four weeks. I couldn't find my pitching rhythm, and the team had so much pitching by then they hardly used me. I felt like the world's biggest asshole. It was really a stupid accident. It screwed up my entire season.

My anguish at the time was more than just physical. Mary Lou and I were going through hard times. We weren't getting along at all. Right after I injured my hip, she took the kids with her to our home in Washington and refused to return to Montreal. When the season was over, I joined her, and we spent an off-again, on-again winter together. When spring training time rolled around in 1981, she said, "See you later."

I suppose our marriage started going downhill after my first road trip in 1969. I think she realized then that being a ballplayer's wife wasn't going to be easy.

After my first couple of road trips, she accused me of running around. At that point, I was innocent, a mere babe in the woods. That didn't last for long. I started taking up with people on the road, rationalizing that as long as I was going to have to hear her accusations, I might as well have some fun for my trouble. Our marriage survived because we played half our games at home. When I wasn't traveling with the club, we had great times. Mary Lou was into a lot of the same things I was: running, camping, and she was concerned with social issues.

But, despite our compatibility, the relationship eroded. We bickered over little things, and these shouting matches eventually grew into real fights, very physical ones. It would be late at night, and I wouldn't want to get into anything, but she would, yelling, "You're not going to bed yet. We're going to have this out."

I would be too exhausted. It was tiring, pitching at the ballpark and catching hell at home. I should have been more receptive to her, but I wasn't. My fault. One night, when I wasn't in the mood for another heavy dialogue and had ignored her, she got frustrated and attacked me with a Tonka toy as I was lying on the bed. As she came at me I reached up and grabbed her with my right hand. I hoisted her up off the ground, and her momentum sent her flying through the air, slamming her into the bedroom wall. It was as if we were practicing for a new Olympic event: the wife/hammer throw. I sprang out of bed, picked her up, and apologized. I felt awful.

The problem was Mary Lou wanted to set down roots, but she had married a nomad. She wanted me to be like Mr. Price, our next-door neighbor. I was expected to come home at five and sit in front of the fireplace, reading the paper while smoking my pipe. I was never that. I was Don Quixote, jouster of windmills. I told her during the first year of our marriage that I would never leave her and that

I would always come home from road trips. That's all I could guarantee.

I knew it was over when she slammed the door on me and told me to go to spring training alone. One other tip-off was her parting line: "Don't come back." I was self-destructing at the time. I was fooling around a lot and had told her so. There was no sense in living a lie. I still loved her as much as ever, but, occasionally, I had to be with people who were more compatible with me in certain ways than she was. We got into a mammoth fight—not surprising, she had every right to want to kill me—and then she threw me out. As I was leaving, my daughter Caitlin came out of her room and sat at the top of the stairs. She said, "Daddy, you don't have to go. I'll hide you in my bedroom." I went out, got into my car, and headed for Florida. I cried all the way.

I almost didn't leave. I thought about giving up baseball, it hurt that much. But, after thinking it over, I decided that baseball wasn't the problem. I was the problem, and I wasn't going to change. At least, not now. As I drove across the country, I thought of everything I might do to make things between Mary Lou and me right again. It was no use. By the time I reached the Florida border, I knew it was all over.

She had a lawyer call me, and she drew up papers for a divorce. I wouldn't sign them, explaining that since I no longer believed in marriage, I couldn't possibly believe in divorce. They were able to push it through without me, though. I told them she could have everything except my Volkswagen camper, my chain saw, and my blue comforter. It wasn't a bad deal for her. She got the duplex in Boston and the house in Washington. One year after the settlement, I crashed the camper after skidding on a sheet of black ice in Saskatchewan. That's when I knew the trials of Job had not ended. I had to remind myself that before things get better, they often get worse.

I don't know how I got through the exhibition season, but I did. I had been hammered into a deep depression. When the Players Association called a strike in June, I couldn't have cared less. I did not vote to strike; I did not want any part of it. We were striking over the issue of compensation for free agency. I didn't believe in free agency, so how could I vote to strike over any facet of it? When the strike question was discussed, I stayed on the fence. The fence is a wonderful place to be, provided you know how to walk it. If you slip while walking that fence, you must make sure that both feet land on the same side of it. Otherwise, it's good-bye gonads.

Steve Rogers was the Montreal player rep, and I was his assistant. I sat in on the first strategy meeting. Our leader Marvin Miller presided, and everybody got a chance to speak. When I stood up, I said, "Screw the owners, Marvin. Who needs them? Why don't we just forget about the season. We'll barnstorm around the country with groups of players, choose up sides, and play in local ballparks in small towns. There will be no admission charged. When the game is over, we'll pass around the hat and divide the proceeds. If we put on a good show, we'll do all right." No one seemed to care for that idea very much.

When the strike was settled, I did not want to come back. My kids and I had traveled cross country from Montreal to Florida to Washington. I had missed them more than I could say. I was also playing basketball and softball everyday, and had put in some appearances with a semi-pro hardball team, the Bellingham Bells, in Washington. I was having a hell of a good time.

The first thing I realized when the season resumed was that Dick Williams was having the skids greased under him, and that his relationship with the Expos was ending. The signs were there. He was near the end of his contract and negotiations over a new one had broken down. Suddenly, we were reading about problems he was having with his players. That was bullshit. He wasn't having any more skirmishes in the clubhouse now than he had had in the past. The club was just laying the groundwork to ease him out. Not too long into what was laughingly called the Second Season, he was replaced by Jim Fanning.

That switch turned the club—which had been spinning its wheels—around, but not for the reasons people think. Everybody assumes we started winning ballgames because Fanning brought a calming atmosphere to the club. Actually, three games after he took over, the players realized that we had to get our act together because Gentleman Jim didn't have a clue as to what was going on out on the field. It would have been tolerable if he had been a nonmanager, someone who just made out the lineup card and allowed us to play. But he was like a hyperactive kid, running up and down the dugout, panicking as soon as we got behind in a ballgame. His ideas on strategy were vague, if not nonexistent. He also held the most disorganized team meetings that I could remember.

After watching him in action, it didn't take long for us to call a team meeting of our own. Fanning and his coaches were not invited. All the players attended. Cromartie acted as moderator of the conclave. When I was called on to speak, I stood up and said, "Williams and McHale hadn't been getting along and that had distracted Dick from managing. But Fanning flat-out can't manage at all. We can all see that. So what it all boils down to is this: We can't afford to be in a position where a managerial decision can cost us the game. We have to take it upon ourselves to get ahead. This team is going to have to battle every inning. Each member of it is going to have to stay alert. We will have to communicate amongst ourselves on when to execute the sacrifice, the hit-and-run, and the stolen bases. We have to make our own strategy decisions."

Fanning never knew what was going on. After the meeting, I told him that he had to settle down and relax on the bench, explaining he just could not panic out of reflex. He said, "I didn't realize how that looked. This is a new experience for me and maybe I get overenthusiastic. But I'm not panicking." He seemed to appreciate the conversation, and he and I communicated well with each other during the rest of the season. Though I hated the split schedule that the owners had come up with, I have to admit that once we started playing, I was having a ball. The team was winning, I was pitching well, and my head was clear. Once again, love had found Andy Hardy.

I met Pam in a bar called the Longest Yard, not long after Mary Lou and I had said our final good-byes. We were introduced by a mutual friend. We didn't say much to each other that evening, and I didn't get the idea she had been dying to meet me. About a week later, she came to a party at my house. I was hammered by nine o'clock and had dragged myself up to bed for some sack. I don't think I had said six words to her the entire evening. I woke up the next morning at seven and came downstairs to make breakfast. As I looked into my living room, I noticed that someone was lying in the middle of it, on a moon-shaped pillow, surrounded by an ocean of beer. It was Pam. Hearing me, she woke up, looked around her, and was startled to find herself in unfamiliar surroundings. Before I had a chance to ask her what she wanted for breakfast, she had slipped out the door. A few days after that, I saw her again and kidded her about leaving her boat in my living room. We started talking, and it was all over for me. She had this mischievous look in her eyes that told me she was as much of a kid as I was. I was hooked.

After winning the Eastern Division's second half title, the Expos had to meet Philadelphia in the first tier of the National League playoffs. This set would determine who would play the Western Division champion for the pennant. We beat Philly in five; Rogers pitched two outstanding games. We were supposed to leave for Los Angeles to face the Dodgers, but I had other plans. On the morning of the fifth game in Philadelphia, I had found out that Pam was ill with pneumonia. Every time I called to talk to her, she was unable to come to the phone. I assumed she was in a coma. As soon as we recorded the final out against Philly, I ran to the clubhouse, got dressed, and left to catch the next flight to Montreal. Running through the parking lot, I was stopped by a bunch of fans from South Philly who yelled, "Hey, you're Bill Lee!" I said, "Yes, I am, but I have no time right now. I have to get to the airport." They offered me a lift in their pickup truck. I arrived at the airport minutes before my flight was due to take off.

I was in Montreal two hours after the game ended. The next thing I knew, I was standing on the sidewalk in front of Pam's house. Pam, who was not as close to death as I had feared, was standing out there with me, in her bare feet, telling me that I couldn't come in because her boyfriend was inside. I was crushed. But then she told me that she was breaking up with him, and that I could see her when I got back from Los Angeles. The following day, I called her mother and said, "Hi, I'm Bill Lee and I love your daughter. I'm going to marry her. Please don't judge this book by its cover. My intentions are honorable." Pam had told me that someone had already told her mother that I was a wild man, and that Pam would just be another notch on my belt. I assured her that I never wore a belt. We hit it off. After her mother spoke to me, she went up and talked to Pam, telling her everything I had said. Pam agreed that she loved me and that if I wanted to marry her it would be no problem.

I did make it to Los Angeles in time for the playoffs, though I did manage to get fined for missing the team flight. That series went the full five games. We lost it in the ninth inning of the final game when Rogers, pitching in relief of Ray Burris, gave up a two-run homer to Rick Monday. Just as I had wanted to pitch in the playoff game against New York, I wanted to be in this ballgame, facing Monday. I almost climbed the bullpen walls to get at him. I was pumped up for that game. When we were finally eliminated, I was pissed.

But, within an hour of the final out, I thought, "Fuck, who cares. Who wants to win a pennant during a split season, anyway?" I was pleased to see that, despite everything that had happened to me over the last year and a half, my powers of instant rationalization were still with me.

After the season, Pam and I planned to get married in Vancouver, but we couldn't come up with all the papers they required. Vancouver is a great place to visit, but it's a tough town to get married in. While vacationing in Jamaica, we told everybody we'd be getting married soon. Someone suggested that we do it while we were down there. We thought that was a great idea, but the first minister we went to turned us down. His wife told me, "We don't do fast marriages for anyone. You might be marrying her so that you can take her to Europe and put her into prostitution." I argued, "But I'm from the States. Do I look like a pimp?" It was no use. They were really paranoid about white slavers down there. We finally found a minister who would perform the ceremony. I'm not sure what faith he was, but I could tell he was sincere. And he ran the only Chicken Burger Palace on the island. We had a Rastafarian band, and one of its members kept asking the minister, "Mr. Preacher Man, can you save me? I have two wives and about twenty kids. Will I go to heaven?" Two girls, Carol and Cynthia, who worked in the house where we were staying made a wedding shirt for me out of the Jamaican flag. They also baked a wedding cake, ornamented with white orchids. David Donald, a friend from Montreal, and most of our friends from the island attended the service. I bought Pam a coral wedding ring. We were married amid the natural wonders of Jamaica, and the ceremony was almost as beautiful as she was.

During the off-season, I was going to Olympic Stadium regularly to work out in the Nautilus room. Fanning would run into me there, and he would spend time picking my brain, looking for ways to improve the ballclub. No matter what elements of the team we focused on, he invariably would turn the conversation into a friendly debate over the merits of Rodney Scott. Sometimes we wouldn't even be talking baseball. I might say, "Jim, did you see where the price of gold has dropped again?" And Fanning would reply, "Yes, but can we afford to keep Rodney at second base next year?" I tried to convince him that we not only could, we had to. I explained that Rodney was an integral part of our defense and that we couldn't afford to replace him. Jim would just nod his head and not mention it again. Until the next time.

The Montreal front office had talked about getting rid of Rodney from the first day he took the field for us. But Williams loved him and wouldn't allow him to be messed with. With Dick gone, everybody knew it was only a matter of time before Rodney followed him out the clubhouse door.

Fanning had already picked Scott's replacement: Wallace Johnson, a second baseman with the Expos' Triple-A farm club in Denver. Fanning had built him up into a combination of Joe Morgan, Babe Ruth, and Frank Buck. He was constantly telling me how Wallace was going to lead us out of the doldrums and that the kid was going to be an instant star. The first time I saw Johnson, I kept checking him out as he walked to and from the shower. I was looking for wings. Fanning had dreams of Wallace hitting nothing but line drives into the power alleys of Olympic Stadium. Funky dreams. I would have loved to find out what herbs he was smoking; I would have gone for several kilos of the stuff.

When the 1982 season opened, Wallace had the second-base job. He hit well at first, but his glove just couldn't cut it. Then, after three weeks, his bat gave up the ghost. Fanning put Frank Taveras in at second. I liked Frank. For years, he had been a starting shortstop for the Pirates and the Mets, and he could do a lot of things to help a ballclub. Unfortunately, playing second base was not one of them. He lasted about a week. Rodney, who was being used for late inning defense, was ready to take his starting job back. But Fanning wouldn't give it to him. Instead, he brought Tim Raines in from leftfield, placing him at second. That had been Tim's position in the minors and Fanning and the front office assumed he could still get the job done.

A few days after the Raines move was made, a team meeting was called by Al Oliver. Oliver had been traded to Montreal from Texas just before the season had started, but he had already established himself as a team leader. He had called us together, hoping to point out that we weren't playing up to our full potential, and that we were making too many mistakes on defense. It was a good meeting. Everybody spoke up, and nobody hurled any garbage. I found it quite constructive.

Midway through it, I noticed that Rodney was absent. I didn't think twice about it; the meeting had been player-organized and had been called on the spur of the moment. I assumed he hadn't heard about it. When it was over, the team prepared to take batting practice, and I went out to do my running. On returning to the clubhouse, I sensed that something was askew. Rodney was at his locker, packing his bags. When I asked him what he was doing, he said, "They released me."

He looked as shocked as I was. I couldn't believe it. I thought, "Jesus Christ, this is *déjà vu*. It's Bernie Carbo all over again." Nobody had to tell me what had to be done. I already knew. It was time for me to walk.

Fanning had a standing rule: in case of an emergency that would force us to leave the ballpark before we could get his permission, we were to leave a note telling him where we could be reached. With that in mind, I wrote a message and placed it on his desk. It read, "I can't put up with this bullshit. I'm going to be at the bar in Brasserie 77. If you want me, come and get me."

When he first took over as manager, Jim had made a speech, telling us that his father had once given him a pair of boxing gloves as a Christmas present, and that he wasn't afraid to put them back on. I added a postscript to my note, inviting him to bring those gloves along. He never showed up. I went back to the ballpark just prior to the start of that afternoon's game. When I asked the trainer if Fanning had seen my message yet, I was told he hadn't. The trainer then handed me my game uniform. After first thanking him, I took it into the manager's office and ripped it down the middle. I layed it across Fanning's desk. Then I went back to the Brasserie and draped little Quebec flags around a picture of Rodney. The customers loved it.

I had three beers while watching our game on television. We were getting jocked, and by the sixth inning, I realized that we were going through an awful lot of pitchers. I hustled back to the stadium in case I was needed. I was mad at management, not at my teammates, and I didn't want to do anything that might jeopardize our chances of winning a ballgame. I got to the park by the eighth inning, but I wasn't needed. We lost by two runs. I went into our workout room and started lifting weights in an attempt to blow off steam.

Fanning called me into his office and demanded to know where I had been. I said, "Right here." He asked why I wasn't in uniform. I told him I had been in uniform that afternoon, adding, "Don't you remember? I was here for the meeting. I took batting practice and did my running. Then, I came into the clubhouse and discovered that you finally found the guts to release Rodney. I went to the Brasserie to wait for you, and, when you failed to show, I came back here in time for the eighth inning."

Fanning said, "Rodney Scott is none of your business."

That set me off. I screamed, "None of my business! That guy gave us everything he had for three years. He helped us win ballgames and was one of the most decent guys on the club. He was my friend. And you say this is none of my business! You never gave Rodney a real shot, and you lied to him constantly!"

Fanning got so upset, he started to tremble. When he finally got hold of himself, he told me, "This is still none of your business. I'm here to tell you that McHale wants to see you first thing tomorrow morning."

I wanted to see John right then and there, but Fanning wouldn't hear of it. Storming out of the clubhouse, I left for home. During the drive back, I thought about how Fanning, throughout our entire argument, could not once bring himself to look me in the face. I could recall similar experiences with other managers. I think it was because, in each instance, we both knew where all the bodies were buried.

10

cHale burst into his office, threw on the lights, and asked, "How did you get in here?" I answered, "Through the door." That reply was another example of my mastery of dazzling repartee. I always believed in giving an immediate answer to a reasonable question. McHale was neither amused nor impressed. He went on the attack.

"You did a bad thing yesterday, a very bad thing."

"Well, that makes two of us."

"Look," he protested, "we released Rodney because we felt he wasn't doing the job and..."

"Wasn't doing the job! Hell, he did the job for three years. No one gave him a chance this season."

"...and you were drunk and disorderly last night. That was a crucial game we lost."

"Bullshit, John. I threw three innings the night before last. Fanning wasn't going to use me. If anything, I would have been the last man used in an emergency situation, and I was ready for that. I was in the clubhouse prepared to pitch if necessary. I was watching the game and knew the situation."

"That's not the issue. We didn't see you. You were supposed to be in the bullpen."

He had a point, but I was not about to slow up while I was on a roll. "Will you please give me a break! I've been up here for fourteen years, and you're going to tell me that! Do you think you have to tell me that? Let's not get off the track. Let's get to the truth. Are you going to claim that you treated Rodney right with all this crap? Are you going to ask me to believe that you couldn't make some sort of deal for him, or that you couldn't have handled his situation better than you did? Whatever happened to 'Love thy neighbor' around here?"

McHale explained that they had tried to trade Rodney, but that nobody was interested. As I would find out later, that shouldn't have been a surprise. The Expos had bad-mouthed him all over the league. I was about to release one more comment on this whole insane episode, but John interrupted me. He had one more thing to say.

"We're releasing you."

I wasn't exactly shocked. "Yeah, sure you are. You've never forgiven me for the time USC beat Notre Dame 55–24. You've never forgotten that game, John, and it will eat your heart out as long as you live. That's right, and so will this day. This day will come back to haunt you. Not because you are releasing me, but because the day will come when you're going to need Rodney's talents. But he won't be there. I've seen this happen before. It will happen again."

I wasn't wrong. It turned out that they could have used both of us. The Expos spent the entire summer trying to fill their hole at second base, and hunting for lefthanded pitching. Despite these shortcomings, they finished only six games out of first place. Rodney and I could have made a difference.

I should point out that I did have "legal counsel" present when I squared off with McHale. Steve Rogers, the Montreal player representative, had joined us in the middle of our meeting. It had been my understanding that Rogers was there to help me with my defense and insure that my rights would not be violated. Some defense. While McHale reiterated his charges against me—absent without leave and insubordination among them—Steve just stood there, nodding his head. He never uttered a word. I thought, "Cy Young, my dick. This guy's seeing to it that I get the same kind of hearing Dreyfus got."

We could have at least mounted a defense against the earlier charge that I had been drunk and disorderly. I was not drunk. I had consumed three beers in three hours at the Brasserie, and that's not enough to give me a light buzz. I also hadn't been disorderly. I may have raised my voice two or ten decibels in the manager's office, but so had Fanning. If I had been disorderly, what about him? None of this made the slightest impression. McHale's idea of considering my side consisted of asking me my name, pronouncing me guilty, and shipping my ass off to Devil's Island.

After leaving McHale's office, I went down to my locker and cleared out my stuff. As I packed, I felt an invisible wall go up between me and some of my teammates. It was as though I had been suddenly transformed into a leper. Only the black ballplayers on our club ventured over to say good-bye. Gary Carter also stopped over. Catchers and pitchers have a special relationship. Of the coaches, only our pitching coach Galen Cisco walked over to tell me that he was sorry to see me go and to thank me for the good work I had done for him. I thanked them all and left. I didn't bother to look back.

When I got home, Pam was still in bed, sleeping. She woke up and asked me why I wasn't at the ballpark. I said, "Hon, I don't have a job there any more."

She thought I was kidding, but when she realized I was serious, she said, "Well, what do you want to do today?" She bounced right back from the news and that picked my spirits up. Pam wasn't into being Mrs. Ballplayer, and so she had no trouble adapting to my new status. The first time she attended an Expo game as my wife, she was introduced to some of the ballplayers' spouses by Scott Sanderson's wife Kathy. Kathy said, "This is Mike Gates's wife, and this is Bill Gullickson's wife, and this is Tim Wallach's wife." Pam later told me she had chatted with them for an hour and that they were very nice, but she never found out any of their first names. Their identities seemed wrapped around their husbands; it was as if none of them had a life of her own. All they talked about was hubby's career and how he was doing at the time. They had nothing to say about their own lives away from the ballpark. Pam thought that it was all very sad.

On the evening I received my pink slip, Rodney and I went out and did up the town. I don't believe it's good to linger in a depression. I started to view my release as a positive thing, reminding myself that I would now have time to go camping with my kids and play basketball with my friends. That's how I am. I've always tried to change a negative into a positive. If I were in a concentration camp, I'd find a broken broomstick, roll up some old twine and tape, and scrounge up a game of stickball. I decided I would explore some new horizons. I didn't have any thoughts about trying to hook on with another team. Yet.

Radio Station CJAD in Montreal offered me a job doing a five-minute sports broadcast in the morning. I accepted and it turned out to be fun. I also got a call from Frosty Deer of the Kanawake Indian Survival School, inviting me to play softball on their reservation. I jumped at that, and it was an outstanding move. The moment I arrived there, I felt a renewal of strength. There's a vibrancy to the place that is energizing, yet peaceful.

I did play some baseball. Semi-pro hardball with the Longueil Senators. I pitched and played first base. I understand that when Dick Young of the *New York Post* heard about it, he wrote that I was up in Canada, bullying a bunch of semi-pros with my pitching. He was so wrong. The Senators asked me to play, hoping they could help keep my arm in shape while at the same time using me as a drawing card. I was still something of a gate attraction in Canada. I would have liked to compete on a higher level, but the majors had been closed off to me.

Playing those semi-pro games was no picnic. It involved a great deal of traveling to a lot of places that were far from the beaten path. I loved the game, and this experience made me realize just how much it meant to me. I had always said that I would play baseball for nothing, and this proved it. It was nice to know I hadn't been bullshitting myself. As for Dick Young, I don't know what he loves. I do wonder, though, based on the way he jumped ship from the *Daily News* just as it appeared to be going under, if he would write sports for free. Somehow, I tend to doubt it.

Most of the players in semi-pro ball spoke very little English, but I found that wasn't important. Baseball has no language barriers. This was the game in its purest form. No agents, no commissioners. Just a bunch of guys hitting, running, throwing, and working up a healthy sweat. Playing without salary, the players in this league showed a professional brand of competitiveness. In one game, against the Quebec All-Stars, I was matched up against a pitcher who threw like Stu Miller. Miller was the pitcher with the Giants and Orioles who threw change-ups off his change-ups, each one slower than the one that preceded it. This pitcher for Quebec had the same repertoire. All I could do with his junk was hit a bunch of hard foul balls. After fouling off about ten consecutive pitches, his catcher looked up at me and said, "He throws like Lefty, huh? Just like Steve Carlton?" I shook my head, and then he said, "You think we should give you a fastball for the fans?" I said, "Great." He replied, "Well, this isn't a show for the fans. We're trying to win." We both laughed, and I ended up going three for five in a ballgame we won, 8–4. I loved every second of it.

I got a chance to play some outfield against Quebec after first ingesting four grams of psychedelic mushrooms. I spent an inning talking to the pine trees in right field. The rest of the time was spent trying to wipe a very big grin off my face. God, did my mouth ache when that game was over. I did very well that day. I snared a ball down the rightfield line that I had almost overrun. I caught it off my chest. I played five games in three days in that transcendent state and the mushrooms did not mess up my fielding at all, though I must admit that there were times when the ball did appear to be dancing when it was hit out to me. It was doing the "Nutcracker Suite." But I caught anything I got to.

The psychedelic mushroom is a natural substance. The Earth Lord put it here so that the high priests of Stonehenge could pound it down their gullets. This enabled them to exert power over the neighboring townspeople. By turning on, they could stay up all night. While everybody in the village slept, the priests sat around the campfire and bullshit with each other. Eventually bored, they sought other ways to amuse themselves. They lined up huge stones, using their shadows to predict the coming of the lunar eclipse. Once they had their forecasts down to a science, they used this knowledge to show the minions who was boss. Gathering the villagers together, the priests would say, "We are going to make the moon vanish." And it would. The people would panic and cry, "Please, give us back our moon!" The priests would retort, "You may have it back on the condition that you vow to heed our words in the future." It was, of course, a trick. They couldn't make the moon disappear; they just knew in advance when it wouldn't be around. The only powers they had were the powers of observation. The priests were like a group of used-car salesmen, displaced in time. In order to pull off their scam successfully, they occasionally needed the assistance of a little graft. Every now and again, the moon would visit them and say, "Give me five dollars and I won't talk."

After a few weeks of leisure, my friend Bill Brownstein said, "Okay, the party is over. It's time we got you back into the pros." He called most of the twenty-six major league teams, telling them I was considering all offers and that if they were interested they should get in touch with me through him. The few responses we did get were all the same: "We have our roster set; yes, it's true we're in last place; yes, it's true we're twenty-five games out of first and it's only June; and yes, it's true we don't have any pitching. But we don't need you at this time." At this time actually meant at any time. Ever.

Dick Lally called the Atlanta Braves for me in early August. At the time, the Braves were in a monumental slump that they eventually came out of before winning the Western Division title. Dick first spoke to Atlanta's assistant general manager Pat Nugent. After telling Nugent that I was available, he bombarded him with stats showing what an effective pitcher I had been in Atlanta, and how I had always thrown well against Western Division clubs, especially the Braves' biggest rival, the Los Angeles Dodgers. Nugent digested the data and promised he'd get back to us.

When he didn't, Dick called John Mullen, Atlanta's vice-president and general manager. Once again, he made his presentation. Mullen's first response was, "We already have our twenty-five man roster set."

Dick told him, "Yes, I understand that. And at the moment they're sinking faster than the *Andrea Doria*, so let's talk business."

Mullen's next response held out some hope for me. He asked about my contract situation with the Expos. That was no problem. Outside of the monies owed me for the present season and my deferred payments, I didn't have a contract situation with the Expos. He wondered what sort of condition I was in (excellent), and said he would talk to Braves manager Joe Torre about me. After speaking with Joe, he assured us, he'd give us a call. We're still waiting. When the Braves met the Cardinals in the 1982 National League playoffs, Joe Torre was quoted as saying that they lacked an experienced lefthanded pitcher. I just want Joe and the Braves' fans to know there was at least one such pitcher only a phone call away.

I became suspicious about all the cold shoulders I had received and began to suspect that I had been blackballed. McHale is a powerful figure in baseball. I asked Marvin Miller about the possibility of taking the Expos to court, charging them with collusion. Marvin, honest as always, said, "If you want to do that we will help you as much as possible. But, I have to tell you, you won't win. Collusion is the most difficult thing to prove in a court of law." The only evidence I had against them was my gut feeling that a conspiracy had been entered into. I did have some proof, however, that Rodney and I were being bad-mouthed around the league. One player told me that he had been speaking to Expo scout Eddie Lopat about me. Eddie told him that the Expos had released me because I hadn't been throwing well. That was a lot of shit. I had given up one run in my final three relief appearances as a Montreal Expo. If I had been throwing much better, Fanning wouldn't have yelled at me that evening. He would have paid for my drinks at the Brasserie, and had a limousine pick me up to bring me back to the stadium.

I was invited to be on *Late Night with David Letterman*, a talk show airing out of New York. I liked the show's energy, so I said sure. Billy Crystal, the actor-comedian, and Tommy John were also scheduled as guests. Backstage, Tommy told me that Yankee vice-president Bill Bergesch had called him, asking him if he knew anything about Rodney Scott. The Yankees were interested in signing him to a contract. Tommy said that Bergesch had heard that Rodney might have a drug problem or that he might be a homosexual. I don't have to think too long to figure out who spread those rumors. Both of them were bullshit. Rodney may have been screwed in the ass a few times, but only by management. I know he wasn't a homosexual because he's attacked my wife on at least four separate occasions. Tommy's response to Bergesch's queries was priceless. He said, "Who cares what he is as long as he can play." That's a player for you. He knows what's important. Management eats all that other crap for breakfast. I did come away from our conversation with one question: "If it was the Expos who were spreading around those lies about Rodney, a player who went off quietly into the night, what sort of garbage could they be spreading around about me?"

I didn't know, and I no longer cared. I resigned myself to the idea that I was not going to be pitching in the majors that summer. I spent the rest of it having a ball, doing my radio show, and learning something of Quebec and its people. It was the best summer I had ever had with my kids. I saw them every day and brought them to my games. We went on outings every afternoon. I got to know them again.

If I learned anything after leaving the Expos, it was that I liked myself. I wasn't always sure whether I did or not. And I learned that people liked me too. Not for being a ballplayer, but just for being me. That was nice. A lot of good things happened.

The Quebec chapter of the YMCA put together a petition, asking the Expos to put me back on the ballclub. It had over ten thousand signatures on it when it was sent to McHale. Members of the media also rallied behind me. Jane Gross of *The New York Times* came up to Quebec and did a piece on me. I respected the way she approached the story of my new semi-pro career. She searched for every detail and gave me the impression that she cared about me as a person, that I wasn't just grist for her journalistic mill. I always like the human approach.

Dick Schaap also came up and did a TV piece on me for ABC. It was a "What is he doing now?" type of story. Dick was a lot of fun. After the filming was over, we went back to his hotel and had a few drinks. And then a few more. At ten p.m., Dick was saying he would do everything he could to get me back into baseball. At eleven, he was calling for a congressional investigation into my charges of collusion. By midnight, we were both seeing God.

I attended a great many sporting events in the months immediately following my release, more than I ever had before. I came away with some eye-popping insights. There was a heavy air of violence in the stands at many of the games I attended. I sensed that a new philosophy had sprouted amongst the fans: "If we can't beat them, let's kill them." It was scary. I attended a basketball game at the Boston Garden, during which a spectator jumped out of the stands and decked a referee. And got a standing ovation. Another fan kept running along the perimeter of the court, screaming, "Oh God, don't let them get the ball! Please don't let them get the ball!" He was gone. I kept thinking, "Boy, I hope he has a big bet on this game, or he is really overreacting." You could have cut this guy's leg off, and he would have never felt it.

Eventually, I stopped watching the game and sat back to watch the fans. It was like watching a Fassbinder film, depicting mankind at its most berserk. The experience made me wonder if we're not breeding a society that lacks self-esteem. I don't think we pat people on the back enough, letting them know that being able to fix a sink is just as much a skill as being able to get Rod Carew out with the bases loaded. And more worthwhile, if you were to ask me. People must be made to feel their value. Otherwise, when they discover they can't find any thrills in religion or in cults, they head out to the ballpark, seeking a vicarious sense of fulfillment. They're tired of long-term reality; they don't recognize what it has to offer them. All they want is one good fantasy. Realizing that really shook me up.

I spent the winter of '82 getting into top physical shape. I had decided to give the majors one more shot. I ran five miles every day and played full court basketball religiously. When spring training time rolled around, I was in the best shape of my life.

I worked out at USC for a couple of days, pitching to their junior varsity team. I was unaware that some scouts from the Atlanta Braves were watching me throw. Apparently impressed with what they saw, they called Henry Aaron, the Braves' director of player development, and told him I was worth taking a look at. Henry called me at my father's home in California. He told me that the Braves were interested in possibly having me come to spring training with them and that they would reach a final decision on the matter after discussing it at a meeting of the team hierarchy. Henry was very cordial, assuring me that he would call back within a few days. There had to be something wrong with the telephone system in Atlanta because he never got back to us.

After a week of waiting for his call, I decided to go to Phoenix, Arizona. I wanted to see if I could hook up with Dick Williams and the San Diego Padres. The day after I left, my father called Henry to ask why we hadn't heard from him. When he reached him, he found Henry was not quite as friendly as he had been in our earlier conversation. He said, "We told Bill we'd get back to him." My dad reminded him that ten days had passed since that phone call. That's when Henry got tough, saying, "The Braves don't owe Bill Lee anything." When I heard that, I flipped out. I mean, Jesus, they were the ones who called me! Henry's last line was the topper. My father had told him that he realized the Braves might be a bit leery of signing someone with my reputation. Henry replied, "I don't know anything about that. That's something Bill will have to talk over with baseball."

Talk over with baseball! What did that mean? Was someone going to lead me into the royal court of the Emerald Palace and bring me before a giant baseball perched on a throne? What would I talk to it about? I guess I could bow down before it and ask, Gee, baseball, what did I do to make you angry at me? Did I let you get hit over the fence too often, or squeeze you too hard on the mound? What's your problem?

That was the last I heard from Henry Aaron, and it convinced me more than anything else that the fix was in. I was certain that someone had gotten to the Braves. I called a few other teams. Steve Boros, the manager of the Oakland A's, told me they wanted to go with their young pitchers. Then they signed lefthanded Tom Burgmeier, a young pitcher who is two years older than I am.

I did call on Dick Williams in Phoenix. I didn't come away with a job, but I did catch a glimpse of the truth. Dick took me in his office, sat me down, and said, "Bill, I want you on this team. I told our general manager that you can help us. But he said we can't touch you. Now that's the way it is. If you tell anybody I told you that, I'll have to deny it." I thanked him and didn't tell anybody what he had said. Until now.

I guess it's over. I think I knew it in my guts the day I walked out of the Expos' clubhouse. A chapter of my life had been closed. I've thought about what I might do with the rest of my life, and the prospects are exhilarating. I'll either go back to college and get my doctorate in political science, or head up a mountain and shoot myself. There's no middle of the road with me. Just kidding. Actually, I might just yet become the forest ranger I wanted to become twenty years ago. I'd like that. I'd work to preserve the salmon. I'll combine modern technology with forestry, creating a bionic fish that will destroy the nets cast by poachers. It would be able to launch a small sea-to-air missile at anybody it caught poaching a salmon.

I am also considering playing in Japan or Venezuela. That appeals to the gypsy in my soul. Of course, you never know when a major league team might need a lefthander so desperately that they might ignore the steel curtain that's been placed around me. Even a team like the Expos. Just the other day, they signed a veteran second baseman to a minor league contract. Fellow by the name of Rodney Scott. It's taking a long time, but they may be learning.

But I don't think I'll be back. I'll still play ball wherever I can, participating in an organized league or competing in whatever sandlot games I can get into. It's always a fun way to spend an afternoon, and it's a great way to stay in shape. It sure beats splitting wood. I also have to admit I can't stay away from it. I have an addiction to resin, and I love the feel of the warm sun on my face as I stand out on the mound, trying to fool yet another hitter. Like Peter Pan, I'll never stop enjoying my games.

The question is often asked of athletes, "How would you like to be remembered when your career is over?" I never really gave it any thought. If I accomplished anything as a player, I hope it's that I proved you could exist as a dual personality in the game. I had to pass through the looking glass every time I went out on the field. Away from the ballpark, I tried to care about the earth, and I wasn't concerned with getting ahead of the "other guy." On the mound, I was a different person, highly competitive and always out to win. Who I was off the field fed the person I became on it. I had to make the stands I did. To be silent in the face of injustice would have made my life and my pitching meaningless. If I was able to keep my compassion while retaining my competitive senses, then I would judge my career a success. I hope I was able to make more than just a few fans smile, while showing them that the game shouldn't be taken too seriously. If I am remembered by anyone, I would want it to be as a guy who cared about the planet and the welfare of his fellow man. And who would take you out at second if the game was on the line.